GREEN HARVEST

A History of Organic Farming and Gardening in Australia

REBECCA JONES

PUBLISHING

National Library of Australia Cataloguing-in-Publication entry

Jones, Rebecca, 1967–

Green harvest : a history of organic farming and gardening in Australia/by Rebecca Jones.

9780643098374 (pbk.)

Includes bibliographical references and index.

Organic gardening – Australia – History.
Organic farming – Australia – History.

631.584

Published by
CSIRO PUBLISHING
36 Gardiner Road, Clayton VIC 3168
Private Bag 10, Clayton South VIC 3169
Australia

Telephone: [+613] 9545 8555
Local call: 1300 788 000 (Australia only)
Fax: +61 3 9662 7555
Email: csiropublishing@csiro.au
Web site: www.publishing.csiro.au

Cover image by iStockphoto

Set in Adobe Minion Pro 11/13.5 and Adobe Helvetica Neue

Edited by Anne Findlay
Cover and text design by James Kelly
Typeset by Desktop Concepts Pty Ltd, Melbourne
Index by Russell Brooks
Printed by Ingram Lightning Source

CSIRO PUBLISHING publishes and distributes scientific, technical and health science books and journals from Australia to a worldwide audience and conducts these activities autonomously from the research activities of the Commonwealth Scientific and Industrial Research Organisation (CSIRO).

Feb26_RP_ILS

Contents

Acknowledgements

There are many people I wish to thank who have assisted me in the research and writing of *Green Harvest*. I am grateful to all the people who participated in interviews for this study and who so generously and cheerfully shared their time, stories, beliefs and experiences with me.

I would particularly like to thank: Janice Chesters who conscientiously supervised the research and writing of this book as a PhD thesis at Monash University, brought different insights to my historical analysis, and from the outset shared my vision. Sue Whyte offered thoughtful and practical advice and shared with me an enthusiasm for organic farming and gardening and an interest in different approaches to the world.

I would also like to thank Anna Jones, Meredith Fletcher, Ted Hamilton and staff of CSIRO Publishing, Libby Robin, John Waller, Tom Griffiths, Tom Stannage, Gary Presland, Margaret Jones and Ivor Jones, and staff of Monash University Department of Rural and Indigenous Health.

I am grateful for financial assistance received from the Commonwealth Government Australian Postgraduate Award, the School of Rural Health Higher Degree Student Support Scheme, Faculty of Medicine, Nursing and Health Science Publication Grant and Department of Rural and Indigenous Health Publication Grant, without which this history would be much more limited in scope and geography.

Staff from the State Libraries of Victoria, South Australia, Queensland and Tasmania, the National Library, the Monash University Library Rare Books Collection, Megg Miller and Graham White all assisted me in obtaining historical sources.

Finally, the broader 'family' of the garden and farm with its floral and faunal residents not only provided welcome distraction and tranquillity but have taught me much about growth, decay and other really important things in life.

Introduction

A city gardener turns her compost, inspecting with delight the moist, dark humus wriggling with earthworms. The manager of an outback station prepares for the muster inoculating the cattle with organically certified tick control remedies. An orchardist is erecting a perimeter fence around a farm wetland, taking time out from pruning to plant native trees. A hobby farmer sows seeds which will, in a few months, supply his family with an abundance of fruit and vegetables. Today, over 12 million hectares of commercial agricultural land in Australia is farmed organically and all types of food production from banana plantations, outback cattle stations and wheat properties to vineyards, poultry farms and home gardens include organic growers.[1] Organic growing is neither a post-1970s fashion nor a pre-industrial anachronism. Australian organic farming and gardening is a phenomenon with an active and engaging history. However, there is limited awareness of the history of organic growing and histories of organic gardening and farming are scarce. This, the first history of Australian organic growing, will show that farmers and gardeners have been growing food in Australia using methods they describe as organic since the 1940s with active organic societies established in three Australian states after 1944. *Green Harvest* explores what it means to farm and garden organically and how this has changed over time. It will identify the key ideas which have defined organic growing from the 1940s. It traces these ideas through to the present day. These defining ideas weave through Australian organic farming and gardening, modifying their form but continuing to bind growers to each other over time.

Organic farms and gardens are earthy, dynamic sites in which people and biological elements co-exist. Like all agricultural and horticultural environments, they are constructed places. Growing food, raising animals and tilling the soil are intense interactions between humans and non-humans such as plants, animals, soil and insects. To borrow American environmental historian Donald Worster's phrase, farms and gardens are 'domesticated ecologies',[2] places where humans are active participants and in which humans mould, work and change their surrounds, and in turn, are changed by them. Beneath organic growers' discussions of soil tilth, animal fodder, revegetation, pest control and land cultivation lie deeply held beliefs about the relationship between the physical environment and human wellbeing. These are the fundamental beliefs that I have attempted to grasp in this history.

What it means to grow food organically in Australia during the last 70 years unfolds as a series of changing conversations about the relationships between human health and land. Australian organic farmers and gardeners discuss organic growing in terms of the dependency of human health on the natural or biophysical environment.[3] The key ideas that define Australian organic growing, throughout its history, are founded on the fundamental concept that human health and the biophysical environment are interdependent and intertwined. To be organic is to produce food in a way that growers believe promotes human health by cooperating with natural processes and enhancing both human and environmental health.

Organic growers' beliefs are inspired by ecological thinking which burgeoned in popularity from the middle of the twentieth century.[4] Ecological thinking is both a science and a philosophy of interrelatedness; a way of thinking about and understanding the world which emphasises the interdependency of all things. Humans are seen as part of, and dependent on, natural systems which are mutual, dynamic and interactive. Animate and inanimate entities and processes are interrelated and interdependent and the context in which something exists has a profound impact on the individual.[5] Therefore changes within the natural environment can impact on human health and wellbeing and human actions that damage the environment can, in turn, have detrimental effects on human health.[6]

Twentieth-century ecological understandings of health echoed some aspects of ancient concepts such as the Hippocratic view of health.[7] Classical Greek and Roman societies as well as ancient Chinese, Arabic and Indian cultural traditions all understood that human health was achieved by balancing the human body with its physical surrounds, particularly the natural environment.[8] Health was a state of harmony between and within the human body and its surroundings and ill-health (or disease) occurred when this harmony was disrupted. In Hippocratic thinking, elements of the biophysical environment, such as climate, seasons, wind, water quality and topography all created conditions for human health and ill health. Disease was addressed by adapting the person to their environment and creating equilibrium between bodily processes and the natural environment. This thinking strongly influenced Western health traditions and formed the basis of Western medicine until the late nineteenth century when a biomedical perspective of health began to prevail.

The defining characteristic of these new biomedical theories was its reliance on 'germ theory' to explain disease.[9] Germ theory was the idea that particular potentially identifiable agents cause particular diseases in individuals. Increasing knowledge of bacteria through the work of Louis Pasteur and infectious diseases such as cholera and tuberculosis through the work of Robert Koch had given people greater understanding of contagion.[10] Disease was now understood to pass between people via invisible micro-organisms. Medical attention focused on bacteria, viruses, parasites and other pathogens as the causes of specific diseases. The focus was on the disease rather than the person and their social and environmental context. 'It was now the details of the foreground rather than the larger constructs in the background that commanded attention', is how Australian epidemiologist and health ecologist Tony McMichael describes it.[11]

Ecological perspectives, while not discounting biomedical theories, placed greater emphasis on the environmental context in which the vector, disease and the human operated. Health and disease were conceived in terms of the natural, social, spiritual and emotional environment as well as the individual body.[12] Increasing interest in ecological notions of health in the mid-twentieth century, of which Australian organic growing was a part, was a reaction against the perceived limitations of a biomedical approach to health as well as a response to evidence of environmental damage. Understanding ecological ideas about the mutual, dynamic dependency of animate and inanimate systems is, I will argue, paramount in understanding the history of Australian organic farming and gardening.

Environmental history is the lens through which I have examined organic growers' changing ideas about health and environment. Environmental history, like health ecology, is founded on ecological thinking and places humans' relationships with the biophysical environment in focus. The prominent and changing role of the natural environment in human life; the interactive processes by which humans are affected by the environment, and in turn, affect the environment and the ways people think about their relationship with the natural environment are preoccupations of environmental history which have inspired this study.[13] For all these reasons, this book will examine Australian organic growing as a set of beliefs about the dependence of humans on the environment and a repertoire of methods for enacting those beliefs.

Green Harvest tells the story of Australian organic farming and gardening from the perspective of the organic growers themselves. It explores the ideas, beliefs and practices of growers who identified their practices as 'organic' from the first use of the word in Australia in the 1940s until the present. My concern is not primarily with public perceptions of organic farming and gardening but with the growers themselves.

History is both fact and fiction[14] and this history is, of course, only one version of events. The driving ideas, the hubs, the fringes, the important issues, the defining moments, and even the crucial people will vary depending on the perspective of the enquirer. Environmental history is one of a number of possible approaches to the history of Australian organic farming and gardening. Research which focused on consumers, organic retailers or processors, rather than on growers would result in a somewhat different history. A social, political or economic history of Australian organic farming may also produce another, equally valid narrative. Similarly, a person who was, themselves, prominent in the Australian organic movement would identify different people and events to discuss.

Although the main focus of this study is those growers who identified as 'organic', I have also sought the ideas of subgroups among organic growers. Australian organic growers are a heterogeneous cluster of organisations and individuals whose beliefs are at times congruent, at other times divergent. The most notable of Australian organic subgroups were the Back to the Landers who were outspoken and active in the 1970s and 1980s but whose prominence among Australian organic growers was to diminish by the 2000s. Other examples are biodynamic growers and permaculturalists. Biodynamic growers followed Austrian Rudolf Steiner's precepts, developed in the 1920s and adapted by German–American Ehrenfried Pfeiffer. Permaculture, a theory of design and local food production, was created by Australians David Holmgren and Bill Mollison in the 1970s. Both permaculturalists and biodynamic growers share many ideas with other organic growers and have influenced, and been influenced by, organic ideas and practice but remain largely separate entities within the broader movement.[15]

My own involvement in organic gardening has, of course, influenced the historical narrative I have woven. This history is a study from both the outside and the inside. Written and oral sources have provided an 'insider's' view of organic farming and gardening – what the growers themselves believed and did rather than how others perceived them. However, I am myself, as the author, in an ambivalent position both as insider and outsider. As a researcher I am an outsider, analysing sources dispassionately. However, as an organic gardener I have, like the people I have written about, discovered the delights of growing food, built compost heaps, grappled with insect pests and planted indigenous flora. First, in inner suburban Melbourne, then as a smallholder in rural Victoria, I have shared with the organic growers in this history a love of working with plants, a dislike of chemicals, a belief in the importance of the physical environment for our wellbeing and a desire to get my hands dirty.

The principal sources for this history are those which reveal the beliefs of organic farmers and gardeners over time. Writings by Australian organic growers themselves, particularly magazines, newsletters and books, as well as interviews with organic growers have been a valuable window into growers' ideas and activities.

Australian organic farmers and gardeners and their societies, have, from their beginnings in the 1940s, been copious publishers of newsletters, magazines and pamphlets. Australia's first three organic societies each had their own publication. The earliest of these was the *Organic Farming Digest,* first printed in 1946 (see Colour plate 1) and renamed *Farm and Garden Digest* in 1950. This magazine was published quarterly by the Australian Organic Farming and Gardening Society of

Figure 1: Masthead of the *Victorian Compost News* in 1950. This magazine was first produced by the Victorian Compost Society from 1947. The Victorian Compost Society remains one of Australia's longest-running organic groups, founded in 1945 and active until the mid-1980s.

(Source: Victorian Compost Society, *Victorian Compost News*, 4, no. 7, 1950)

New South Wales. The Living Soil Association of Tasmania produced occasional newsletters and booklets during the early 1950s and the *Victorian Compost News,* renamed *Good Earth* in 1965 was produced by the Victorian Compost Society from 1947 (see Figure 1).

The New South Wales and Victorian magazines were produced quarterly, monthly or bi-monthly. Each magazine was over 40 pages long and included editorials, opinion pieces, debates, letters, reports of lectures and tours, descriptions of organic methods, news snippets, and material syndicated from other Australian and international organic publications. The New South Wales *Farm and Garden Digest* ceased publication in 1954. The Victorian publication was published continuously for nearly 40 years, from 1947 to 1983, and provided a valuable barometer of change and continuity during the first four decades of Australian organic growing.

These early magazines were 'no-nonsense' publications dedicated to improving farming and gardening methods and public health. They were earnest, passionate, polite and energetic with little time for frivolity. The densely typed pages were usually enlivened only by the cover illustration. Inspired by the desire to reinforce organic beliefs among members as well as 'convert' non-organic farmers and gardeners, these publications at times edged close to propaganda. Contributors included farmers and gardeners as well as the editors, presidents and other society office bearers. While some differences of opinion, debate and dissent nestled in their pages, contributions were generally indicative of the organisational 'party line' rather than of individual thinking. Organic farmers and gardeners who had divergent beliefs and were not motivated to educate others through the organic societies were unlikely to be found as contributors to these society magazines.

From the early 1970s the number of organic society publications proliferated.[16] I have selected for analysis a range of these post-1970 publications which represent organic growing in different climatic and environmental conditions.[17] While some of these magazines were slim and concentrated solely on society activities, other more weighty publications discussed, reported on and debated organic issues and methods and used illustrations to convey their ideas. One of the most comprehensive of this generation of magazines was *The Organic Gardener and Farmer* published by the Tasmanian Organic Gardening and Farming Society from 1976.[18] This magazine was similar in content to the publications of the New South Wales and Victorian societies in the 1940s and 1950s. It included discussion of pertinent issues, reporting of relevant news, descriptions of organic methods, reports of society events, opinion pieces and letters. Although *The Organic Gardener and Farmer* included more illustrations and light-hearted anecdotes it too, like its predecessors, had proselytising intentions. In the 1990s organic farming and gardening magazines that were commercial enterprises rather than society publications began to be published. Examples include *Organic Gardening,* for home gardeners and small landholders and *Acres Australia* aimed at commercial organic farmers. Like their predecessors, these magazines profiled organic growers, provided detailed discussion of organic methods and debated current issues in organic farming and gardening.[19]

While the organic societies' magazines and newsletters tended to be indicative of organisational preoccupations, publications by individual organic growers have provided alternative and at times dissenting interpretations of organic growing. A very small number of publications by Australian organic growers existed in the 1950s and 1960s but from the early 1970s the number of published books by individual organic growers increased.[20] These books, mostly aimed at the gardener, described organic methods and educated readers about organic gardening techniques and their adaptations to particular environments.

Other important sources of post-1970s organic growers' writings are the magazines *Earth Garden* and *Grass Roots.* These two magazines were unaffiliated with organic farming and gardening societies. They were produced by and for Back to the Landers, a subgroup among organic growers, people who were creating self-sufficient lives in rural Australia. Unlike the organic societies' publications, these magazines were not dedicated solely to organic farming and gardening issues.

As well as information about organic beliefs and practices, these magazines included other self-sufficiency material such as alternative energy production and alternative building materials. *Grass Roots* and *Earth Garden* were more experiential and included less commentary on public affairs and policy. Unlike the organic society publications, these magazines were often playful and humorous and were infused with wide-eyed youthful discovery and optimism. They were also more inward-looking, pursuing personal transformation rather than public improvement.[21]

There are few government or official sources relating to organic farming and gardening prior to the 1980s. For much of the history of organic farming and gardening in Australia, growers were articulating ideas which were out of step with government policy. Many members of the organic societies were middle-class professionals and they tried to engage bureaucratic interest in their ideas but organic farming and gardening was almost completely ignored by state and federal Departments of Agriculture until the 1980s. One notable exception to this is the Victorian Royal Commission on the Bread Industry in 1949 to which members of the Victorian Compost Society gave evidence.[22] From the late 1980s Australian state and federal governments became more involved in organic production. In the 1990s Australian standards regulating the commercial production of organic food were published. These standards reveal the beliefs and philosophies which underpin organic farming today and have informed my understanding of themes in Australian organic growing in the last 20 years.

My second major source of insights into the beliefs and practices of Australian organic growers are interviews with farmers and gardeners. I interviewed organic farmers and gardeners who were significant or representative figures of the last 70 years of Australian organic growing. I also spoke to current organic farmers and gardeners from around Australia who practised different types of organic production in various environments. Like the magazines and books written by organic growers, interviews provide direct insight into the beliefs, experiences and interpretations of the subjects of investigation themselves – the organic farmers and gardeners – rather than external commentary on these subjects. Again, like the magazines, interviews provide valuable source material for ideas and activities which are not officially recognised or documented.[23] However, unlike the magazines and books, interviews can provide insight into the ideas and activities of people who do not have the inclination to write or contribute to a public newsletter. This was the case with many of the current organic farmers interviewed for this study. These farmers were selected to represent diverse production types and geographic environments rather than for being particularly prominent or outspoken.

All of the growers interviewed for this study relished the opportunity to speak about organic beliefs and practices. For them, farming or gardening organically was not just work but a commitment. The interview was part of the process of the organic grower 'making and remaking'[24] individual and collective organic beliefs. In informing me (and through me, others) the interviewees were reinforcing collective ideas and identities; the interview itself being part of the meaning-making.[25]

As a source for this history, interviews with organic farmers and gardeners provided rich, in-depth insights into organic growers' beliefs, experiences and perceptions. Interviewees were wholeheartedly subjective informants rather than sources of facts about the history of organic farming and gardening. As many oral historians have noted, the subjectivity of the oral record is not a cause for concern or a bias to be avoided but is the strength and virtue of the interview.[26] The oral record is not only a dialogue between two historians – interviewer and interviewee[27] – but it is a many layered narrative influenced by individuals' subjective perception, time and subsequent experience and the circumstances of recollection; an interplay between interviewer, informant, past, present and memory.

This history of Australian organic farming and gardening is organised around the key ideas which define organic growing, gleaned through my interviews with and writings of Australian organic farmers and gardeners. I have identified four key principles, each founded on organic farmers' and gardeners' belief in the dependence of health on the biophysical environment. These four principles are: soil, chemical free growing, ecological wellbeing and back to the land. The emergence and establishment of each of these four principles in Australian organic farming and gardening is discussed in the four theme chapters. Following each thematic chapter is a case study profiling a particular Australian organic farmer or gardener.

The farmers and gardeners discussed in this history are all active examples of Australian organic practice. The case studies which follow each thematic chapter illustrate the key ideas discussed in the preceding chapters. Each profiles an organic farmer or gardener who, although they may not always be the most well-known or influential organic growers of the period, exemplifies the key principles of Australian organic growing and practically applies these principles to their specific local environment. These growers practise a variety of farming and gardening types including livestock, horticulture, broadacre cereal and gardening. They are located in a range of Australian environments including subtropical highlands, cool moist temperate, semiarid Mallee and inland temperate.[28] The three farmers represented in these case studies were, or are, all commercially successful organic farmers, for whom farming was their sole income, while the gardener described in the final case study is a non-commercial small landholder.

The first thematic chapter, 'Soil', explores the original key principle of organic growing: that human health depends on humus-rich fertile soil. Fertile soil, as the basis for nutritional food, was, organic growers believed, the most basic requirement for human health. This was the idea upon which Australia's first organic farming and gardening societies were founded. Australian organic growers' societies imported European organic ideas about human health and methods to increase soil humus, initially, with little questioning but then modified and adapted these methods to the particularities of the Australian environment. Harold White, the subject of the first case study, was one of the most prominent Australian organic farmers in the 1940s and 1950s and represents the application of organic beliefs to a large commercial broadacre grazing property. Like his fellow organic growers of the time, Harold White believed that increasing the organic content of the soil would not only be healthy for the plants and animals on his farm but also improve the health of those who consumed the farm's produce. Between 1910 and 1960 he developed a method for increasing soil humus which adapted British organic growing techniques to his northern New South Wales farm.

'Chemical free' is the second key principle of Australian organic growing, described in Chapter 2. This chapter describes the promotion of organic growing as 'natural' and healthy because it is 'chemical free' and the condemnation of agricultural chemicals as 'unnatural' and therefore unhealthy for all life forms including humans, plants and animals. Organic growers' opposition to chemicals began as a rejection of chemical fertilisers such as superphosphate, a fertiliser increasingly being used by non-organic farmers as a means of increasing soil fertility. This rejection of chemicals broadened in the 1950s to include pesticides, most particularly DDT, a position subsequently supported by Rachel Carson's revelations about its dangers in *Silent Spring* in the 1960s.[29] Confirmation of the hazards of agricultural pesticides inspired Australian organic growers in the 1970s to develop their own organic pest and disease remedies. Tasmanian dairy farmers Ray and Elma Mason, profiled in the second case study, practised chemical free organic growing and increased soil humus on their farm. Health crises among the cows and in Ray himself inspired the Masons to convert to organic and biodynamic farming methods in the early 1970s and they believed that their organic methods improved the health of all life on their farm.

The third principle of organic growing, 'ecological wellbeing', discussed in Chapter 3 was a broadening and deepening of the first two principles 'soil' and 'chemical free'. During the 1950s, Australian organic growers began to argue that organic growing was not just about improving human health by being chemical free and growing food in humus-rich fertile soil but that human health also required ensuring the health of the 'non-productive', 'natural' environment. The methods they advocated for increasing ecological wellbeing initially focused on preserving native flora and fauna on farms and by the 1970s encouraging ecological wellbeing had broadened to include conservation of native habitats beyond agricultural areas. Wheat and sheep farmer Anthony Sheldon, the subject of the third case study, illustrates the combination of the three principles of organic growing on his Mallee property. He has increased soil organic matter, farms without chemical fertilisers and pesticides and has improved the ecological wellbeing of the farm by increasing native flora and fauna habitat. Anthony Sheldon describes these methods, and his own conversion from conventional farming techniques, as being about increasing animal, plant, human and ecological health.

The fourth thematic chapter, 'Back to the Land', explores another important element in Australian organic growing: that human health depends on people living and working in close association with the natural environment. Back to the Landers argued that growing food organically for self-sufficiency was the way to achieve wellbeing and to rebel against the unhealthy influences of urban industrial society. The Back to the Land theme was an aberration in the history of Australian organic growing. Unlike the other three themes, which evolved in tandem and were advocated by organic farmers and gardeners associated with the Australian organic growers' societies, Back to the Land ideas arose from the counterculture and its advocates formed a parallel group within organic growing during the 1970s and 1980s. Back to the Land growers and members of the organic farming and gardening societies cooperated and influenced each other but remained separate and at times uneasy allies in the Australian organic growing movement. Jackie French, the fourth and final case study, exemplified the Back to the Land organic grower. She moved from the city to rural southern New South Wales where she grew food organically and lived self-sufficiently on what she could grow in her large garden. Jackie French's story of going Back to the Land then modifying her organic self-sufficient ideas during the 1990s and 2000s illustrates the evolution of Back to the Land ideas over 30 years.

The final chapter examines the integration of these four key elements into Australian organic farming and gardening in the 1990s and 2000s. It revisits each of the themes and explores whether the ideological basis for organic farming and gardening in the past remains relevant today. It examines whether these principles have been eroded by increased government regulation and industrialisation of organic growing, a question frequently raised among sociological researchers of current organic farming.[30] This chapter discusses the continued prominence of soil, chemical free and ecological wellbeing in Australian organic growing, reinforced by the certification standards for organic farming. However, Back to the Land, while still an important thread running through organic growing, has been further marginalised by certification standards. While the values of rebellion through self-sufficiency remain relevant today, the reality of going Back to the Land and growing food organically for self-sufficiency has changed.

By exploring the key principles of Australian organic growing and illustrating them with case studies I trace continuity and change in what it meant to be organic from the 1940s to the 2000s. The 1940s is the starting point for this history because at this time Australian farmers and gardeners first identified themselves as 'organic'; as people united by common beliefs and practices and an alternative to 'non-organic' growers.[31] The framework for this history is thematic rather than chronological and, in exploring each of the themes, there is overlap in the time period covered. Each theme does not obliterate previous themes; rather, as each new theme unfolds, a more complex picture emerges of what it means to be organic in Australia.

1

Soil

Dark, crumbly, moist, friable soil, bursting with organic matter, rich in nitrogen and other minerals, and crawling with microscopic soil creatures: humus-rich soil was the vision upon which Australia's first organic farming and gardening societies were founded in the mid-1940s. This chapter explores Australian organic growers' preoccupation with the dependence of human health on humus-rich fertile soil, the first key principle of Australian organic growing. The country's first organic societies were founded to promote methods for increasing soil organic content in farming and gardening as a way of improving human health. They were responding to a crisis of soil erosion and decline in soil fertility and were inspired by an increasing interest in the dependence of human health on soil fertility and the techniques for increasing soil organic content developed by British agricultural scientist Albert Howard. Initially, the organic societies promoted methods for increasing soil humus such as composting, manuring and sewage recycling, methods adopted from Britain and applied to Australian conditions without questioning their appropriateness. However, through the 1950s and into the 1960s Australian organic growers began to adapt and modify these imported methods to suit the particularities of their own local environment and soils, creating their own home-grown version of organic farming and gardening with soil humus as the central principle.[32]

The fermentation of organic beliefs

Most Australian native soils differ markedly from the fertile, humus-rich ideal described above and have inherently different characteristics from agricultural soils in the northern hemisphere. Native Australian soils are often described as infertile. Yet they are perfectly fertile for indigenous flora, which is adapted to Australian conditions,[33] although they lack many of the minerals essential for the cultivation of European crops. The most well-known mineral 'deficiency' of Australian soil is phosphorus, required by plants for production of new growth including flowers and fruits. With the exception of the Darling Downs in southern Queensland and adjacent parts of northern New South Wales, almost all native Australian soils have low levels of phosphorus.[34] Nitrogen, associated with organic matter, is also low. Other trace elements are present in different proportions in Australian soils, when compared with northern hemisphere soils. Most minerals, particularly copper and magnesium are at lower levels in sandy soils, so common in Australia. Copper and magnesium are required by plants to produce chlorophyll which they use to photosynthesise and convert sunlight into plant energy. Boron, essential for plant cell structure and division and hormone regulation, is deficient across the length of the Great Dividing Range from north Queensland to southern Victoria as well as Tasmania.[35]

Most native Australian soils are characteristically low in soil organic matter. Soil is composed of broken-down particles of rock and sand, clay, decayed plant and animal matter and microscopic soil fauna. Soil fauna and moisture help to decompose surface organic matter and create soil humus. However, naturally sparse vegetation means that surface organic matter is low while relatively dry conditions and inherently low levels of soil fauna mean that decay of organic matter is slow, soil creation is slow and there is a low level of humus in most Australian soils.[36] Soils dominated by clay or sand predominate in Australia. These soils have a very different tilth from loamy soils common in agricultural areas in other parts of the world, being too heavy or too light, respectively, for European cultivation techniques.

The agricultural techniques, brought to Australia with European occupation, exacerbated naturally low levels of soil organic matter and soil fertility. Settlers cleared native vegetation, ploughed, sowed and reaped European staples such as potatoes, wheat and vegetables. They introduced sheep and cows as well as rabbits and, in some areas, reconfigured the topography of the land. As historian Paul Carter describes, settlers glided over the surface of nature, neutralising its uniqueness rather than adapting to, and engaging with the particularities of the environments they encountered.[37] While on the surface of the land settlers were attempting to domesticate and Europeanise the environment, beneath the surface, in the soil itself, imported farming techniques further compounded the differences between Australian and European soils. Farming and gardening continually removed plants and animals (with their inherent components of minerals) from the land depleting the already meagre supply of soil nutrition and leaving less available for the next crop. Nitrogen, phosphorus and other minerals became severely depleted in intensively farmed areas.[38] Ploughing the soil accelerated the rate of decomposition of organic matter and soil researchers have estimated that after only 15 to 20 years of cultivation, Australian soils would have lost half of their stored organic matter.[39]

The top 15 to 20 centimetres of soil – the most fertile layer of soil and the layer upon which shallow rooted pastures and crops depend – is also the most vulnerable to erosion. Clearing the vegetation, the hard hooves of cows and sheep and the incessant burrowing and nibbling of rabbits broke the structure of the soil, leaving it exposed to wind and water. After 100 years of European occupation many agricultural areas were experiencing significant erosion as stock damaged river and creek banks and wind whipped up the dry, sandy, exposed and damaged soil. Just as in the United States' Midwest where erosion rendered formerly productive agricultural areas almost uninhabitable, during the inter-war years the Mallee district of Victoria and South Australia faced its own 'dust bowl'. Three severe droughts between 1937 and 1945 compounded the problem.[40] In the final years of the Second World War, the years the first Australian organic societies were established, vast quantities of soil in semiarid south-eastern Australia eroded. Without organic matter, the powdery degraded topsoil blew as far away as New Zealand and soil erosion became a national preoccupation for farmers, governments and agricultural scientists.[41]

While some Australian farmers sought solutions in the increased application of agricultural fertilisers (discussed in Chapter 2), British agricultural writer Albert Howard – whose books were available in Australia – offered an alternative solution. Sir Albert Howard was a botanist, agricultural scientist, farmer, writer and agricultural adviser to the British government in India in the inter-war years. With his botanist wife, Gabrielle, he was researching ways to increase food production for India's expanding population.[42] They were particularly interested in developing ways to maintain soil fertility and increase plant and animal disease resistance. Through their research in India, the Howards became convinced of the importance of humus for plant growth and its role in encouraging disease resistance. Their theory of disease resistance was reinforced by the medical doctor Robert McCarrison who conducted his own research into nutrition and degenerative diseases among the people of northern India. He concluded that human health and resistance to disease depended on the consumption of nutritious food.[43]

The ideas of both agriculturalist Howard and physician McCarrison were brought together by the launch of *The Medical Testament* in England in 1939. *The Medical Testament* was a call to action against malnutrition and disease prepared and signed by British medical doctors, agriculturalists and educationists. They argued that the way to prevent illness was to consume food grown in humus-rich soil:

> *Nutrition and the quality of food are the paramount factors in fitness. No health campaign can succeed unless the materials of which the bodies are built are sound... We conceive it to be our duty ... to point out that much, perhaps most, of this sickness is preventable and would be prevented by the right feeding of our people. ... [T]he better manuring of the home land so as to bring an ample succession of fresh food crops to the tables of our people, the arrest of the present exhaustion of the soil, and the restoration and permanent maintenance of its fertility concerns us very closely.*[44]

Albert Howard reiterated the same points a year later in *An Agricultural Testament*, in which he argued that health, whether plant, animal or human, was dependent on nutritious food grown in fertile soil and he detailed methods for achieving this on a large scale.[45] Howard demonstrated these points again, with even greater emphasis on human health, in his 1945 publication *Farming and Gardening for Health and Disease.*[46]

The Medical Testament and Howard's publications were part of a widespread renewed interest in the connections between human health and the biophysical environment – the ecological perspective on health.[47] Humans were seen as permeable to their surrounds and attaining health was about achieving rapport or balance with the environment. Ill health occurred when this balance was disturbed. 'Let food be your medicine and medicine your food', sums up the emphasis the Hippocratic philosophy placed on diet. Food was an important site of interaction between a person and their living conditions and was a crucial way of maintaining equilibrium between people and their environment. It was a crucial element in what medical historian Warwick Anderson describes as, 'the physiological flow between body and land'.[48] The importance of this interaction had been recognised in the nineteenth century by medical doctors who treated disease by adapting people to their environment or changing the environment to suit the people.[49] However, by the 1940s this approach to health and disease had become unfashionable among the mainstream of the medical profession, having been replaced by a biomedical or 'germ theory' model of health. The pendulum had swung the other way and belief in disease or malaise caused by imbalance with the environment had been replaced by belief in specific agents causing particular diseases in particular individuals. Increasing knowledge of infectious diseases such as cholera and typhoid had given people greater understanding of contagion and medical attention now focused on bacteria, viruses, parasites, poisons and other pathogens as the causes of specific diseases in individuals. While germ theory held sway, there was also resistance to its hegemony. Tony McMichael describes the 1940s as a time in which people began to react against the over-zealous application of germ theory at the expense of a holistic or ecological approach.[50] There was growing awareness that germ theory told only part of the story and that factors such as diet also played an important role in disease, as seen by the launch of *The Medical Testament* in Britain.

The founding of the Australian organic societies

Resurgence of popular interest in the importance of the environment to human health; the specific solutions offered by Albert Howard and *The Medical Testament;* the inherent challenges of Australian soils and the crisis of erosion and declining soil fertility combined to provide the catalysts for the founding of Australia's first organic farming and gardening societies. The Australian Organic Farming and Gardening Society of New South Wales established in 1944, the Victorian Compost Society founded in 1945 and the Living Soil Association of Tasmania established in 1946 were among the first organisations in the world dedicated to organic farming and gardening.[51]

All three societies comprised both farmers and gardeners, but the Victorian and Tasmanian societies directed most attention to home gardeners and small farmers while the New South Wales society made graziers their area of special interest. Biodynamic farmers were loosely affiliated with and occasionally contributed to the New South Wales and Victorian Societies. A small, separate and largely closed biodynamic society was established by Alex Podolinsky in Victoria in 1953.[52] The covers of the Victorian and New South Wales magazines illustrate the societies' different orientations. *Farm and Garden Digest* in 1950 depicts an iconic Australian pastoral scene (Colour Plate 2). By contrast, the masthead of the *Victorian Compost News* in the same year shows a small farm in gently rolling agricultural land and a suburban home garden (Figure 1). After only two years of operation, the Victorian Compost Society (the only society to publish membership numbers) had over 450 financial members, increasing to 600 by the early 1950s. For every financial member there would most likely also have been a 'submerged network' of unaffiliated supporters[53] as is suggested by 800 requests for information to the Victorian Compost Society following an article about composting in the Melbourne *Herald* in 1958.[54] These members lived not only in metropolitan and rural Victoria but in all states of Australia.

These early organic growing societies drew membership from the middle-class social establishment. Metropolitan membership of the Victorian Compost Society clustered in the wealthier eastern suburbs of Melbourne and included doctors, high ranking military officers, a 'sir' and a 'lady' and rural members included many well-off landholders.[55] The president of the Living Soil Association of Tasmania, Henry Shoobridge, was a member of a landowning Tasmanian pioneer family. Members of the societies deliberately canvassed the support of official organisations, hoping to influence government policy as well as individual farmers and gardeners. Initially they received some official endorsement and the first edition of the *Organic Farming Digest,* the journal of the Australian Organic Farming and Gardening Society, was supported by the New South Wales Premier W.J. McKell and the journal cited its postal address as 'care of' the Primary Producers Union. Similarly the Living Soil Association of Tasmania was allied to the Tasmanian Farmers' Federation, Education Department of Tasmania, State Fruit Board, Hobart City Council and the Royal Agricultural Society. However, official endorsement of the Australian organic societies was short-lived as organic ideas about human health and wellbeing and its dependence on the soil differed markedly from mainstream models of health and disease.

Soil as the key to health

Members of the Victorian Compost Society, the Australian Organic Farming and Gardening Society and the Living Soil Association of Tasmania were all inspired by the ideas about soil and health advocated by Albert Howard. The Victorian Compost Society was formed by Victorian farmers and gardeners who were so impressed by the writings of Albert Howard that they called a public meeting to discuss his work at which the Society was born.[56] In the early editions of their newsletters, all three societies frequently quoted the writings of Albert Howard and *The Medical Testament* and Howard was patron of both the Victorian and New South Wales societies, until his death in 1947.[57] Australian organic farmers and gardeners believed that Howard provided a solution to what they perceived as a crisis of human malnourishment and disease. Writings in the early Australian organic newsletters echoed his views, reiterating that disease was caused by poor nutrition. At a talk to the Victorian Compost Society in 1947, the speaker, dietician Dr Hearman, claimed it caused 85 per cent of human disease.[58] Specific diseases such as arthritis, stomach ulcers, heart disease, cancer, high blood pressure, kidney and gallstones, vascular and respiration diseases (to name but a few) were attributed by organic growers to poor nutrition.[59] Some articulated, in *Organic Farming Digest*, a more extreme view that 'there is only one major disease and that is malnutrition'.[60] Organic farmers and gardeners were disgruntled about the dominance of a biomedical contagion approach to health. While most did not reject biomedical theories, they argued that they were limited by ignoring environmental factors, particularly diet and food-growing techniques. 'Our uncritical acceptance of the germ theory – that superstitious excuse for all physical ills – has had far reaching effects upon our whole philosophy of life. Us and our day to day habits are not to blame but the germs', organic growers complained in *Farm and Garden Digest* in 1951.[61]

These early Australian organic growers, again echoing Howard and *The Medical Testament,* argued that the means to attain good nutrition was growing food in humus-rich fertile soil. Healthy soil, they argued was a dynamic living system comprising minerals, bacteria, fungi and organic matter all working together. They believed that human health was not only enhanced by but was derived from healthy soils. 'A sick soil produces crops and livestock lacking in nutritional values and this lack is directly reflected in the rising statistics of disease and the ever increasing demand for hospital beds', writes the *Organic Farming Digest*.[62] Reiterating these ideas, the Victorian Compost Society published a pamphlet called *Healthy Soil is the Key to Good Health*.[63] The objectives of these societies emphasised the connection between humus-rich soil and human health. The Tasmanian group's objectives elaborate on this connection:

> *It is only when properly prepared humus is available in the soil that plants can be truly healthy, and can have that full nutritive value, by which they are able to pass on this health to animals. It is only when prepared from healthy plants and healthy animals, that our own food can have true nutritive value, which enable us to enjoy robust health, so that we can resist disease.*[64]

The methods that Australian organic farmers and gardeners used to work towards human health reflected their belief in humus-rich soil as the key to health.

Organic methods – the Rule of Return

Although the destruction of Australian soils in the inter-war and war years was achieved largely by imported agricultural techniques, the solutions adopted by the first Australian organic growers were also imported. These methods were intended to make Australia's organic-poor, so-called infertile, dry soils more reminiscent of temperate northern European humus-rich soils. They adopted Albert Howard's techniques as the best and favoured organic practices and transferred them to Australian conditions, initially with little questioning. The basis of these methods was 'the Rule of Return'. This was the theory that all organic wastes, such as plant matter and animal manure must be returned to the soil to decay and replenish soil humus. In the 1880s research in the biological content of soil had revealed the importance of symbiotic soil fungi (or mycorrhiza) to plant growth and soil bacteria's significant role in converting nitrogen in the air to soil nitrogen in a form useful to plants. Soil was, they claimed, a living biological system rather than inert matter.[65] Versions of the Rule of Return had been part of traditional agricultural practices worldwide.[66] Howard, in his work in India, observed it practised with success by Indian peasants in traditional farming methods and he incorporated it into his own system of agriculture, describing it in detail in his publications. [67]

Returning organic matter to the soil to decay and replace lost fertility was given the authority of a 'Rule' by these early Australian organic growers. It was promoted as one of the fundamentals of life: everything of plant and animal origin that was once alive must be 'returned' to the soil to decay. Organic growers believed that it

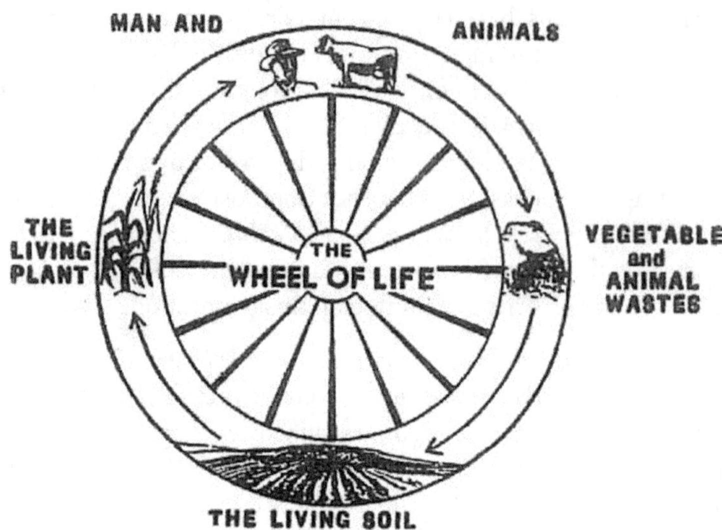

Figure 2: The Wheel of Life depicted in a Victorian Compost Society publication in 1951 illustrates the link between decaying plant and animal wastes, 'living' soil, plants, humans and animals.

(Source: Victorian Compost Society, *The Compost Heap: The Principles and Practice of Making Compost by the 'Indore' Method as Originated by the Late Sir Alfred Howard.* Melbourne: Victorian Compost Society, 1951, p. 17)

was neglect of this Rule that had resulted in erosion and loss of fertility in Australian soils.[68] The Rule of Return was a 'virtuous' cycle[69] – virtuous in that it sustained life as well as being a morally uplifting practice; health was a moral as well as a physical state. Practising the Rule of Return was the key to life:

> *The most amazing results that have been obtained, by obeying this law of return ... are found in the improvement of human health. Where the food has been supplied from grains, vegetables, and fruit, milk, eggs and meat produced in obedience to this cycle, the general health, energy and power of resisting disease has been built up to an amazing extent.*[70]

Early Australian organic growers illustrated the dependence of humans on cycles of growth and decay through the Rule of Return by the image of the Wheel of Life (Figure 2). The Wheel of Life first appeared in Australian organic literature in *The Compost Heap,* a pamphlet produced by the Victorian Compost Society in 1951.[71] The insignia had been adopted from Albert Howard who had, in turn, adapted it from the Mandala of Life which appears in Tibetan Buddhist imagery in many different forms.[72] The wheel illustrates the continuous cycle of birth, life and death, although the elements of the cycle chosen by organic growers are different to those depicted in the Buddhist mandala. The organic growers' wheel of life depicted decaying organic wastes nourishing the soil, upon which grow plants, which feed humans and animals whose wastes and decaying matter, in turn, nourish the soil.

Compost

For the first years after the establishment of the Australian organic societies, composting was the key method which Australian organic growers used to undertake Howard's Rule of Return. As the society's name suggests, the promotion of compost was the primary reason the Victorian Compost Society was founded. The compost bin takes pride of place in the foreground of the *Victorian Compost News'* masthead (Figure 1). Compost was an old term derived from Middle English and Old French words for mixture or compound, and prior to Albert Howard's research and for many non-organic farmers and gardeners, compost referred to a decaying pile of organic matter, as much waste disposal as fertility enhancement.[73] However, Howard had created a means of composting which systematically and deliberately created humus as a fertiliser which he named 'the Indore Process' after the north Indian town in which it was developed. Indore composting techniques combined Indian and Chinese traditional methods with British agricultural science, creating a systematic, scientific process from ancient farming and gardening practices.

Indore was the specific composting method advocated by the Australian organic societies. Following Howard's prescription they mixed diverse plant materials with other organic matter such as animal manure, sawdust and waste paper and arranged it in a moist layered heap, leaving it uncovered and regularly turning it to ensure mixing and oxidation. Australian organic growers also practised an adaptation of the Indore process made by Lady Eve Balfour, British farmer, agricultural scientist and founder of Britain's first organic society The Soil Association. Balfour's version incorporated air vents and more animal dung into the heap.[74] The Victorian and Tasmanian societies (the organic groups more oriented to the home gardener and small commercial farmer) were particularly strong promoters of Indore composting, presenting public lectures on compost making and publishing 'how to' educational pamphlets for the general public (Figure 3).[75] The Old Colonists' Home, an elderly people's home in North Fitzroy, Melbourne, became a showpiece and demonstration site for the Victorian Compost Society's Indore composting methods. The superintendent Richard Weller built 12 brick and timber compost bins in which he composted biodegradable waste from the homes and used the compost to fertilise the institution's extensive flower gardens (Figure 4).[76]

Members of the Victorian Compost Society considered themselves experts on the connection of compost-raised plants and animals to human health. Melbourne doctor Isabella Younger Ross, one of the founding members of the Society, exemplified early organic belief in compost-raised food as the key to health. Dr Younger Ross was an expert on maternal and child health and one of the creators of the Victorian Baby Health Centre networks.[77] Her expertise in health and nutrition led her, like the signatories of *The Medical Testament,* to advocate

18 THE COMPOST HEAP

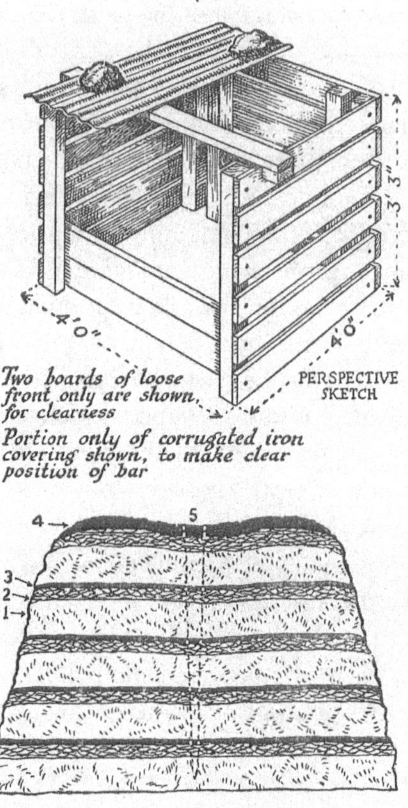

1. Layer of plant waste (straw, weeds, etc., etc.) 6-8 in.
2. Layer of animal manure—2 in.
3. Sprinkling of soil plus limestone or wood ash.
4. Final layer of soil—2 in.
5. Ventilating hole made by driving in a crowbar or building the heap round a stake and subsequently removing it.

Figure 3: Diagrams illustrating the Indore composting method from the Victorian Compost Society's publication *The Compost Heap* in 1951.

(Source: Victorian Compost Society, *The Compost Heap: The Principles and Practice of Making Compost by the 'Indore' Method as Originated by the Late Sir Alfred Howard.* Melbourne: Victorian Compost Society, 1951, p. 18)

growing food in humus-rich soil. In 1949, Younger Ross gave testimony on behalf of the Victorian Compost Society to the Victorian Royal Commission on the Bread Industry in which she explains to a confused enquirer, Mr Pape, the connection between health, humus and compost:

Mr Pape: *You are a doctor of medicine, are you?*

Younger Ross: *I am, yes.*

Mr Pape: *Are you practising?*

Younger Ross: *I am practising in South Yarra.*

Mr Pape: *Forgive my ignorance, but what precisely is this Society whose views you have put to the Commission?*

Figure 4: Victorian Compost Society member, Richard Weller, creating large compost heaps at the Old Colonists' Home in Melbourne in the 1950s.

(Source: The Organic Farming and Gardening Society (Aust.), *Good Earth*, 26, no. 3, 1973, p. 39)

Younger Ross: *It is the Compost Society.*

Mr Pape: *Would you mind spelling it?*

Younger Ross: C-O-M-P-O-S-T.

Mr Pape: *I would have thought it was a thing in the backyard where one puts the leaves?*

Younger Ross: … *We use it in the ordinary way.*

At this point the Commissioner intervenes to clarify the situation: *What Mr Pape wants to know is what is compost?*

Younger Ross: *Surely to goodness, you do not want that explained at this stage?*

Mr Pape: *I really want to find out precisely what are the objects of this society?*

Younger Ross: *Health.*

Mr Pape: *That is a broad generalisation.*

Younger Ross: *I can tell you all about compost.*

The Commissioner again intervenes: *It is a process of returning to the soil organic waste which forms the compost. There are various ways of treating it. It is used as manure for the soil.*

Mr Pape: *I thought so, and I could not appreciate how it came into this inquiry.*

The Commissioner: *This organic waste of the soil is said by devotees of the system to greatly enrich the soil and make the product of the soil much better and more nutritive than anything that can done by artificial manures. There is a grave controversy on that.*

Mr Pape: *By and large, the real object is to improve the quality of the wheat?*

Younger Ross: *Yes.*

Mr Pape: *And secondly to improve the quality of the bread?*

Younger Ross: *Yes.*[78]

For Isabella Younger Ross the connection between decayed plant matter and human health was palpable and her exasperation with Mr Pape's confusion reveals how obvious and profound she feels this connection to be. This interaction illustrates a polite but fundamental discord between Younger Ross's ecological perspective on health and Mr Pape's more conventional views.

More light-heartedly, the organic newsletters were also a forum in which members exchanged hints and anecdotes about composting. J.S. Lennie writing in the *Victorian Compost News* in 1951 described the day he and his wife consigned his many-times-darned army socks to the compost heap:

> *... with great solemnity we laid the socks to rest in the very centre of my next heap. That was an extra specially well-made heap, and when I opened it later on, everything – even the rose prunings – had rotted away nicely, that is, everything except the Army socks. My wife wanted to wash and darn them again and replace them in my drawer, but I was firm and I interred them in my next heap. They've been in six other heaps since then, and only now are they showing signs of wear. When they finally decompose, the vitality they put into the compost is going to be something worth watching.*[79]

Stories such as these were designed to demonstrate the positive life-giving quality of compost which played such a central role in early Australian organic growers' belief in soil humus as the key to human health.

Animal manure

Incorporating animal manure into the soil was another key method of practising the Rule of Return. As animal manure is plant matter partially fermented in the animal's gut, it is ideal organic matter for increasing soil fertility. Manure from cows, sheep, horses and poultry was an important ingredient of Indore compost as a source of nitrogen and organic matter. Like compost, animal manure was an ancient fertiliser, still used by non-organic farmers and gardeners,[80] although it had become less fashionable and in conventional farms and gardens was being replaced by artificial fertilisers which were praised by non-organic growers for being cleaner and easier to handle than manure.[81] However, organic farmers and gardeners were still avid promoters of manure as fertiliser. In 1947 Violet Hancocks, an active member of the New South Wales society, published an ode extolling the health and life-giving properties of manure which illustrates the reverence with which manure, as a source of soil fertility, was held:

Tribute to Dung

Songs of Beauty I have sung
In my callow days.
Now I chant of lowly dung,
Raising words of praise.
Do not draw your nostrils tight,
Pull aloof your dress.
In that muck is prospect bright
For our world of stress.
Mixed with garbage from your dump,
Dung will serve you well.
It will leaven all the lump:
Leave no sordid smell.
Nourish Nature with good muck,
Then fine food you'll gain.
Body, brain and sinews buck,
Banish ache and pain.
Dust to man a warning brings,
Sudden, swift yet clear.
When the earth has taken wings,
You'll grow yours I fear.
Werribee has shown the way,
Lush with pastures green:
Cattle sleek and children gay:
Men with open mien.
Compost, then with honest dung
Furnish Nature's need.
Bells of Peace have truly rung,
When these truths we heed.[82]

Violet Hancocks' poem draws a direct link between soil and human health. It illustrates the connections made between the use of manure as fertiliser and production of nutritious organic-grown food, banishment of sickness, protection from erosion and even societal peace and harmony. This poem again illustrates the authority given to the Rule of Return and the importance placed on the connection between human wellbeing and the soil.

Humanure[83]

Human manure provided the third method for practising the Rule of Return for early Australian organic farmers and gardeners. Utilisation of human sewage was enthusiastically adopted by Australian organic gardeners and farmers who argued that the Rule of Return should apply to human waste as assiduously as animal waste. Although always coy and tasteful, referring to sewage as 'household waste', 'manure' or 'nightsoil', organic farmers and gardeners did not shy away from discussing human excrement as a fertiliser and the Victorian Compost Society, particularly, were staunch advocates of the composting of sewage as part of the Indore process. Inspiration for the reuse of human manure as fertiliser, again, came from Albert Howard for whom the composting of sewage and biodegradable household garbage had been a pet project and under whose influence sewage composting was practised on a large scale in South Africa.[84] Organic gardeners also cite Chinese–Australian market gardeners as inspiration for reusing sewage to enhance fertility.[85] The Chinese were major commercial producers of fruit and vegetables in Australian regional towns prior to the Second World War and they regularly used human sewage to fertilise crops.[86]

In the matter of sewage reuse, organic groups turned their sights away from individual gardeners and farmers and focused on lobbying municipal councils to systematically compost the euphemistically named 'nightsoil'. An entire issue of the *Victorian Compost News* in 1954 was devoted to municipal composting of sewage[87] and members of the Victorian Compost Society lectured about the importance of composting sewage to replenish fertility, at municipal councils in Victoria including Mornington, Hawthorn, Richmond, Brighton and Mildura.[88] Chelsea and Mornington City Councils in Victoria, Canterbury City Council in Sydney and Fremantle City Council in Western Australia all trialled pilot programs for recycling municipal waste assisted by information from the organic societies.[89] In the Victorian society's only foray into direct political action, they supported Alex Finlay in his successful campaign for election to the Melbourne City Council, promoting the composting of town waste.[90] Superintendent Richard Weller of the Old Colonists' Home demonstrated the composting of dehydrated sewage sludge supplied by Melbourne's sewage treatment plant at Werribee.[91] Werribee Sewage Treatment Plant, west of Melbourne was the city's main sewage processing area and the plant had an associated farm fertilised with recycled sewage. This farm was revered by organic growers as an exemplar of the potential for human sewage. Organic farmers such as New England grazier Harold White (the subject of the first case study) travelled to Werribee to view the methods used on the farm and Violet Hancocks was inspired to serenade it in her 'Tribute to Dung'.

Despite organic growers' enthusiasm for human manure, in matters of human excrement, organic growers were people out of step with their times. The use of sewage for crop fertilisation brought the mainstream germ theory and the organic ecological viewpoint into conflict and organic growers' promotion of sewage recycling, albeit composted sewage, was an anathema to ideas of contagion and avoidance of pathogens. It was the indiscriminate disposal of sewage near the Broad Street Pump in London in the nineteenth century that had inspired John Snow's now famous observation that human excrement contained a contagious pathogen which caused cholera.[92] By the late nineteenth century the connection between sewage and transmission of cholera, typhoid and other bacterial infections was generally accepted among health professionals. With greater emphasis on contagion came a preoccupation with public sanitation and domestic hygiene and health reformers attempted to educate the public about the dangers of sewage.[93] Health workers and doctors successfully campaigned for the cessation of nightsoil dumping in Melbourne's Yarra and against the irrigation of the grounds of the Alfred Hospital in Melbourne with sewage.[94] During the inter-war and post-war years the focus of hygiene campaigns shifted to the home and Australian households were inculcated with ideas of 'sanitary sensitiveness' and awareness of personal, domestic hygiene and disposal of wastes.[95] People were discouraged from disposing of nightsoil on gardens and farms and the popular mainstream gardening books ceased recommending the incorporation of 'waste water, slops and liquid manure', including the contents of chamber pots, into the garden in the 1920s.[96]

Authorities remained sceptical about the desirability of recycling sewage, despite the persistence of organic growers' arguments. Experimentations with sewage in compost at the Old Colonists' Home in North Fitzroy were conducted under the close supervision of the State Department of Health.[97] Organic growers' campaigns for the reuse of sewage continued to be met with suspicion. Fremantle City Council ceased its brief experimentation with municipal waste recycling in the early 1950s and in Victoria, the use of sewage as soil fertiliser was illegal by the beginning of the 1960s.[98] So strong was public antipathy to the use of human excrement as fertiliser that in its annual reports of 1957 the Victorian Compost Society admitted defeat on this issue and acknowledged its failure to interest municipalities and the general public in sewage reuse.[99] Humanure was an issue where organic growers' ecological perspective on health and promotion of soil humus as the key to health clashed directly with mainstream biomedical germ theories. Concern about sanitation and popular fear of contagion, encouraged by the prevalence of the biomedical theories of health, meant the organic perspective was firmly sidelined from official endorsement.

Adapting to Australia

Although compost, manure and human sewage remained the primary ways for early Australian organic growers to increase soil humus, some organic farmers and gardeners of the 1950s were beginning to question if they were the best and only ways to practise the Rule of Return and increase soil humus. As they applied these methods to their own farms and gardens, many realised that specific environmental conditions required specific responses which did not always mirror imported organic techniques such as Indore composting and the use of animal manure. Panton Hill farmer Eric Butler emphasised: 'The application of these principles must, I believe, be modified to suit Australian conditions', when speaking to the Victorian Compost Society in November 1951.[100] Although the first organic societies were established in Australia's three most temperate states, New South Wales, Victoria and Tasmania, moist, organic-rich soils were not a reality for many Australian farmers and gardeners. Organic growers began writing to the *Victorian Compost News*, *Organic Farming Digest* and *Farm and Garden Digest* protesting that organic methods developed in Britain and India were not always appropriate to Australian conditions. 'It is because we are dealing with such a variety of soils and climates that it is impossible to lay down hard and fast rules', writes a contributor to *Victorian Compost News* in the late 1940s, 'each individual farmer to a great extent being an explorer'.[101]

The Indore composting method came from a 'one size fits all' approach that insisted that Indore composting was possible and beneficial for all environments. However, this process had been developed in India and used extensively in Malaya and parts of South America and other countries where labour was cheap, the climate was wet and organic matter was plentiful.[102] The sheer diversity of environmental soil and climatic conditions in Australia challenged the practicality of Indore composting. The dry Australian climate and slow rates of decay made composting for large grazing properties unfeasible. Australia's mild winters meant that farmers did not over-winter cattle and sheep in barns as did many British, northern European and North American farmers. Therefore, Australian farmers did not have access to large supplies of manure in spring for Indore composting. As mechanised transport overtook horse drawn vehicles, and as cities expanded, urban gardeners also had less access to a ready supply of manure.[103]

Australian organic farmers and gardeners began adapting methods of practising the Rule of Return such as composting to their own idiosyncratic natural environments. By the mid-1950s many organic growers were experimenting with methods of composting and manuring more suitable to Australian farming conditions. In Roma, in central Queensland, L.R. Petrie, farming sheep, wheat and cattle, writes of the imperative of thoroughly covering compost heaps to prevent evaporation of moisture in the hot Queensland sun.[104] At Whittlesea in Victoria, farmers practised large-scale composting methods using tractor powered mechanised compost turners.[105] Australian organic gardeners also experimented with plants such as yarrow, stinging nettles, valerian, camomile and dandelions as compost 'accelerators', which (although they did not always acknowledge it) were techniques borrowed from biodynamic approaches.[106]

Broadacre organic farmers – farmers of sheep, beef and cereals – of the inland and the semiarid interior were particularly active in adapting organic production methods to Australian conditions. The incompatibility of British organic methods to Australian conditions was magnified in these environments and, although these broadacre organic farmers still strove for the ideal of humus-rich, fertile soil, they modified their organic techniques to suit their local conditions. The New South Wales society was dominated by graziers and the society took a particular interest in organic methods for the broadacre farmer. The Victorian Compost Society, although located in Melbourne, also had members in the dry interior, for example in Alice Springs and Katherine in the Northern Territory and in western Queensland.[107] These graziers, broadacre farmers and residents of the arid inland played an active role in developing methods for increasing organic content of soil without relying solely on Howard's methods by adding organic matter directly to the soil rather than through compost and manure.

One of the most influential organic farmers to develop organic techniques for broadacre Australian conditions was New England grazier Harold White, the subject of the first case study. Another example, was the Butcher family, farming a 24 000-acre sheep station in Western Australia who developed organic techniques suitable for their hard-pan clay soil and low rainfall. They broke the surface of the soil with a tractor to maximise water penetration and ploughed in weeds to increase organic matter.[108] Other broadacre organic farmers grew nutrient-rich crops such as legumes (the pea and bean family) specifically to be ploughed into the soil and allowed weeds to grow spontaneously then slashed them prior to seeding, leaving them on the surface of the soil as mulch.[109] Others used waste vegetative matter (such as cereal stalks) as mulch on the surface of the soil.[110] Many Australian growers also found that, unlike the seasonal deluge of compostable leaves that northern hemisphere deciduous trees provided, the ubiquitous sparsely foliaged eucalypts produced a gentle drift of leaves which decayed slowly due to their high oil content. Some recommended using eucalypt leaves as mulch on the soil surface to reduce evaporation and cool the soil, rather than as compost.[111]

Another Australian broadacre farmer who developed ways of increasing soil organic matter which were not based on British or European techniques was Percival Alfred ('P.A.') Yeomans. Yeomans' 'Keyline' system was specifically designed to retain moisture in Australia's dry soil, to accelerate pasture growth and increase organic matter and soil fertility. Some Keyline advocates claimed that the system could create an inch of fertile topsoil in two or three years, a feat that would take 500 to 5000 years to achieve naturally. Yeomans' Keyline design also aimed to retain water on the farm by slowing its flow and redistributing it according to the contours of the hills through dams and plough lines. Annual chisel ploughing during pasture establishment then aerated the moist soil and allowed water to penetrate without destroying the soil structure. These techniques combined with nutrient-rich grasses and intermittent grazing encouraged growth of thick pasture which, after ploughing, rapidly built up soil organic matter creating dark, humus-rich soil with plentiful soil life.[112]

An integral part of Yeomans' techniques was his redevelopment of the plough. In 1952, P.A. Yeomans and his son Allan began manufacturing an Australian version of the American chisel plough. The chisel plough, unlike the mouldboard plough traditionally used by Australian farmers, bored into rather than bulldozed through the soil and did not invert or disturb its structure. P.A. and Allan Yeomans modified and improved the design of the chisel plough to work better in heavy Australian soils. An attached vibrator broke up clayey compacted soil which reduced machinery wear and allowed smaller, lighter vehicles to plough, thereby reducing soil compaction.[113]

Although Yeomans did not identify himself as an organic farmer, his Keyline system was admired and adopted by Australian organic growers as a method of soil creation and improvement and water retention. Yeomans' *Keyline Plan,* published in 1954 was sold through Soil and Health Publications, the sales arm of the Victorian Compost Society and was written about extensively in the *Victorian Compost News.* Chisel ploughing became a core organic practice during the 1950s and Keyline continued to be discussed intermittently by the Victorian magazine for the next 30 years.[114] British organic advocate Lady Eve Balfour visited Yeomans' properties on her tour of Australia in 1958–1959 and later claimed Yeomans was making the single biggest contribution to sustainable agriculture in Australia.[115]

In the first two decades following the founding of Australia's first organic farming and gardening societies in the 1940s, soil humus became established as the first principle of organic growing. Good human health, organic growers claimed, depended on food grown in humus-rich soil and organic farmers and gardeners adopted and adapted methods for achieving this. Motivated by erosion and loss of soil fertility, a belief in an ecological model of health and inspired by the British agriculturalist Albert Howard's methods, increasing and maintaining soil organic matter by practising the Rule of Return became the primary aim of Australian organic farming and gardening. Growers initially adopted methods of increasing soil humus such as composting, manuring and using human sewage as developed by Albert Howard and his associates. However, faced with the idiosyncrasies of the Australian environment these growers adapted the Rule of Return to suit their own farms and gardens. The importance of soil humus to human health was firmly established as the first defining principle of Australian organic growing. One of the most vocal exponents of the importance of soil humus was New South Wales grazier Colonel Harold White. White's lifetime farming work was dedicated to the development of his organic beliefs and agricultural methods and he is the subject of the first case study.

Case Study 1: Harold White

The White family grazing property, Bald Blair, lies on one of the highest parts of the New England plateau in northern New South Wales. The nearest town, Guyra is on the watershed of the Great Dividing Range over 1300 metres above sea level and 160 kilometres inland (Figure 5). When I visited the farm in late autumn the grass was scorched fawn by frost. The temperature the previous night was –6° Celsius and at

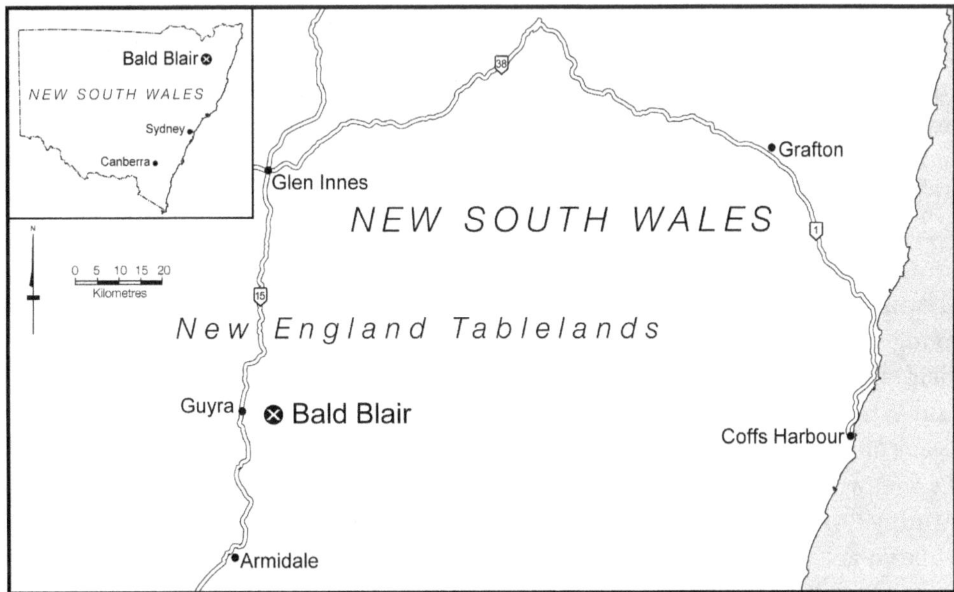

Figure 5: Map showing the location of Bald Blair.

(Source: Arts Imaging Unit, School of Geography and Environmental Science, Monash University)

dawn a crisp white frost clothed the ground. Looking across the property from the Bald Blair homestead, the land is gently undulating with wide hills, low ground crossed by small creeks and distant stony rises (see Colour plate 3).

Trees cluster around the homestead, fence lines and windbreaks leaving the paddocks open. Tips of distant forested ranges are visible in the east. Deciduous trees have already lost their leaves. Winters arrive early and are long and cold with frequent frost and occasional snow on this high plateau. Summers are warm and moist although drought is frequent. Rainfall is over 800 mm annually[116] with spring and summer being the wettest seasons, as the plateau catches the warm subtropical rainfall. The soil is deep and heavy and overlays hard basalt and ironstone.

Grazier Harold White, who farmed Bald Blair from 1911 until his death in 1971, is remembered by his family as a man of strong convictions and forthright views who was direct and unwavering in pursuit of his beliefs about soil and health. 'He had very pale blue eyes and you'd stand up when he came into the room. His eyes would not leave your face and they would not blink. So it was a battle of the wits. We talked cattle and pastures and if he didn't believe in what you were talking about he'd just not talk to you', recalls Elizabeth White of her father-in-law.[117] At Bald Blair, Harold White applied his convictions about the importance of soil humus to plant, animal and human health. Like the organic growers discussed in the previous chapter, he perceived a crisis of soil and pasture quality on his farm and connected this to problems in human health. He selected British and European methods for undertaking the Rule of Return which he gradually adapted to this large commercial grazing property and the particular New England environment of Bald Blair. He was a practical and influential example of an organic grower whose beliefs about the connection of human health to the environment shaped his organic farming practice. Through his work at Bald Blair and his writings about this work he became one of the giants of Australian organic farming in the 1940s and 1950s – a broadacre farmer who created a distinct form of Australian organic farming.

Conversations with the White family and Harold's own publication have informed this case study. Son Graham, who worked closely beside his father from a young age, and two daughters-in-law, Elizabeth and Mary each discussed with me their memories of Harold and his farming methods. Bald Blair's current owner, Sam White, grandson of Harold, showed me around the property, explaining the legacy of his grandfather's methods on the farm today.[118] Harold White's *Life from the Soil,* written in 1953, was the first Australian book describing organic farming.[119] In it White documented his practical methods of organic agriculture while co-author Stanton Hicks, Professor of Human Physiology and Pharmacology at the University of Adelaide and nutritional adviser to the Australian military during the Second World War, provided the biological and theoretical explanations for these methods.[120] Later in the 1950s, White published two more booklets: *After*

Figure 6: The cover of White's booklet *After 50 Years* published in 1959 depicting the author standing in a lush pasture of phalaris and white clover.

(Source: H.F. White. *After 50 Years: Human Life and the Food Chain.* Guyra: H.F. White, 1959)

50 Years (Figure 6) and *The Why and Wherefore of Cultivation,* and made numerous contributions to the organic newsletters *Farm and Garden Digest, Organic Farming Digest* and *Victorian Compost News.*[121]

Harold White developed his organic methods over 60 years. He and his wife Evelyn, recently married, settled at Bald Blair in 1911 (Figure 7). The New England plateau had been occupied by European farmers since the 1830s, and by the 1910s the Bald Blair pastures had already fed generations of cattle and sheep and the deep soil and native vegetation had been transformed by the hungry hard-hoofed interlopers. Unlike native marsupials, which nibble the grass and leave the seed

Figure 7: Harold and Evelyn White in about 1961.

(Source: Graham and Mary White)

heads standing, cattle and sheep ate the seed heads as well as the leaves, damaging plants and 'trampling the soil into a dust heap', limiting the grasses' ability to reseed.[122] In drier years, sheep also pulled at the roots, destroying the plants.[123] Cattle and sheep favoured some grass species over others, and by the time Harold and Evelyn settled at Bald Blair native pastures were limited to those species of tufted and rhizomous plants that can withstand heavy grazing through having tissue below ground. Trampling hooves and chewing mouths disturbed the soil and also increased the amount of light reaching it, allowing weeds and annual grasses to germinate and dominate.[124] Harold White noted that the perennial native grass species which remained were the 'tough old red grasses' – rough and dry species that stock found unpalatable: tussocky poa, spear grass, red leg, and wild sorghum.[125] These grasses grew rapidly with spring and early summer rains, crowding out other more nutritious species. When the weather was hot they ceased growing but remained standing rather than falling to the ground to decay.[126]

Bald Blair was a 'veterinarian's paradise'. Low soil fertility and vegetation lacking in nutrition left sheep and cattle vulnerable to parasites. 'Breeding sheep was not viable in New England as the sheep were malnourished. I was never happy tending stock on the natural pastures. It all seemed so futile and aimless, trying to control something which was never very good', wrote White.[127]

At the same time as the sheep, cattle and pasture of Bald Blair were ailing, Harold was grappling with his own health problems. He was diagnosed with a mystery ailment that his son Graham was to later describe as 'something like diabetes'.[128] The symptoms are now unclear as Harold did not readily speak of personal issues, but he and a friend suffering from the same condition turned to a naturopath in Toowomba, Queensland, who pointed to diet as the cause of the problem. The White family attribute this event to the beginning of his interest in human nutrition. On the naturopath's advice, Harold altered his diet and, apparently, cured the condition.[129]

The First World War took Harold White away from Bald Blair and Australia to fight in Belgium and France as an officer of the AIF.[130] While Harold was in Europe, Evelyn gave birth to their first child, a boy, who was sickly and died shortly after birth. Harold White did not speak of this event[131] and it is not known if Harold associated the child's failure to thrive with poor nutrition, but it is possible that this event further confirmed his belief in the importance of nutrition to human health.

During active service, and a lengthy convalescence in Britain in 1917, White observed European agricultural environments, which were very different from northern New South Wales and southern Queensland where he had previously travelled. Comments he made in his later writings indicate that he observed the European landscape with a grazier's eye and was very impressed by British methods: 'those wonderful pastures in England. How carefully they were tended.'[132] In Belgium he observed the use of dairy manure as fertiliser and also noted the apparent infertility of unimproved pastures on the eastern escarpment of the Salisbury Plain in southern England.[133]

When he returned to Australia in 1919, now a colonel, he brought back to Bald Blair his medals[134] and a greater understanding of, and interest in, European pastures. His observations while in Europe had rekindled an interest in exotic pastures and he returned home with an increased conviction that animal health could be improved by changing the pasture vegetation and increasing soil fertility. Establishing exotic pastures was his first step in addressing the nutritive problems of his cattle and sheep at Bald Blair and he turned to the Mediterranean pasture grass *Phalaris tuberosa*.[135] This action was the beginning of the development of White's organic farming techniques. Prior to the First World War, his father Francis John had sown experimental plots of *Phalaris tuberosa* (then called Toowoomba Canary Grass), importing seeds from New Zealand.[136] After his

Figure 8: The exotic pasture pictured here at Bald Blair in 1935 was a mixture of phalaris and lucerne.

(Source: H.F. White and C.S. Hicks. *Life from the Soil.* Melbourne: Longmans, 1953, after p. 64)

return from Europe, Harold cut roots of this grass and planted them in rows at Bald Blair. He also acquired phalaris from the Toowoomba botanical gardens:

> *The gardener there was throwing away this 'rubbish' as he called it: big tusks of grass that he couldn't handle. They bundled up a few bags full. It was phalaris and they put it in the orchard at Bald Blair where it survived, then ultimately went out to the paddocks.*[137]

It is possible that the Whites were the first to introduce phalaris, now a common pasture grass, to the New England area. The grass spread and Harold noticed the stock relished it (Figure 8).

In the 1920s the White family sold over 13 000 hectares of land in New England for closer settlement, including part of the Bald Blair property, which allowed Harold to concentrate on improving the remaining 2000 hectares of the farm. After he had drained low-lying swampy ground, he concentrated on the establishment of exotic pasture grasses, or 'pasture improvement' as it was known. Bald Blair, unlike more arid areas, could support exotic pasture plants that were lush, nutritive, grew rapidly and produced masses of organic matter. A mix of *Phalaris tuberosa* and white clover and other herbs, formed the basis of his pasture.[138] Clover, like other legumes (such as peas and beans) when grown in the presence of particular soil bacteria, has the ability to bring nitrogen from the air into the plant roots. If these plants are allowed to decay in the soil the nitrogen is returned to the soil rather than the air and is available for use by subsequent plants.[139] Phalaris is deep-rooted and can survive New England's frosty winters, hot summers and droughts.

Harold White had, in the 1920s or 1930s, been introduced to the artificial fertiliser superphosphate. Agricultural scientists and other graziers were at the time heavily promoting this manufactured phosphorous fertiliser as necessary to provide nutrients for the establishment and growth of non-native grasses.[140] White sowed pasture seed with superphosphate and then 'top dressed' the pasture every four years. 'The initial results were most spectacular; you could track the super cart by the better and greener growth.'[141] However, after a few years, he began to notice that the superphosphate ceased to further improve his pasture growth. 'I was nonplussed and blamed the seasons and stepped up the applications.'[142] Increasing the quantity of super had no effect on the quality of his pastures and the application of other chemical fertilisers, such as sulphate of ammonia containing nitrogen, gave an initial growth spurt but no sustained pasture growth or higher nutrient content of the pasture. The missing factor in his pasture improvement, Harold was to reflect, was the humus content of the soil.

> *And so I came to the realisation of the neglected factor in our soil use, the organic matter of the soil; the thing that had been the basis of the husbandry of our forebears, and then neglected for the apparently easier and more spectacular early results of artificial fertilisers.*

He explains this revelation:

> *... decomposing organic matter is fundamental to soil use; it is the starting point of all living matter, as well as the end result of all living matter.*[143]

Although he continued to use superphosphate when sowing exotic grasses, he rejected its ongoing use on established pastures.

During the Second World War White, now in his fifties, remained at Bald Blair farming and experimenting with methods for increasing soil humus and collecting and reading every book he could find on the subject. By this time, his interest in animal health had concentrated his interest in human health:

> *My work originally was concerned with animal husbandry, merging with agriculture and improved pasture. However, one cannot study animal functions without merging into the function of the human being.*[144]

In 1944, he was among a group of farmers and gardeners who founded the Organic Farming and Gardening Society in New South Wales. In the opening edition of the society's newsletter, White wrote an explanation for organic growing based on Albert Howard's ideas:

> *We see increasing ill health in the community, not necessarily sickness, but physical and mental disability, leading to social disorders and unrest. In the animal and vegetable world the incidence of disease and pests is an ever growing burden, our land is being laid waste by loss of soil fertility, followed by erosion and leading eventually to sterility. The medical profession, veterinary and agricultural authorities have made spectacular strides in curing disease and destroying pests but that does not prevent them. There is ample evidence from all over the world to support the statement of that great agricultural research worker, Sir Albert Howard, 'that the health of plant, animal and man is based on a fertile soil; and a fertile soil is one rich in organic matter'.*[145]

White also joined the Victorian Compost Society and the British Soil Association and became a copious contributor to both the New South Wales and Victorian societies' newsletters during the 1940s and 1950s.

To further develop his organic methods, White again turned to British agricultural techniques for inspiration. He read *The Medical Testament* and the work of British organic farmer Lady Eve Balfour, whom he was to quote liberally in later writings. He became friendly with Eve Balfour who, with her companion Kathleen Carnley, stayed at Bald Blair when touring Australia and New Zealand. Graham White, who was then in his late teens, recalls their long and interesting conversations about organic farming techniques. 'She was a stately old lady but she'd get down on her hands and knees and scratch around in the soil', he remarked.[146] Two other British agriculturalists who had a profound influence on Harold White's organic farming methods were Englishman George Stapleton and Scot Robert Elliot who both successfully raised agricultural production in Britain during the Second World War using ley farming techniques of rotating grass and legumes with crops.[147]

Harold White's own organic methods, developed at Bald Blair, were influenced by British ley farming methods. They centred on 'the plough down' which increased soil organic matter by periodically ploughing the thick, nutrient-rich exotic pastures into the soil. Ploughing the pasture at approximately 10-year intervals aerated the soil and encouraged the roots and dense grassy mass to decompose, improving the heavy soil structure, retaining moisture, adding fertility and breaking pest cycles.

The manure from the sheep and cattle that had been grazing the pasture sped up the decay of the grassy organic matter. Once established, Harold was careful to protect both pasture and soil. He restricted the number of cattle and sheep on his property to maximise production but minimise damage to the pasture and soil and

Figure 9: A photograph taken at Bald Blair in the 1940s compares exotic pasture in the background in which a horse is almost obscured, with sparser native pasture in the foreground.

(Source: H.F. White and C.S. Hicks. *Life from the Soil.* Melbourne: Longmans, 1953, after p. 64)

allow some reserve pasture to be available for bad seasons when the weather was too dry, too cold or too wet for good grass growth.[148]

In the years following the 'plough down', pastures at Bald Blair were impressive. 'You could always see where the boundary fence was, I can tell you that now. It was quite incredible', recalled daughter-in-law Elizabeth.[149] Photos taken at Bald Blair in the late 1940s show a comparison between the exotic pasture in the background where the horse is almost buried in phalaris and sparse 'unimproved' native pasture in the foreground (Figure 9). The quality of the pastures at Bald Blair were well recognised with the property winning the New England champion in the Royal Agricultural Society pasture and fodder competition in 1954. By 1953, 75 per cent of pasture at Bald Blair was being farmed using the organic ley farming techniques.[150]

The plough used by Harold White was the traditional mouldboard plough. He set it in such a way so that it partially inverted the grass, allowing the leaf matter to decay but regrowth to occur from the grass roots. White was aware of P.A. Yeomans' chisel plough methods and admired them but felt disc and chisel ploughs were not appropriate for his heavy soil and thick pasture. The chisel plough brought the subsoil to the surface to dry out while the heavy soil pulled the disc plough to pieces.[151]

Harold White was as meticulous about nutrition for his family as he was about his pasture. His four children were given daily supplements of lucerne pills and ground bonemeal with their porridge. He believed that bonemeal, coming from animals' skeletons, was the perfect food containing calcium and phosphorus and other necessary nutrients, but it was remembered by his son as 'a bit hard to digest in the morning'.[152] Influenced by other members of the organic societies, the Whites grew a large vegetable garden fertilised with Indore compost. Evelyn and a paid gardener tended the one-acre vegetable patch but composting was Harold's preserve and his son Graham recalls numerous bales of compost scattered around the garden.[153] From this garden they fed the family and workers and at times supplied the Guyra hospital with vegetables. White was interested in the use of composted sewage as fertiliser and three times he visited the Melbourne Metropolitan Board of Works sewage processing farm at Werribee to observe its fertilising practices.[154]

Harold White's commitment to organic farming and gardening was not only about improving his property and his own and his family's health; White also believed organic farming was about creating a better nation. Grazier, large landholder, military officer, Member of Parliament, councillor and executive member of many community organisations, Harold White was part of 'the directing class' who comprised a form of aristocracy in New South Wales at the time.[155] White believed that the ruling classes must take the lead to ensure national health. He appealed to other graziers to heed their civic responsibility to the nation to improve the nutritive content of food: 'We appeal, to all land users and point out that they hold the health of the community in their hands.'[156] In an article titled 'Whither civilization' in the *Organic Farming Digest*, he states that preventing erosion and loss of soil fertility and recognising the importance of nutrition and the way food is grown is necessary to advance civilisation.[157]

Improving human health was, according to White, about achieving national productivity and stability. He was deeply concerned about securing farm productivity through increased soil fertility, not only for the prosperity of individual landholders but also to ensure a strong society.[158] White writes cryptically, '... if we are to hold this country we must make it produce much more, while at the same time preserving its fertility and increasing it.'[159] Written in the 1950s in the aftermath of the Second World War, it is possible that 'holding this country' refers to foreign invasion. However, it is more likely, in the context of his other writings, that the force Harold feared was internal social unrest.[160] Poor population nutrition and unproductive farming would, he believed, lead to social instability.[161] He was a member of the Old Guard Movement, an organisation comprised of the elite of the AIF, graziers and Sydney financial powerbrokers formed in 1930.[162] Its aim was to assist the civil authorities in the event of popular unrest, defending key strategic points such as bridges, transport centres and telephone exchanges. The organisation was motivated by a fear of Bolshevik revolution, civil unrest as a result of widespread unemployment and the economic depression and a distrust of the Lang New South Wales State Labor Government. The Old Guard was officially disbanded in 1932, although historian Andrew Moore speculates that it may have continued into the 1950s.[163] Harold White was also a member and vice president of the New States Movement, a group formed with the goal of creating new states within the Australian federation. The New England New States Movement was active in agitating for a separate state for northern New South Wales.[164] Harold White's involvement with the Old Guard and the New States Movement reinforces that his organic beliefs reflected his concern about national stability and security and his belief in his own – and other graziers' – responsibility to ensure population stability.

Harold White's story is a tale of the transformation of a property by organic methods, over 60 years, to become a healthy environment in which soil and in turn plants, animals and people were vigorous and strong. Through his work at Bald Blair and his publications, Harold White was an important member of the Australian organic farming community in the 1940s and 1950s. Like his colleagues in the Australian organic farming and gardening societies, the organic methods White developed at Bald Blair changed the structure and composition of the soil by adapting European farming techniques to the specific Australian environment. Again, this was not driven by nostalgia for the homeland but by a firm belief in the importance of the soil environment to human health. His organic methods reflected the belief that human health could be enhanced or compromised by the soil in which food was grown and that organically grown food, food grown in soil rich with organic matter, would convey health and combat disease. His doubts about artificial fertilisers such as superphosphate, which he articulated in his descriptions of his organic methods were a foretaste of the preoccupation with 'chemical free' growing which, as we shall see in the next chapter, Australian organic growers adopted in the 1950s and 1960s.

2

Chemical free

In 1952 an organic farmer wrote to the organic newsletter *Farm and Garden Digest* lamenting the corruption of healthy food by agricultural chemicals.

> *Dear Sir, – How is this for something really artificial. I refer to our Queen of Fruits, the Pineapple, which once was truly a choice fruit and could cure sore throats and always be a sure cure for stubborn coughs. The artificial practice is: four doses of '10-6-10'*[165] *per year and one or two applications of sulphate of ammonia to help along as well, until the whole area is choked up with fertiliser.*
>
> *In the meantime, the land has probably been given a dressing of sulphur and the pineapple plants within the first years have received through the leaves a spraying of sulphate of iron and possibly some ammonia dissolved in the spray. Now the plant is persuaded to flower four to seven months prematurely by the addition of carbide dissolved in water and poured down its neck, or some hormone, which has the same desired effect. A regular spraying of Pent-a-chlorophenate,*[166] *which kills all small weeds and the residue on the surface prevents any further germination of seeds. Sometimes a fruit remains on the plant and is not even injured, but ferments and the juice bubbles out and after a while all that remains is skin and fibre.*
>
> *The consumer buys them in good faith, believing he has a wholesome article, sun-drenched and healthful food and yet it is so entirely artificial that it is of little value. – Sincerely yours, B.M.*[167]

This letter illustrates early opposition to the use of agricultural and horticultural chemicals by Australian organic growers. 'Chemical' was used as a shorthand term by organic growers to describe manufactured fertilisers, pesticides, herbicides and fungicides created in a laboratory; molecules that did not exist in a natural form except through human synthesis: 'the synthetic creations of man's inventive mind, brewed in his laboratories, and having no counterparts in nature'.[168] As synthesised substances, chemicals were an anathema to organic growers because they were seen as 'unnatural' and contradicted their belief that human health was derived from a 'natural' biophysical environment. It was fertilisers that were the first type of chemical to attract their attention. During the 1950s Australian organic growers' rejection of fertilisers broadened to include other types of chemicals. Aversion to the pesticide DDT launched organic societies' campaigns against chemical pesticides in the early 1950s, views which they felt were vindicated by the publication of Rachel Carson's *Silent Spring* in the 1960s. By the 1970s, Australian organic growers were energetic and vocal in opposing a wide range of pesticides and developing their own organic 'chemical free' pest controls. During the 1950s, 1960s and 1970s 'chemical free' became a catchcry of organic growing, sitting beside soil humus as the second of the key principles of Australian organic farming and gardening.[169]

Chemical fertilisers

During the first few years after the founding of the Australian organic farming and gardening societies, organic growers were preoccupied with promoting humus-rich fertile soil as the key to human health (as discussed in Chapter 1). However, by the late 1940s, organic growers were also becoming outspoken in their opposition to agricultural chemicals and this opposition began with a rejection of artificial fertilisers. In 1948, the editor of the *Victorian Compost News*, stated firmly:

> *The Victorian Compost Society stands 4-square in its advocacy of organic methods as a means of maintaining and increasing fertility of the soil. The principles of sound husbandry are the same whether applied to farms and gardens and the difficulties can be overcome without resorting to inorganic chemical fertilisers.*[170]

Chemical fertilisers had been available to Australian farmers and gardeners since the 1860s.[171] The theoretical basis for the development of artificial chemical fertilisers was formulated by German chemist Justus von Liebig. In the 1840s von Liebig argued that plants rely on elemental minerals in the soil for their nutrition.[172] These ideas led to the identification of nitrogen (N), phosphorus (P) and potassium (K) as important minerals for plant nutrition. They also led to the manufacture, in Britain, of the first artificial fertilisers (then called 'patent manures') containing the elements N, P and K. This was the beginning of a lucrative and influential artificial fertiliser industry.[173]

Manufactured fertilisers became a symbol of progress. They were described by gardening books as 'clean and easy to handle' compared to aromatic and cumbersome compost and animal manure.[174] Chemical fertilisers were promoted as an essential part of good farming practice. Fertiliser manufacturers such as the Melbourne Nitrogen Fertiliser Pty Ltd promoted Sulphate of Ammonia (a high nitrogen chemical fertiliser) as 'Public Friend Number One' (see Colour plate 5). Speaking on behalf of the 'Public Friend', the company claimed that farm and garden productivity depended on artificial fertilisers:

> *... just throw me around on the surface and I'll show you returns ... that you never thought possible before. You may prepare your ground in any way you like. You can add compost or animal manure of any kind, you can lime, you can dig and fallow ... but they are not enough, I am still required. I am the Key that unlocks the door to Success.*[175]

Promoters of chemical farming argued that growing food was now about supplying the right chemicals to feed the plant.

By the beginning of the 1950s, chemical fertilisers had become an integral part of conventional farming practice. Australian farmers used well over a million tons of artificial fertilisers on a quarter of a million acres of crop and pasture land in the 1950s. This amount was to increase steadily during the next 20 years.[176]

Phosphate fertilisers were the chemical fertiliser used most heavily by conventional Australian farmers in the 1940s and 1950s. Most Australian soils have a lower level of naturally occurring soil phosphorus than Europe and North America[177] and superphosphate, it was hoped, would rectify this 'deficiency'. Superphosphate is made by chemically treating phosphorus with sulphuric acid. Sulphuric acid was readily available in Australia as a by-product of industrial processes and during the 1950s a rich source of phosphorus was mined in Nauru and the Gilbert and Ellice Islands in the Pacific and from Christmas Island in the Indian Ocean.[178] These were sites where thousands of years accumulation of bird manure had formed a rock-like substance called guano. The product of treating guano with sulphuric acid is the chemical superphosphate – a form of phosphorus that is soluble, reactable and easily absorbable by plants.[179]

Chemical fertilisers, organic growers claimed, led to ill health in all life forms. As the use of chemical fertilisers by conventional growers increased, and as organic growers noted the heavy promotion of these chemicals by Departments of Agriculture, chemical manufacturers, seed merchants and the press,[180] organic farmers and gardeners became more strident in their opposition. The New South Wales society printed an article in the *Organic Farming Digest* in 1947 that argued that an increase in human disease in the first half of the twentieth century was associated with the use of chemical fertilisers and in a later edition claimed that it was able to demonstrate the nutritional superiority and therefore inherent healthiness of crops grown organically: 'organic farmers are demonstrating the superiority of plants cultivated by their means over those whose growth has been stimulated by chemical fertilisers'.[181] Tasmanian organic gardener, Leicester Jones lamented the level of ill health which he attributed to chemical farming:

> *I see suffering people everywhere. I see veterinary bills that were breaking farmers. I see crop failures, pastures that couldn't stand any stress at all. I see outbreaks of brucellosis; all because of chemical farming. Human health has been suffering since. We ... are sick because of it.*[182]

One of the strongest opponents of chemical fertilisers was organic gardener Peter Bennett. Peter Bennett was a South Australian ecologist, broadcaster and agricultural adviser. At the beginning of the 1970s he conducted a public lecture tour of Tasmania, advocating organic agricultural methods. He claimed that:

> *Artificial fertilisers, are poisoning our farms and gardens. Run by the chemical industry and cheered on by governments, it is just more of the same, more of the same, with farmers getting into more and more trouble; retained afterbirth, infertility, you name it, and of course the vets were having a ball.*[183]

Fellow organic grower Leicester Jones recalled the strength of Peter Bennett as a speaker, locking eyes with the audience and confidently accepting no opposition. 'It was like sending the artillery in before the infantry. He is a very powerful, challenging man.'[184] So strongly did Peter Bennett lampoon the chemical industry and so defensively did they respond that the Tasmanian tour became open warfare with each side attempting to discredit the other. Bennett recalls that outside one public hall a young organic potato farmer grabbed a man distributing anti-organic pamphlets and shook him by the collar.[185]

The source of Australian organic farmers' and gardeners' opposition to chemical fertilisers was that they were artificial and unnatural and were an anathema to the organic belief that human health was derived from the natural environment. 'Health is from the garden and farm, never from the chemist', cried the *Victorian Compost News*.[186] Organic growing was about creating a symbiotic relationship between plants, animals, humans, soil life, and soil humus: 'Artificial manures do not and *cannot* produce humus which is to the soil what healthy blood is to the human body.'[187] Organic growers juxtaposed organic methods as 'natural' against chemical farming as 'artificial' with relative worth assigned to each. An essential part of organic growers' opposition to chemicals, as explained by Henk Verhoog and his colleagues (Dutch researchers of European organic farming),[188] was the association of natural with life, alive (or once alive) and therefore healthy and life-giving compared to 'artificial' which was never alive, and therefore unhealthy or lifeless. Composted plant and animal materials 'are living substances. Inorganic chemicals are inert', claims the Organic Gardening and Farming Society of Tasmania.[189] As a writer to *Farm and Garden Digest* suggests, 'doctoring the soil with chemicals is an affront to nature'.[190]

According to organic growers, the 'unaliveness' and unnaturalness of artificial fertilisers disrupted the natural functioning of crucial life processes. Organic farmer Harold White advocated minimal and judicious use of superphosphate, claiming that the use of artificial fertilisers rendered the soil sterile and lifeless.[191] Chemical fertilisers 'throw spanners in the works of nature's machinery', writes Peter Bennett.[192] Organic growers condemned chemical fertilisers for damaging worms and other soil life and disrupting the decay and regrowth of plants.[193] In 1950, quoting a New York medical doctor, the *Farm and Garden Digest* claimed that artificial fertilisers chemically transformed plants which, in turn, had the potential to transform the functioning of the human body.[194]

Artificial fertilisers, based on the elements nitrogen, phosphorus and potassium were derided for reducing soil fertility to three agents rather than a complex relationship between plants, humans, animals and their environment, as depicted in the wheel of life. Organic growers condemned the use of chemical fertilisers as 'the NPK mentality'.[195] British organic pioneer Eve Balfour explained in *The Organic Gardener and Farmer* that composted plant materials 'have a far more complex and comprehensive formula than N, P and K'.[196]

The difference between 'the NPK mentality' and organic growing is explained by Henry Short:

> *... members who understand the holistic nature of organic husbandry are certain that nature will win the battle with the chemist in the end. Further scientific study may well mean that micro-biology and similar sciences will supersede chemistry as the most important science in agriculture.*[197]

British historian Philip Conford named these contrasting perspectives on agriculture 'The Great Humus Controversy'.[198] The chemists, working from Liebig's theoretical base, believed that minerals (particularly nitrogen, phosphorus and potassium) were the most important aspect of plant nutrition, while the biologists (organic farmers among them) drawing on agricultural biological research argued that soil organic matter was a crucial reservoir of nutrients and was additionally important as a promoter of bacteria and fungi necessary for plant growth. This controversy was, in essence, a philosophical battle between ecological and biomedical perspectives on health. Organic growers' ecological view was that health was achieved by working with biological processes such as decay and regrowth and preventing disease by assisting biological cycles between plant and animal waste, decay and growth, animal health and human health. By contrast, supplying individual elements through the addition of manufactured chemical fertilisers provided a 'quick fix' rather than systemic prevention. Artificial fertilisers were like a drug, supplying a response to a nutrient deficiency rather than creating a soil environment which would support healthy, nutrient-rich plants and animals.

Chemical pesticides

The second group of agricultural chemicals that came under the disapproving eye of Australian organic farmers and gardeners were chemical pesticides. The use of chemical pesticides, like chemical fertilisers, was contrary to organic growers' ecological view of health. They provided a remedy to destroy the pest on an individual plant or animal – reflecting again a biomedical rather than ecological approach to health. Again like chemical fertilisers, chemical pesticides were manufactured synthetic substances and their unnaturalness therefore was equated with unhealthiness.

Chemical pesticides had been available in Australia at least since the late nineteenth century.[199] They were promoted assiduously by non-organic gardening and horticultural manuals, usually without handling precautions. Many chemical pesticides commonly used in gardens and orchards prior to the Second World War were based on arsenic, the most common being lead arsenate, a compound of lead and arsenic. Promotion of chemical pesticides, like the promotion of chemical fertilisers, was linked to modern efficiency and growers who did not adopt a routine of chemical spraying were derided as old-fashioned, lazy or thoughtless: 'it is only the won't-be-convinced, non-thinking orchardist who will not put spraying into practice. This gives the energetic and progressive man an advantage.'[200]

Soon after the end of the Second World War the arsenic-based chemical pesticides were being replaced by a new generation of complex chemicals: the organochlorides, chemical compounds of carbon, hydrogen and chlorine. The most notorious member of this family of chemicals was DDT (dichlorodiphenyltrichloroethane).[201] DDT was first synthesised in 1874 in Germany but it was not until 1939 that its insecticidal properties were realised.[202] Two of its first applications as an insecticide were during the Second World War to eradicate mosquitoes in swampy land and to dust soldiers, refugees and prisoners to control lice. DDT was first used in Australia in 1945[203] and by 1949 was available for both gardeners and farmers.[204]

Organochlorides were used widely by Australian farmers during the 1950s to kill pests on both plants and animals.[205] DDT and its sister chemicals dieldrin and lindane were highly effective pesticides that were poisonous to insects both on contact and ingestion. They had broad toxicity to a wide range of insects and they were 'persistent', that is they did not break down easily and therefore remained poisonous for a long time. Organophosphate pesticides, compounds of carbon, hydrogen, phosphorus and oxygen such as malathion and parathion, were even more toxic to insects than organochlorides as they were absorbed by the plant's roots and leaves and spread around the plant. This meant that feeding insects were poisoned by the plant itself rather than the pesticides on the plant's surface. Tasmanian dairy farmer Ray Mason (who later became organic) recalls, like all farmers in his district, spraying organophosphates and organochlorides such as DDT on pastures in the 1950s:

> *DDT was marvellous. Magic. We were handling it with bare hands and all. Then when we learned about it, oh dear ... We didn't notice any bad effects. We had bare hands and no mask, sitting on an open tractor. We thought we were doing a good job, particularly when the grubs came out and died. It appeared to be a wonderful thing. But it wasn't, was it?* [206]

The application of DDT peaked in Australia in 1958–1959.[207]

DDT was the first pesticide to galvanise Australian organic growers' attention as public enemy number one.[208] Most people associate the beginning of the campaign against DDT with the publication of Rachel Carson's *Silent Spring* in 1962 but Australian organic growers were condemning DDT over 10 years before *Silent Spring*'s publication. Within three years of the chemical's release in Australia, organic societies launched a concerted and increasingly vocal campaign against DDT as the epitome of all that was wrong with chemical pesticides. In 1948, the Australian Organic Farming and Gardening Society of New South Wales reported the killing of beneficial insects such as parasitic wasps and ladybirds by DDT and remarked on DDT resistance developing in houseflies.[209] Later that year the Victorian Compost Society (reporting information from the British organic press) questioned the threat of DDT to human health.[210] The New South Wales society, in a cover article about pesticides in 1950, reiterated the dangers to human health of DDT consumption:

> *If fruit trees need to be drenched with poison sprays before they can produce a crop, what is the effect of such fruit on the health and wellbeing of the people who have to consume it?*[211]

This magazine also reported that in the United States, traces of DDT had been found in meat, milk and butter from cows dusted with the powder.[212] In the following year it reported that organochloride powder, used to kill flea beetle on turnips and kale and consumed by dairy cows, was subsequently traced in the cows' milk. 'Seen through clouds of DDT billowing down our crops is the depressing picture of more and bigger and better hospitals', the magazine trumpets.[213]

Organic growers also issued dire warnings about the health consequences of organochlorides and organophosphates for farmers working with the chemicals. A report in the *Victorian Compost News* in 1957 claimed that organophosphates had killed at least three farmers and hospitalised many others. They reported that pesticides were believed to have caused an array of acute health problems for farm workers such as giddiness, headaches, chest tightness, blurred vision, sweating, nausea, vomiting, abdominal cramps, convulsions and even coma. The *Victorian Compost News* added that danger to people continued even after the spray had evaporated.[214] Tasmanian organic gardener Leicester Jones recalls with outrage the ill health of Tasmanian orchardists, which he claimed was a result of working with pesticides: 'I saw men who lost their fertility, lost all the hair off their body, got squeaky voices and all out of those orchards.'[215] Organic gardeners were also concerned about the use of the organophosphate parathion and the organochloride chlorodane in households and gardens resulting, they feared, in the emergence of unspecified new diseases.[216]

The Australian Organic Farming and Gardening Society of New South Wales enshrined opposition to all chemical pesticides in its objectives. It stated that:

> *the Society ... condemns the use of poisonous sprays and dusts as such preparations injure the soil by killing its micro-organisms, also the earthworms, bees and birds that are in the vicinity.*[217]

The use of chemical pesticides was contrary to organic growers' ecological view of health. Organic growers considered pesticides, like chemical fertilisers, to be unnatural, their artificiality reinforced by unpronounceable names, such as *pentachlorophenate,* the herbicide used on the once healthy pineapple. Pesticides, herbicides and other agricultural chemicals provided a short-term remedy rather than a systematic method of prevention of pests and disease. By contrast, the organic methods of practising the Rule of Return attempted to prevent disease by creating healthy plants, animals and people.

While the main organic response to pests and diseases was to grow plants and raise animals on humus-rich soil, as described in Chapter 1, organic growers also promoted other systemic preventative measures to avoid pest and disease concentration. These solutions were based on the idea that nature as a whole was self-regulating and in a state of equilibrium or constantly evolving towards stable equilibrium. Individual organisms contributed to the overall balanced state of the environment.[218] Organic growers criticised insecticides for 'upsetting Nature's balance' by indiscriminately killing beneficial as well as harmful insects, destroying predator insects as well as the pests.[219] Organic methods for avoiding accumulation of pests and diseases promoted a diversity of species. This included rotating crops to avoid a build-up of diseases. An organic wheat farmer wrote to *Victorian Compost News* in 1961 about his method for alternating wheat with oats to prevent the accumulation of the fungal infections in his wheat.[220] Similarly a Queensland organic orchardist combined bananas, pineapples, citrus and dairy cows to minimise the chance of infection and Eric Butler of Panton Hill, Victoria encouraged a wide range of pasture plants including many species of grasses, clover, lucerne and chicory to maximise pasture diversity.[221]

The publication of *Silent Spring* vindicated Australian organic growers' opposition to chemical pesticides, solidified their concerns about the health effects of DDT and justified their 14-year campaigns against chemicals. Rachel Carson was an American ecologist, marine biologist and writer who, in the 1950s, had published the bestselling natural histories, *The Sea Around Us* and *The Edge of the Sea*.[222] She became interested in the effects on wildlife of persistent pesticides such as DDT while working for the United States Fish and Wildlife Service during the 1940s. In 1957 her interest in pesticides was again piqued both by a lawsuit attempting to prevent blanket aerial spraying of Long Island as well as a United States Department of Agriculture's program of fire ant eradication. The spray program caused widespread damage to wildlife, particularly birds, and the lawsuit conveniently accumulated a large amount of scientific literature documenting devastating environmental and health effects of organochlorides and organophosphates. Rachel Carson began synthesising and analysing the scientific research.[223] She confirmed that DDT as well as its decomposition products are poisonous and that, being fat soluble, they accumulated in the bodies of birds, animals and humans. They became concentrated through the food chain, with predators acquiring DDT from the fish, insects, birds, amphibians and even soil that they consumed. This stored DDT was thought to be a carcinogen and an endocrine disruptor, with effects on the reproduction of animals and humans.[224]

Silent Spring engaged public attention internationally and in Australia. The book was not only thoroughly researched, it was engagingly and accessibly written and remained on the *New York Times* bestseller list for 31 weeks.[225] Rachel Carson had taken discussion of DDT out of the scientific literature and brought it to the dinner tables of the general public. She became the subject of fierce condemnation by chemical manufacturers who launched a counterattack of personal vilification. However, this attack further strengthened support for the book.[226]

Despite the publication of *Silent Spring* and widespread public concern about pesticides, organochlorides and organophosphates continued to be recommended by mainstream gardening books throughout the 1960s and into the 1970s.[227] The 1965 edition of *Yates Garden Guide* promoted DDT and organophosphates as safe, effective pesticides and illustrates gardeners applying pesticide dusts without gloves or other protective clothes.[228] There were also official scientific publications which continued to dismiss health concerns associated with DDT, sometimes on spurious grounds. One example is the Australian Academy of Science report *The Use of DDT in Australia* which states that: 'as breast feeding is declining and in any event only continues for six months, no hazard from DDT was likely to result'.[229]

Rachel Carson herself argued against *indiscriminate* use of pesticides rather than a total ban on pesticides and was careful to distance herself from organic farming[230] but her arguments and evidence provided organic growers with valuable ammunition. The *Victorian Compost News* (the only one of the original Australian organic magazines still in operation in the 1960s) published reviews and discussions of *Silent Spring* and cited Carson's evidence for the harm associated with DDT.[231] Rachel Carson died in 1964 but the impact of *Silent Spring* continued to resonate among Australian organic growers throughout the 1960s and 1970s. Australian organic growers continued to fight against the use of chemical pesticides: 'So widespread has the use of these poisons become that even if you raised all your own food [organically] you would still find it difficult to avoid them', writes a member of the organic society.[232] By 1968 'food grown without the use of artificial or synthetic chemicals at any stage of production' had become an essential part of the definition of what it meant to be organic.[233] Organic farmers and gardeners wore their rejection of chemical pesticides as a badge of pride. Tasmanian organic gardener David Stephen recalls a local vegetable farmer selling lettuces crawling with slugs in Hobart: 'There is proof that I didn't use poison', the farmer gloated.[234] Displaying marked and damaged produce was a visible sign of his 'chemical free' status, although it did not present an appealing view to consumers.

The Victorian Compost Society's strong opposition to chemicals through the 1960s coincided with a rapid increase in membership.[235] By the mid-1970s new organic gardening and farming societies had formed in all Australian state capitals as well as many regional areas. The establishment of some of these groups can be directly attributed to opposition to agricultural chemicals. For example, Mr Friend and Dr Adams, founding members of the New South Wales organic group the Henry Doubleday Research Association, were motivated to set up the association by bad experiences they attributed to agricultural chemicals. Reading *Silent Spring* shocked Dr Adams into noticing the absence of small birds in Australia while entomologist Mr Friend believed that his own illness could be attributed to working with chemical sprays.[236] The first survey of Australian organic farmers conducted by Jeanette and Arthur Conacher in 1982 found that belief in the detrimental effects of agricultural chemicals was cited by farmers as a primary reason for conversion to organic methods (Figure 10).[237]

The new organic societies established in the 1970s made promoting chemical free farming and gardening a primary activity. The Brisbane Organic Growers Group collected and itemised pest remedies which they considered compatible with organic practice and published these as a guide for organic gardeners. *Pesticides and Alternatives. A Guide to Safer Pest Control for Gardeners and Householders* was first published in 1978.[238] This collection of organic pest control remedies was produced by growers in subtropical Queensland where fruit fly and other insect pests were particularly troublesome. Jeanette Conacher from the Organic Growers Association of Western Australia quickly followed with her own list of organic remedies, *Pests, Predators and Pesticides: Some Alternatives to*

Figure 10: This cartoon illustrates organic sentiment about pesticides in the 1970s as the spray-happy man metamorphoses into a giant mutant bug.

(Source: Conservation Council of Victoria, *Pumpkins, Poisons and People*. Melbourne: Conservation Council of Victoria, 1979, pp. 22–23)

Synthetic Pesticides in 1980.[239] Gardener Peter Bennett included a list of organically acceptable remedies in one of the first Australian organic gardening books, *Australia and New Zealand Organic Gardening* first published in 1979 and the Victorian organic society (renamed the Organic Farming and Gardening Society) published a short list of organic remedies in their magazine *Good Earth* in 1981.[240]

The base line for pest control remained growing plants and raising animals on humus-rich soil but the organic societies' inventories of pesticides also established a new organic practice that included pest control remedies. They organised remedies into a hierarchy based on their organic acceptability. The most acceptable pest control methods were barrier or deterrent interventions such as squashing and trapping, tree banding, netting and encouraging natural predators such as birds and beneficial insects. The second group of products were made from plant and animal material, such as pyrethrum made from the flowers of *Chrysanthemum* (or *Tanacetum*) *cinerariaefolium*; garlic spray; a solution made from rhubarb leaves; derris dust, derived from the roots of *Derris* and *Lonchocarus* plant species; and quassia chips, aromatic wood chips made from the bark and root of *Picrasma quassioides*. A small range of manufactured chemicals such as Bordeaux mixture (a solution of copper sulphate and lime) and Burgundy mixture (a solution of copper sulphate and sodium hydroxide) were tolerated but their use was discouraged.[241] Chemical pesticides such as organophosphates and organochlorides and arsenic sprays were firmly excluded from organic practice. However, there was some disagreement between organic growers about what substances were acceptable and what were not. For example Peter Bennett recommended lime sulphur as a suitable fungicide but Conacher condemned it for being a manufactured substance which killed too many beneficial insects.[242]

Organic growers' incorporation of pest remedies into their organic farming and gardening practice blurred the definition between 'natural' and 'chemical', 'healthy' and 'unhealthy'. For example rhubarb leaves, a natural plant product, can be highly toxic to humans and animals if ingested, and similarly derris dust, although not toxic to humans can kill beneficial insects such as ladybird larvae, lacewings and bees and can harm fish.[243] By contrast Bordeaux and Burgundy mixtures – artificial chemical compounds – are less toxic than both rhubarb and derris to plants, animals and humans, and they break down quickly with oxygen and light. What is natural is not always non-toxic and what is chemical is not always toxic.

By incorporating pest control remedies into their organic practice, organic farmers and gardeners were relying on cures rather than systematic prevention, an aspect of organic growing which was not completely consistent with the ecological view of health and more akin to the biomedical model which they strongly criticised. Substituting one unacceptable product for another acceptable one, as well as relying on disease prevention through an increase in soil organic matter and maintaining balance and diversity in the farm and garden, was to become in later decades an important but disputed aspect of Australian organic farming and gardening.[244]

The organic magazines show that throughout the 1950s, 1960s and 1970s, opposition to agricultural and horticultural chemical fertilisers and pesticides became a crucial aspect of Australian organic farming and gardening. 'Chemical free' now sat beside humus-rich soil as the second defining principle of Australian organic growing. Opposition to chemicals, like organic belief in the importance of humus-rich soil, concerned the dependence of human health on natural cycles of growth, decay and plant and animal resistance to disease rather than on manufactured chemical inputs. The key to health, organic growers claimed, was working with the natural environment to prevent disease rather than administering 'quick fixes' that were unnatural and therefore potentially harmful to life. The next case study will tell the story of Ray and Elma Mason, Tasmanian dairy farmers who converted to organic methods in the early 1970s. They embraced chemical free growing and organically acceptable remedies as well as humus-rich soil as a way of preventing animal diseases and improving their own health.

Case Study 2: Ray and Elma Mason

The emerald green country around the small town of Penguin on the northern Tasmanian coast is soft, lush and fertile. When the sun shines the country is warm and sparkling, although at other times the sky is heavy with grey clouds. Ray and

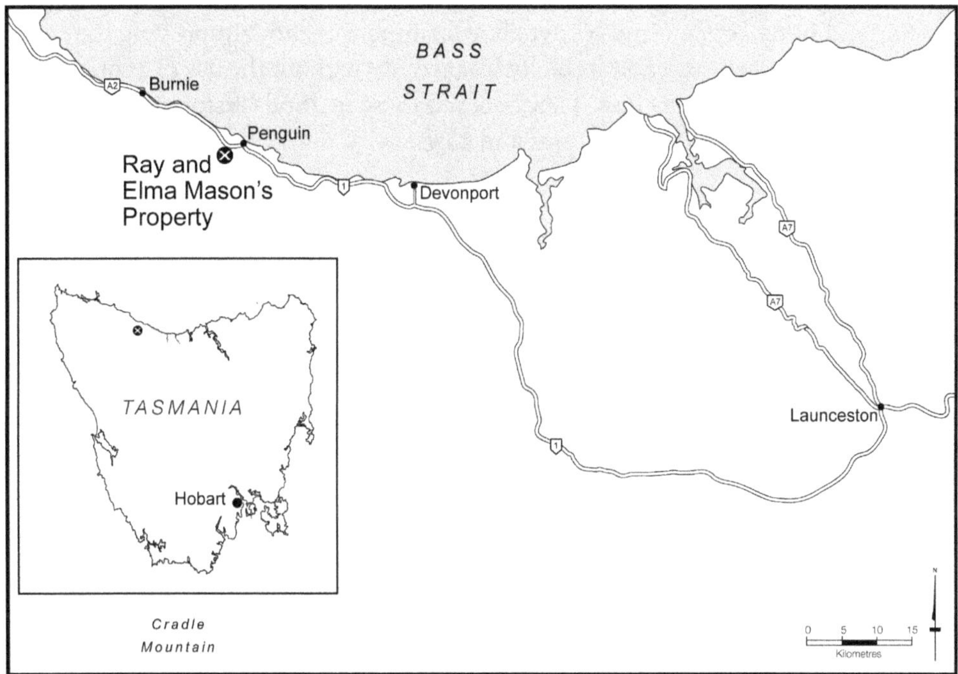

Figure 11: Map showing the location of the Masons' dairy farm.

(Source: Arts Imaging Unit, School of Geography and Environmental Science, Monash University)

Elma Mason, now in their late seventies, have retired from farming and live in Penguin, but for most of their married life they worked a dairy farm a few kilometres from town (Figure 11). The day I visited the Masons in June 2006 a cold blustery wind was blowing from Bass Strait to the north. The ocean moderates the temperature which is neither very hot in summer nor very cold in winter. Rainfall is high, being approximately 1000 mm annually and falls regularly throughout the year.[245] From their home in town overlooking the hills Ray and Elma told me the story of their conversion to organic methods of farming in the 1970s (Figure 12).

Ray and Elma purchased the Mason family farm when Ray's parents retired. In 1970, Ray and Elma, then in their mid-thirties, had 30 cows which was an average-sized herd for the time. Like most other dairy farmers in the district they sold milk to the Cadbury Chocolate factory near Hobart. They farmed conventionally, fertilised with sulphate of ammonia, muriate of potash and copious quantities of superphosphate and used pesticides and herbicides.

Two events occurred on the farm which alerted the Masons to the ill health of their cows and to Ray's own poor health. These events shocked Ray and Elma into deeply questioning the way food was produced by conventional farming practices and propelled them on a lifetime's journey through organic and biodynamic farming. Their conversion to organic and biodynamic methods involved adopting two defining themes of organic growing: soil fertility and chemical free growing. For Ray and Elma, organic and biodynamic farming was about improving the nutrient content of the soil and its biological activity without the use of artificial chemical fertilisers or pesticides. They believed these methods restored Ray's health and the health of their pastures and cows.

Conversion to organic farming

The two events which caused Ray and Elma to reassess conventional farming methods occurred in 1971. In that year things hit rock bottom for the Masons:

> *I [had] had it by 1971. Yeah, I was done. We had ten cows down in one afternoon; couldn't get up. That was a third of the herd crook in one afternoon.*
>
> The cows had magnesium deficiency, known as 'grass tetany'.
>
> *We knew then that there was something wrong, something wrong with the way we were farming. I know there were lots and lots of farmers in serious trouble with their cows because of the soil imbalance. Brucellosis was running pretty hot and we had manganese toxicity from over-liming of the pastures. A complete imbalance and the cows just couldn't live anymore. We*

Figure 12: Ray Mason in his garden in Penguin, Tasmania in 2006.

(Source: Rebecca Jones)

couldn't afford to buy superphosphate and our pastures were terrible, back to deep rooted weeds, dandelions, daisies, docks and plantain.[246]

Things were to get worse for Ray and Elma that year:

One day I went to get out of bed and it stabbed me there, my heart stopped. I lay back down and luckily my heart got going again but I was only thirty-

eight. I had three days in intensive care. We had sick cows, a big mortgage and I was crook. That was a lot of pressure.[247]

When Ray had recovered enough to return to work he decided he had to change both his farming practices and his diet. He attended a talk at the local hall in Penguin by South Australian organic adviser Peter Bennett. Ray heard Peter Bennett's views on organic methods for improving the balance and fertility of the soil and ways to dispense with chemical pesticides, herbicides and chemical fertilisers. Bennett spoke about the composition of the soils, challenging farmers to understand that if they balanced the minerals in their soils and increased organic matter in the soil then animal, plant and human health would follow. 'You must get the soil right because we are so dependent on the soil. If you get the soil right then everything else starts to fall into place', he claimed.[248] Peter Bennett was known by Tasmanian organic growers as 'the dolomite man'[249] as spreading dolomite was one of the methods he advocated for improving soils made acidic by artificial fertilisers. Dolomite is a naturally occurring rock mineral containing calcium carbonate and magnesium carbonate. It added calcium and magnesium to the soil which, Peter Bennett believed, was depleted by the use of artificial fertilisers, and were the minerals in which the Masons' cows had become dangerously depleted.

Peter Bennett came at just the right time for us. 'Nope, no more superphosphate, no more inoculations', he told us. He hit the nail on the head. We knew there was something wrong so we took up organic farming. We used the money we were saving for superphosphate to buy dolomite. We put dolomite all over the place and my word did that make a difference. That was the changing point. We had so much clover and growth. You could stand on top of the hill and you could just see the difference. Something happened. So pronounced.[250]

After the initial dolomite application Ray concentrated on improving soil and pasture without the use of artificial fertilisers. 'Artificial fertilisers were growing the plant but only on those three elements, nitrogen, phosphorus and potassium.'[251] He believed more comprehensive soil fertility could be achieved by improving the biological activity of the soil – 'the life of the soil' – and that artificial fertilisers, particularly superphosphate and fungicides had killed the soil life. He reasoned that soil fungi, bacteria and micro-organisms were essential to plant nutrition and disease prevention. 'If you can get the biological activity balanced, well they will gobble up the disease.'[252] Ray noticed that the incidence of mastitis halved and grass tetany did not return. Other common diseases of dairy cows, such as blackleg and pulpy kidney, also declined. Increasing soil life improved the nutritional quality of the pasture, which, in turn, improved the health of the cows. 'Organic farming was good for animal health', Ray concluded.[253]

After converting to organic practices, the Masons had their soil analysed each year for 25 years. Biological activity steadily increased and with it soil fertility. Initially phosphorus levels declined but then rose again without any addition of phosphorus fertiliser. Ray Mason explains:

> *... mycorrhiza is a phosphorus factory in its own right. It just produces phosphorus. I reckon that happened to us. The chemical companies had it all tied up with superphosphate: knock the life of the soil on the head then sell the phosphorus to you.*[254]

The Masons also ensured the pastures contained a variety of different plants so that many trace elements were present in the cows' diets.

> *We had comfrey planted around the dairy and at certain times, when they were calving and needed something, they would chomp it off. We let blackberry grow around the fence. It didn't look too good but it was for roughage and weaning the calves. When the calves are going off the milk they pick up the tummy worms. We had particular blackberry patches and we found that the calves would prune every leaf off. That stopped us from having to drench. We didn't drench and we didn't use poisons or sprays. We conquered that one too. The other way, where the farmer will spray every weed and leave only the grass is like us living on cream cake.*[255]

'A good organic lifestyle'

Ray and Elma believed that Ray's health, like the health of the cows, could be improved by diet. For the Masons this meant eating organic food.

> *It meant organic vegies, organic food, everything. We raised our own meat and vegies and dairy products. It was just a complete change of life. No cream cakes. We used to have a lot of cream cakes before that. We changed right around and battled on with a good organic lifestyle.*[256]

Ray didn't want to take the tablets the doctors prescribed, nor climb upon what he saw as 'the treadmill of surgery', so he consulted naturopath, organic gardener and active member of the recently founded Tasmanian Organic Gardening and Farming Society, Leicester Jones.[257] 'Take responsibility for what you put in your mouth', Leicester exhorted.[258] Leicester Jones believed that good health was not about remedies but was about people's relationship with plants, animals and the soil. Like the organic growers of the 1940s and 1950s discussed earlier, he believed that taking responsibility for one's own health extended to good stewardship of the land, particularly the soil. Leicester encouraged everyone to get a garden and grow food organically on humus-rich soil without the use of chemical fertilisers and pesticides.

Through Leicester Jones, Ray Mason became an active member of the Tasmanian Organic Gardening and Farming Society. Ray recalled:

> *The first organic meeting I went to, my wife didn't go. I came home and she had this big pot of superphosphate. I said, 'You have got to get rid of that super.' She jacked up a bit and said, 'Oh no, you can't grow peas without that.' (I thought he was mad, recalled Elma dryly). But those peas grown with super, well they didn't look too good. In the finish we got dolomite on them and the garden looked a lot better. My word, we had a wonderful vegie garden.*[259]

As a member of the Tasmanian Organic Gardening and Farming Society, Ray travelled around the state with ABC gardening broadcaster Peter Cundall, speaking about his organic farming techniques.

> *We [Ray and Peter] spoke about our successes; what we had done, how we had done it, what should be done. There was plenty to speak about. We would help them form their branch of the society then I'd travel home that night and milk cows next morning.*[260]

The atmosphere at the society's meetings was enthusiastic. One member recalled:

> *The enthusiasm boiled over and it just catches on. It was standing room only; they were hanging from the rafters.*[261]

By 1975 the Tasmanian society had 1000 members, both farmers and gardeners.

The highlight of the organic society's year was the annual festival. The first festival was in 1975 in Tomahawk in the state's north-east. Ray and Elma rented a caravan and travelled to the festival for a three-day weekend. They continued to attend these festivals each year for the next 31 years. An active member of the society recalled:

> *Fun! Oh wow! Quite a buzz. Lots of like-minded people, locked in groups talking enthusiastically, night and day, their voices booming out around camp fires.*[262]

When the festivals found a permanent home in Penguin, Ray helped to establish a demonstration vegetable garden and organised the planting so that the vegetables could be harvested on the day of the festival.

The support of the Tasmanian Organic Gardening and Farming Society was important to Ray and Elma, providing an opportunity to share ideas about organic growing and receive support for their activities. There were no other organic farmers in the Penguin district in the 1970s and 1980s so the festivals and meetings gave the Masons contact with other growers. Despite the activities of the organic group the Masons, at times, felt isolated and were ostracised by some members of the local community for their organic farming practices. In the 1970s the north coast of Tasmania was a conservative place where deviations from accepted farming practice were viewed suspiciously. Elma recalled:

> *You would go out and you would feel funny. I used to go out to the CWA [Country Women's Association] and there was only one lady who ever talked to me about it. I felt terrible really. But I didn't give up because of that did I?*
>
> *Ray: No you stuck to it. But yeah it was hard. Of course at the time we had neighbours who reckoned we were mad. It was just too hard. It was. But after you say a certain amount you are not going to back down if you are viable. It changed ... eventually.*[263]

Biodynamic farming

In the late 1970s Ray and Elma Mason took organic farming to a new level. Ray attended a talk in the Burnie Town Hall by Alex Podolinsky, one of Australia's first biodynamic farmers who had adapted biodynamic techniques to Australian conditions. Ray recalled that after hearing Podolinsky speak, 'We thought well, yeah, this is something a bit better so we grabbed that and ran with that.'[264] Podolinsky arranged for Ray to study biodynamic farming techniques at a dairy farm in Gippsland.

> *Before you become a member they always sorted you out to see if you were fair dinkum and had what it took to carry it through because there is such a lot in biodynamics. This Gippsland farmer rang Podolinsky up and I heard him say, 'This bloke is going to be alright.' And that was me.*[265]

Following his return to Tasmania, Ray and Elma practised biodynamic techniques on their own farm. The precepts of biodynamic cultivation were set out by Rudolf Steiner in the 1920s, then developed by European farmers. Biodynamic growers shared with other organic growers beliefs in the importance of soil humus and chemical free production. Like other organic growers, they saw soil fertility as having a biological basis. However, unlike other organic growers, biodynamic farmers and gardeners believed in the importance of cosmic and holistic forces for plant and animal growth and health. Many biodynamic methods were intended to stimulate cosmic energy and attain equilibrium between the earth and cosmos and harness lunar and astrological energies. Biodynamic farmers and gardeners applied special preparations made from small amounts of herbs, minerals and manures to plants, soil and compost.[266] These preparations were developed by Ehrenfried

Pfeiffer in the 1920s and 1930s. Application of the preparations according to season, time of day and lunar cycle was a way of stimulating and harmonising plant growth, compost decays and different earth and cosmic forces.[267] Ray purchased two biodynamic preparations called 'Preparation 500' and 'Preparation 501' from Podolinsky. Preparation 500 was made from fermented cow dung prepared with specially selected cow horns and stirred in a particular way which was believed to stimulate soil life, promote root development, and strengthen the energy in the soil. Preparation 501 was made of finely ground quartz or feldspar and was sprayed in a mist on the foliage of actively growing plants to stimulate light, warmth and cosmic forces. Both were applied in very dilute amounts, approximately 60 grams per acre of land.[268] Ray recalls,

> *... my word, it livens the ground up. I still make the preparations, sometimes for my vegie garden. I get cow manure that I know is good. Put it in a drum and put a few cow horns with it and sit it in the sun. Like cow manure tea. You get that crust that comes on top of it and you whip that off and spray it around.*[269]

Ray also harrowed his land in a way recommended by Podolinsky:

> *We spread the dung completely by pasture harrowing both ways. We had to do it in the evening when the ground was moist and there wasn't going to be a frost.*[270]

In the 1970s organically and biodynamically grown produce was not sold at a premium price. The Masons never sold their milk specifically as organic but continued to supply Cadbury as they had done all their farming life. Following their conversion to organic and biodynamic methods, the Masons had greatly increased milk production and they were able to pay off the mortgage, buy more land and expand the herd. Reflecting on their years of organic farming Ray remarks:

> *Yes. I would never do anything else. It was good. And we were viable. We did alright whereas a lot of others were going broke. We came through and proved that it can be done. We were at maximum debt when we converted but we converted and paid it all off. Two hundred and seventy acres we finished up with, with 120 cows. And my heart didn't catch up with me for 34 years. I must have been doing something right.*[271]

When Ray and Elma retired from farming they sold their farm and cows to another organic dairy farmer who regularly delivers milk and yoghurt to them. In their garden in town Ray still grows organic vegetables and fruit. Ray and Elma Mason's conversion to organic and biodynamic farming was inspired by a simultaneous crisis in both Ray's health and the health of the Masons' cows, due, they believe to conventionally grown pasture and food. The organic and biodynamic farming practices they adopted combined the creation of humus-rich soil while rejecting the use of chemical fertilisers and pesticides. This combination of organic and biodynamic techniques allowed the Masons to reverse the declining health of their animals, improve Ray's health and enabled them to create a more productive, and commercially viable organic farm.

3

Ecological wellbeing

> *The wellbeing of man is bound up with that of the animal and insect kingdoms, the trees and plants and with the living soil itself. All are inter-related and mutually dependent upon each other.*[272]

This statement by the editor of *Farm and Garden Digest* in 1950 illustrated the development of a third principle in Australian organic growing. Organic growers, through their books and newsletters, argued that maintaining ecological wellbeing with a robust native environment was necessary to achieving plant, animal and ultimately human health. These ideas developed among organic growers in the early 1950s and became more prominent during the subsequent 20 years. Initially this new organic principle focused on the preservation and planting of native flora and fauna in organic farms and gardens. Organic societies then became involved in lobbying for the preservation of plants and animals beyond the farm and garden. By the 1970s, organic growers' concern about the native environment broadened to include the conservation of entire ecosystems and the application of ecological principles to the design of organic farming and gardening systems.[273]

Ecological wellbeing was emerging as a third principle of Australian organic farming and gardening at the same time as soil fertility and chemical free growing were consolidating as major principles. Organic growers' interest in the preservation of native flora, fauna and habitats reflected a broadening of organic growers' belief in the connection between human and environmental health to include so-called non-productive elements of the environment. Soil humus and chemical free approaches to organic growing had encouraged farmers and gardeners to focus exclusively on domesticated, non-Australian agricultural plants and animals. As discussed in earlier chapters, the soil humus approach changed rather than preserved the native environment of the soil and relied on indigenous pastures being replaced by exotic species. By contrast, organic growers' new-found conservation ethic encouraged them to preserve rather than change the native Australian environment. Organic growing societies formed links with the Australian conservation movement in their efforts to conserve native habitats. However, human health remained the ultimate goal of these societies and differences of opinion among organic growers about the degree to which organic growing should embrace a conservation ethic eventually contributed to the demise of Australia's longest running organic growing society in the 1980s.

Native trees, plants and animals

Native flora and fauna caught the attention of Australian organic farmers and gardeners and began to feature in their societies' newsletters during the 1950s. Organic society newsletters explained the importance of trees in regulating water flow, curbing erosion, tempering climate, controlling wind, circulating minerals and providing wildlife habitat. Trees, they claimed, were 'not merely a form of wealth to be exploited but an essential link in the great chain of life. No link in this chain can be jeopardised without its effect being felt upon mankind.'[274] The Australian Organic Farming and Gardening Society made tree planting one of its primary objectives: 'the Society advocates large-scale tree-planting operating to temper the natural aridity, conserve moisture, foster bird-life, and provide wind-breaks'.[275] The society newsletters profiled farmers who were revegetating parts of their properties. A.J. Gray, writing in the *Farm and Garden Digest* described reforestation projects in the Wimmera region of Victoria using indigenous species such as buloke, yellow gum, native pine, she-oak, yellow box and grey box.[276] P.A. Yeomans, profiled regularly in the organic newsletters, used native trees extensively in his 'Keyline' farm designs. He placed trees strategically along the contours to provide shelter and aid water retention and soil formation.[277] His work inspired other organic farmers who set up 'Keyline' associations, the most active of these in the Kiewa Valley in north-eastern Victoria.

Native trees became an emblem of the sound organic farm. The profile of a towering eucalypt framed the cover of the *Farm and Garden Digest,* signifying its importance in the organic system (see Colour plate 2). Trees had symbolic as well as practical importance for organic farmers and they were anthropomorphised as partners and co-conspirators in the organic endeavour. 'Arboreal homicide!' cried the *Organic Farming Digest* in response to the felling of trees.[278] A writer in the *Farm and Garden Digest* in 1950 emotionally lamented that 'an all too frequent sight is the ringbarked tree whose ghostly white and twisted arms point to heaven as if in anguish at man's mistreatment'.[279] In the *Victorian Compost*

News in 1962 British organic farmer Eve Balfour decried the ringbarking of trees on Australian farms.

> *Ring-barked tree cemeteries [are] so poignantly sad ... the gaunt white corpses are an ever-present reproach ... Trees do something to you ... they speak ... they are 'people', that's the point!*[280]

The presence of trees was, for Australian organic growers of the 1950s and 1960s, evidence of an untrammelled robust natural environment.[281] Trees were emblematic of the organic approach because they were a counterpoint to non-organic practice. During the 1950s and 1960s tree clearing was still strongly encouraged by government departments of agriculture throughout Australia, as it had been through the nineteenth and early twentieth centuries.[282] The price of agricultural produce was high in the decades following the Second World War. Large areas of native forest and scrub were cleared to make way for agricultural land, for example in southern Western Australia, in the Queensland Brigalow country and the Heytesbury forest in south-western Victoria. Agricultural policies encouraged farmers to intensify productivity, enlarge areas of 'improved' pasture and remove paddock trees and perimeter woodlots.[283] This was occurring on conventional farms at the same time as organic growers were beginning to plant and preserve trees.

Organic growers' infatuation with native flora was not limited to trees but also included native shrubs and wildflowers. Wildflowers were recognised for their important role in attracting pollinator insects such as bees and native wasps. The Victorian Compost Society encouraged gardeners to grow native plants and to mix native and exotic plants in the home garden as a way of improving the garden environment.[284] This was in 1959, 10 years before native plants became fashionable in Australian home gardens. At this time non-organic gardening books such as *Yates Garden Guide* were still largely preoccupied with exotic garden plants and suggested only a small number of native flowering shrubs for home gardeners.[285]

In the 1950s, native fauna began to be preserved by Australian organic farmers and gardeners as a valued part of the native environment. The 1952 objectives of the Australian Organic Farming and Gardening Society recognised the role wildlife played in maintaining a well-functioning farm environment: 'the Society holds that the natural function of birds is to keep insects in check. It deplores the wanton destruction of birdlife now prevalent, which gives rise to periodic plagues of insects e.g. locust[s] etc.'[286] Conserving native wildlife on the farm was 'a new element in farming' claimed Jim Mauger, a contributor to the *Victorian Compost News* in 1965.[287] Mauger had preserved natural bushland on 15 per cent of his New South Wales farm. He gazetted his property as a wildlife reserve which he combined with cattle and cropping. This, he claimed, had increased the numbers of native bees for pollination and reduced the destructive cut-worm population.

Ecological influences

Australian organic growers' opposition to the destruction of native plants and animals in the 1950s and 1960s was influenced by ecological sciences. Organic growers acknowledged the inspiration of ecology in their beliefs: 'each life contributes its own individual part in the great symphony of nature. The science of ecology teaches us of this co-operation', remarked the founder of the Living Soil Association of Tasmania, Henry Shoobridge in 1952.[288]

One of the most eloquent and popular ecologists of the period who inspired Australian organic farmers and gardeners was American forester and environmental philosopher Aldo Leopold, cited by contributors to the organic newsletters in the 1950s and 1960s.[289] Leopold's writings were informed by his observations of the destruction of environments and over-hunting of large predators. Leopold's *A Sand County Almanac*, published posthumously in 1949, proposed a 'Land Ethic' which encouraged people to see themselves as part of a community with the non-human world. He argued that human wellbeing depended upon this circle of interrelatedness in which humans were equal members rather than conquerors. Human actions were therefore limited by responsibility to the rest of the community and curtailed to those actions which promoted the integrity and stability of the whole community. Leopold described this as 'enlightened self interest' and argued that seemingly non-productive elements of this community, such as wildflowers, birds and microscopic life, were essential to the healthy functioning and stability of the whole.[290]

Echoing Leopold's land ethic, Australian organic farmers and gardeners pleaded for the recognition of the interdependency of all life. A speaker to the Victorian Compost Society in 1957, proclaimed: 'Man is an animal. He shares this world with other humans and members of other species, both plant and animal, all drawing on its material and energy resources.'[291] Similarly, nutritionist Stanton Hicks, adviser to the organic societies, described life as 'a vast complexity of interlocking phenomena that defy definition'.[292] In 1962, the president of the Victorian Compost Society, reflecting Leopoldian humility towards nature, wrote that 'all forms of life are dependent on one another and that the laws of nature evolved over millions of years must be followed as closely as possible to achieve plant and animal health'.[293]

Destroying native plants and animals damaged the balance of natural systems of food production which, organic growers argued, could lead to human ill health. The 1952 objectives of the Australian Organic Farming and Gardening Society warned that significant damage to the agricultural environment through non-organic methods could result in human disease:

> *The Society is convinced that by upsetting the balance of Nature ... disease will continue to take a heavy toll of crops, animals and man, despite palliation by medicaments, which attempt to cope with the effects while neglecting causes.*[294]

A year later the Victorian Compost Society predicted dire consequences from environmental damage.

> *We are only just beginning to realise the full significance of gross interference of man with the landscape that supports him ... does anyone sincerely believe that this sort of approach to food production can in the end have no serious boomerang result? Fifty years hence, we will face an entirely new set of degenerative diseases together with unexplained variations in other diseases.*[295]

That human interference with the environment could lead directly to human disease was proposed by microbiologist René Dubos in the 1950s. Dubos was one of the most prominent post-war scientists to take an ecological perspective on human health. He made explicit connections between human-induced ecological change and the potential for the emergence of new infectious diseases through habitat change.[296] Although Dubos' ideas were not directly discussed in the organic newsletters, organic growers' belief in the connection between human health and the agricultural environment echoed his theories.

Reaching beyond the farm and garden

In the 1950s and 1960s, Australian organic growers extended the first tentative feelers beyond the perimeters of the farm and garden to support the preservation of flora and fauna on non-agricultural land. They reasoned that preserving plants and animals in their natural environment enhanced the broader wellbeing of the whole environment, including farms and gardens. The Victorian Compost Society and the Australian Farming and Gardening Society of New South Wales both lent support to campaigns for the establishment of wildflower and faunal reserves.[297] Organic growers also called for the protection of native animals in national parks. For example, the Victorian Compost Society expressed concern about the accidental poisoning of native wildlife by sodium monofluoroacetate ('1080') rabbit poison in Wyperfeld National Park in the 1950s.[298]

In their concern about the preservation of native plant and animal life in their natural environment, organic societies formed links with nature preservation organisations dedicated to the protection of flora and fauna. Examples of such organisations included Save the Forests Campaign, the Conservation Committee of the Field Naturalists Club of Victoria, the Victorian National Parks Association and the Sydney conservation organisation Men of the Land. The Victorian Compost Society became an organisational member of Save the Forests Campaign. It promoted other nature organisations' activities, advertised their meetings and, in the case of the newly formed Victorian National Parks Association, appealed for funds on their behalf.[299] The Victorian Compost Society regularly reported on the activities of the Native Plant Preservation Society, an organisation established in the 1950s by Winifred Waddell to preserve native plants in their natural environment.[300] The Compost Society circulated advertisements devised by the Native Plant Preservation Society aimed at halting wildflower gathering. When the Australian Farming and Gardening Society of New South Wales ceased printing *Farm and Garden Digest* in 1954 it passed responsibility for organic advocacy to the Sydney conservation group Men of the Land,[301] suggesting that it was to this local conservation organisation that the organic society most strongly aligned its interests.

Ecosystem conservation

During the 1970s organic farmers and gardeners further deepened their attention to the native Australian environment and its wellbeing. Organic groups now strove not only for the preservation of particular elements such as trees, plants and animals but for the conservation of whole habitats. The Victorian Compost Society, now renamed the Organic Farming and Gardening Society (Aust.)[302] recognised that farms and gardens were not patches of land that ended at the fence but were part of whole ecosystems connected to the regional, national and even global environment. The society expressed concern about conservation issues with no direct connection to agricultural land such as climate change, the effect of deforestation on the 'greenhouse effect', preservation of the Great Barrier Reef in Queensland and pollution of the Mordialloc Creek in Melbourne.[303] In 1971, Vice President of the Victorian Organic Farming and Gardening Society, S.W. Newman, made a submission to the Commonwealth Government House of Representatives Select Committee on Wildlife Conservation. In this submission he expressed the society's support and respect for habitat conservationists and concluded that 'the public aim should be to make the country viable for the natives [flora and fauna] that remain; and to make the whole an ecological entity'.[304]

A new generation of organic societies which proliferated in Australia in the early 1970s also adopted ecological wellbeing, alongside soil fertility and chemical free growing, as the fundamental tenets of organic growing. The Brisbane Organic Growers Group defined organic gardeners as those who 'have changed to a method whereby nature is worked with and not against'.[305] Colleen Russell, president of the

Soil Association of South Australia, made a similar distinction between organic and non-organic growers in the society's newsletter:

> *We in the organic movement may be leading the way to a new system where Man will live in harmony with nature. At present Man does not see himself as part of nature's scheme but, rather, as an outside force destined to improve on or conquer. He even talks of battle with nature, forgetting that if he wins the battle, he may well lose the race ... and Mother Earth records her disapproval by the steady growth of disease in crops, animal and mankind.*[306]

The Tasmanian and South Australian organic newsletters, produced by two of the most active societies of the 1970s, reinforced ecological belief in the interconnection of farms and gardens with the wider native environment. The masthead of the Organic Gardening and Farming Society of Tasmania described organic growing as *ecology* as well as natural growing and nutrition.[307] The cover of the Soil Association of South Australia's newsletter depicted a tree with roots

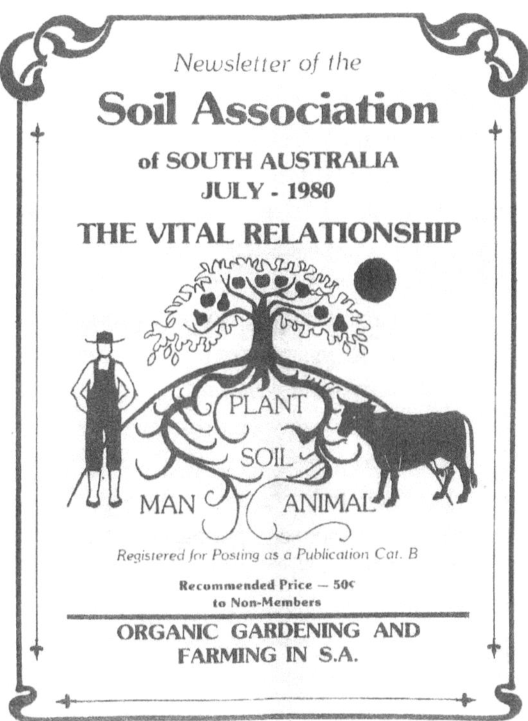

Figure 13: The cover of the Soil Association of South Australia's newsletter in 1980 depicts the interweaving of humans, domesticated animals and plants.

(Source: Soil Association of South Australia, *Newsletter* July, 1980)

intertwined around a person and a cow overlooked by the sun (Figure 13). This illustrated organic belief in the interrelationship of humans, plants, animals, soil and climate.[308]

Organic societies' recognition of the importance of conserving entire ecosystems mirrored a shift within the broader Australian conservation movement. Environmental historian Libby Robin has suggested that in the late 1960s the emphasis of conservationists shifted from concern about protection of particular species to protection of whole ecosystems.[309] The defining campaigns of the 1970s were for the preservation of ecosystems such as Lake Pedder in Tasmania, Fraser Island in Queensland and the Little Desert in Victoria. Conservationists now claimed that the natural environment should be protected and managed in a way which did not privilege human need for resources over the needs of other biological entities. Conservation, Robin argues, was no longer only about resource protection but had become eco-centric.[310]

Australian conservationists of the 1970s were influenced by international thinking about the natural environment, argue Drew Hutton and Libby Connors, in their *History of the Australian Environment Movement.* They remark that international apocalyptic scenarios, such as that generated by the British and United States publication *Limits to Growth*, profoundly influenced Australian consciousness of environmental damage.[311] *Limits to Growth,* published in 1972 by the intellectual association known as the Club of Rome, was a hugely popular book selling over 30 million copies in 30 languages. It argued that economic growth could not continue without significant depletion of natural resources and outlined a scenario in which shortages of resources such as oil, and pollution would cause widespread environmental breakdown.[312]

Australian conservationists and organic growers' increasing interest in habitat protection and ecological wellbeing was part of a widespread interest in ecological thinking in the 1970s. Donald Worster describes the 1970s as 'the Age of Ecology', a time when environmental concerns became a prominent part of popular consciousness in many Western countries.[313] In his history of ecological thinking, *Nature's Economy*, Worster argues that increasing interest in ecological thinking in the 1970s was a reaction against the sense of human omnipotence over nature prevalent in the 1950s and early 1960s. In the post-war decades, he argues, people had a vision of the world remade by scientific and technological ingenuity to serve human needs; a vision similar to that promised by Francis Bacon in the seventeenth century. However, by the 1970s, people were beginning to question this confidence. They feared that over-zealous human manipulation of nature at the expense of systemic prevention had created as many problems as it had solved. Many people now doubted that humans had dominion over nature.[314] The threat of nuclear destruction, oil spills, petrol shortages, depletion of fish stocks, air pollution and heavy metal poisoning, as well as the widespread poisoning of birds and humans revealed by Rachel Carson, all seemed to confirm fears that humans might potentially destroy all life.[315] This same way of thinking among Australian conservationists in this period is described by Libby Robin as 'techno-pessimism'.[316]

Models of organic ecological systems

Native plants and animals, habitat conservation and ecological principles became the framework for three Australian organic cultivation systems, demonstrating the importance of ecology as a third principle of organic growing. The first of these systems was Peter Bennett's gardening method described in *Organic Gardening* first published in 1979.[317] Peter Bennett described himself as an ecologist and studied ornithology, biology and zoology. He was involved with both the South Australian and Tasmanian organic societies, had a large garden near Adelaide and ran an organic farming and gardening advisory service. His book was one of the earliest and best known Australian organic gardening texts. Bennett claimed that ecology was the future of humankind and the interdependence of organisms one upon the other as 'the organic imperative'.[318] Bennett's gardening system relied on the ecological principle of diversity conveying stability.[319] He argued that organic gardens and farms must include diverse plant and animal communities which created a symbiosis of insects, birds, wildlife, micro-organisms and native and exotic plants. Diversity, he explained created a healthy, vigorous ecosystem for growth, decay and disease resistance. Gardening, he argued, was about creating and maintaining 'a stable life support system ... upon which man may depend for a vigorous and healthy life-cycle'.[320]

Permaculture was the second and best known system of organic growing which adopted ecology as a defining principle. Permaculture was developed by David Holmgren and Bill Mollison, in Tasmania, and first published by Holmgren and Mollison as *Permaculture One* in 1978.[321] Permaculture was based upon a framework of interrelationships and interdependencies between elements in an ecosystem. In formulating his design, Holmgren was influenced by, among others, P.A. Yeomans, organic writer and agriculturalist Sir Albert Howard and biodynamic grower Ehrenfried Pfeiffer. Permaculture recognised the efficiency and productivity of natural ecosystems and used them as a model for constructing systems for intensive human food production. The design of permaculture properties took particular note of local environmental forces such as patterns of sunlight, rainfall, shadow and frost. They incorporated diversity of plants and animals and each individual element in the system performed multiple, mutual roles. For example a greenhouse adjoining the kitchen at David Holmgren's property in Hepburn, Victoria provided food throughout the year, shade in summer when its exterior was clothed in climbing plants and warmth in winter when the climbing plants had been removed. Similarly, a chicken in a permaculture system provided eggs, meat, manure for compost, cleared slugs and insects in the orchard and processed kitchen scraps. The permaculture production system aimed to be self-sustaining and used minimal resources for maximum benefit. David Holmgren's property was divided into zones varying in intensity of production. These zones were similar to those in a traditional subsistence farm; the house and vegetable garden are located together, the orchard is a little further away from the house, and the dam and woodlot are at the further reaches of the property. These zones emphasised multifunction and incorporated layers of production. Chickens foraged beneath shrubs which grew beneath larger productive fruit trees mimicking a forest ecosystem. Although permaculture was originally conceived as a design system for large as well as small-scale food production, its advocates were more usually gardeners and small landholders.[322] By the late 1970s there were at least seven gardening groups in Australia dedicated to permacultural practices and affiliated with both organic growers' organisations and conservation organisations. The aim of permaculture, as stated by the newsletter for the Maryborough permaculture society, was: 'to produce an efficient, low-maintenance productive, integration of plants, animals, structures and man, with the ultimate result of on-site stability and food self-sufficiency in the smallest practical area'.[323]

Coralie Whitby's 'Eco-Gardening', devised at the same time as permaculture, was another system of organic gardening influenced by ecological principles. Eco-gardening shared many of the same bases as permaculture but never received the same attention as its well-promoted cousin. Coralie was editor of *Good Earth,* the newsletter of the Victorian Organic Farming and Gardening Society (the new name for the Victorian Compost Society) during the 1970s and early 1980s. She had trained as a biologist and ecologist and described herself as a 'conservation minded scientist'.[324] Whitby developed the eco-gardening system while she was a member of the Organic Farming and Gardening Society.[325] Like permaculture, eco-gardening used ecological systems as design principles but eco-gardening had a stronger focus on native flora and fauna. Whitby's methods aimed to provide subsistence food production in a manner that mimicked and was incorporated into a native Australian forest ecosystem. Developed at her home in Gembrook in the moist temperate rainforests of the southern Victorian Yarra Ranges, Whitby used the Mountain Ash forest as a model for the eco-garden. She aimed to create a food-producing garden which was part of the equilibrium of a forest ecosystem. 'In the eco-garden man stops parasitizing the environment and becomes multisymbiont', she wrote in *Good Earth* in 1982.[326] Her garden mingled native plants and animals with introduced food-producing plants. Like permaculture she advocated a diversity of annuals, perennial and tree crops and used 'traditional' organic methods of chemical free production and increasing soil organic matter.

Coralie Whitby had been drawn to organic gardening because she felt that it recognised and promoted the maintenance of the interconnectedness of humans and the environment. However, during the nine years of her editorship of *Good Earth* she became increasingly interested in native flora and fauna and as she did so she became impatient with organic growing. Despite the incorporation of native flora, fauna and habitat protection into organic farming and gardening during the 1950s, 1960s and 1970s, Whitby felt that organic growers still over-emphasised human health rather than the native environment's intrinsic right to exist. But although Australian organic growers had absorbed ecological thinking, they had not become eco-centric or conservationist to the degree which Whitby desired and in the end Australian organic growing was not 'ecological' enough for her. In October 1983 she wrote her final editorial for *Good Earth* stating that:

> *... quite apart from its use to us and the delight and sense of peace it gives, the local natural environment has its own intrinsic right to exist around us in its full variety. The idea of valuing the whole natural environment complex, not its soil component alone, goes far beyond the organic concept as it was put forward in our early magazines. Will you the individual member, at least make room for a group of local native plants in your own farm or garden? – if you do that, then you really love the good earth because you will be doing what is best for it.*[327]

And with that plea she bade the magazine and the society goodbye. Soon after Coralie's farewell, the Victorian Organic Farming and Gardening Society disbanded. Differences between Whitby and other members of the society about the degree to which ecological principles were adopted had contributed, at least partly, to the society's demise.[328]

The Victorian Organic Farming and Gardening Society published its last newsletter in 1983 after 40 years of continuous operation. By then, Australian organic growers had travelled a long way from their single-minded focus on soil humus, the principle upon which the first Australian organic societies were founded in the 1940s. Organic farmers and gardeners had taken up the fight against chemical farming and embraced the idea that all of life is interconnected; the health of the whole affecting the wellbeing of individual elements. They had adopted an ecological understanding of the interdependency of elements in an environment and the importance of maintaining native flora and fauna and native ecosystems. These ideas were compatible with soil humus and chemical free agriculture, derived from the same belief that human health was dependent on the biophysical environment, but they were also a significant expansion of what it meant to be organic. Organic growers now embraced robust native flora, fauna and whole habitats into their definition of health and wellbeing. If organic growers were to have again drawn the Wheel of Life, the insignia of the early organic movement, the mandala would now depict an intricate web of connections, featuring native plants and native animals beside humans, plants, domesticated animals and soil. But while organic societies were influenced by the eco-centrism of the conservation movement, they remained farming and gardening organisations primarily devoted to the production of human food and the promotion of human health. Australian organic growers remained at heart, anthropocentric, closer to Aldo Leopold's call for 'enlightened self interest' rather than the eco-centrism of the conservation movement. In the pursuit of plant, animal and ultimately human health, organic farmers and gardeners now negotiated three main principles: increasing soil humus, chemical free growing and enhancing native ecosystems. The integration of all three principles defines the organic farming methods practised by Mallee sheep and wheat farmer Anthony Sheldon, the subject of the next case study.

Case Study 3: Anthony Sheldon

The Victorian and South Australian Mallee is a region of huge horizons, flat beige wheat fields stretching as far as the eye can see, blue skies and grey-green mallee scrub. Anthony Sheldon's 1027-hectare wheat and sheep farm lies between Pinnaroo in South Australia and Murrayville in Victoria (Figure 14). This part of the Mallee is made up of long low sand dunes overlaying clay loam. Seen from the

Figure 14: Map showing the location of Anthony Sheldon's property.

(Source: Arts Imaging Unit, School of Geography and Environmental Science, Monash University)

Figure 15: Anthony Sheldon with the wide horizons of his Mallee farm in 1997. (Source: Museum Victoria)

air, the dunes are a series of long shallow ripples across the country. The Mallee lies on the margins of the semiarid temperate Australian Commercial Cropping Zone, a band of cereal growing country stretching from the Victorian Mallee, through South Australia and into Western Australia.[329] Rainfall in this area is low, between 250 and 310 mm annually.[330] Summers are hot and very dry and winds coming off the deserts in the north and west can be searing hot. Despite a dry climate, low soil fertility and loose sandy soil, Anthony believes that, if farmed responsibly, the Mallee is good reliable farming country (Figure 15). I visited Anthony's property in early April 2006. Although the day was cool and there had been an overnight rain shower, the air was clear and dry. We sat on the verandah of his house overlooking the home paddocks and discussed organic farming in the Mallee, then spent the day driving around his large property.

The Sheldon family have farmed in the Mallee since the 1880s, selecting and clearing land in the local area in the 1910s. The property now combines four of the '640 acre' blocks taken by selectors in the 1910s. Anthony grew up here, working for his father Huebie. After inheriting the farm at his father's death in 1985, Anthony changed his farming practices, gradually incorporating organic methods and he became registered as an organic grower in 2004. For many years after he began using organic techniques he continued to sell his wheat and sheep on the general market. After registering as an organic grower in 2004 he began to sell his wheat to an organic cereal wholesaler. Anthony is a broadacre commercial cereal and sheep farmer working in a semiarid environment who converted to organic farming to enhance the wellbeing of both people and the environment. Anthony's story of his gradual adoption of organic farming methods and their application to the particular, challenging environmental conditions of the Mallee demonstrates the integration of the three principles of Australian organic growing: soil fertility, chemical free growing and ecological wellbeing. For Anthony, improving and maintaining soil fertility; farming without chemicals; and developing robust native ecosystems, all enhanced plant, animal and food production and ultimately human health and wellbeing, with his main emphasis being on the wellbeing of the whole environment.

Preventing soil erosion

Anthony Sheldon's first venture into organic farming methods was to protect the soil from erosion. Like the early organic farmers of the 1940s and 1950s, Anthony considers the soil as the first priority on the farm, enabling abundant crops and healthy animals. The Sheldon farm is made up of two soil types: clay loam which is the most productive for cereal growing and sandy dune areas which, at the crest, are almost pure sand overlaid by a thin layer of vegetation. In 1986, shortly after his father's death, Anthony Sheldon's first step towards organic methods was to improve the low-lying clay loam areas of his property that were potentially productive but had become compacted and hard. He spread gypsum, a rock-derived mineral containing calcium sulphate, which breaks up the clay, improving workability, drainage and fertility.

Anthony Sheldon then turned his attention to the more difficult and vulnerable sandy areas of his property. Mechanical cultivation of the soil and the grazing habits of sheep, pulling at the grass roots and damaging the ground with their hard hooves, can leave sandy areas denuded of vegetation and vulnerable to wind erosion. Anthony has seen the strong westerly winds that are common here, leave paddocks 'scrubbed flat and sandblasted' with pasture blown away or covered

Figure 16: Abandoned farm machinery lies partially submerged in drifting sand in the Mallee during the 1940s drought.

(Source: Argus Newspaper Collection of Photographs, State Library of Victoria)

by loose sand.[331] Since the region was cleared by farmers in the early twentieth century, controlling erosion of the sandy soil has become part of Mallee farming. Selectors cleared the Mallee scrub, many with the Mallee Roller, a timber or metal ball or cylinder dragged through the scrub crushing and uprooting trees and bushes; the early twentieth-century equivalent of the bulldozer. The Mallee eucalypt, a low, multi-stemmed tree with a large tenacious root could survive wind, fire, and drought and even survived the smash and crush of the rollers, re-shooting again and again until finally grubbed out. Mallee roots and other covering vegetation had bound the loose sandy soil and had, albeit slowly, maintained the organic content of the soil. Clearing the vegetative cover left the sandy soil exposed to wind, and cultivation of the soil to sow crops or pasture broke the soil structure and accelerated the rate of decomposition of organic matter, further depleting soil organic matter. After only 15 to 20 years of cultivation, Mallee soils had lost half of their stored organic matter even further destabilising the structure of the soil and making it vulnerable to erosion.[332] In the early years of Mallee settlement many farmers practised 'bare fallow' – leaving paddocks free of vegetative cover and therefore vulnerable to wind erosion.[333]

During the three decades after selection the Mallee experienced a series of intense droughts.[334] The newly cleared farmland came adrift with sand engulfing fences, water channels, train lines, roads and even farm houses. Many farms became unproductive due to loss or inundation of productive soil and others were abandoned (Figure 16). Anthony recalls family stories from the 1930s of children digging out roadways to get to school, only to find the tracks sanded over again on their return home at the end of the day.[335] Between Ouyen and the South Australian border the Melbourne *Herald* reported in 1940 that on one 10-mile stretch of road eight wheat farms lay abandoned due to drifting sand.[336] The severity of the erosion in the Mallee made many question if the Victorian and South Australian Mallee was too marginal for farming.[337]

With such a history of erosion in this part of the Mallee, stabilising the loose dune soil to prevent erosion was an early priority for Anthony's organic farming regime. He ceased to cultivate the dunes, planting some with wide shelter belts of native trees to reduce wind velocity and reserving others for permanent sheep pasture. He has created 'living haystacks' from the dunes, planting strips of saltbush and acacia interspersed with deep rooted perennial pasture plants such as lucerne, evening primrose, veldt grass and clover. He has planted over 50 000 shrubs which provide permanent feed as well as shelter for sheep, and their deep roots help to stabilise the loose sand.

Improving soil humus

Through the 1980s and 1990s Anthony experimented with maintaining soil fertility through a three-year rotation of cereal, pasture and fallow.

> *The technique is really no different to the way we used to farm before we started using the chemicals. Fallow early, control your weeds, work your ground, and get a good medic pasture in the break.*[338]

The three-year rotation was a farming system practised in the Mallee earlier in the twentieth century. Medic is a pasture plant introduced to the Mallee in the 1920s. Like clover, it is able to bring nitrogen from the air into the root zone of the soil. While clover flourished when the soils were moist, medic thrived in dry soils.[339] Other deep-rooted perennial pasture plants brought up nutrients from deep in the soil and sheep grazing on the pasture added manure to the mix. 'I always liked the idea that the pasture phase with stock processes it through and that is your fertiliser',[340] remarks Anthony. When all this was ploughed into the soil it increased organic matter, added nutrients to the soil, increased water retention and fertility. Alternating cereal and pasture also prevented build-up of harmful fungi and pests in the cereal crops.[341] Weeds turned into the soil after the fallow phase added further organic matter. Anthony Sheldon's system of turning pasture plants into the soil was, like Harold White's techniques, a variance of ley farming methods although Anthony rotated crops and pasture more frequently than Harold White's 10-year 'plough down'.

Clover and medic, claims Sheldon, are the key to organic production on his farm. Clover was sown extensively in the Mallee after the Second World War. Anthony recalls his father being 'the big clover man', introducing clover in the 1950s. 'I remember stands of clover that you were struggling to run through as a kid'.[342] However, by the late 1960s and 1970s all the clover was destroyed. 'By the time Dad died in 1985, you could send out a search party and you wouldn't find a clover plant.'[343] During the 1990s Anthony reintroduced clover to the farm. 'If you can get good strong stands of clover and medic over your country, then you are seriously back in business. It has done the trick here.'[344] The improved fertility from clover and medic made pasture more nutritious for sheep and when cereal crops are subsequently grown in the soil the protein content of the grain increases. However, unlike the organic growers in the immediate post-war period, he does not link organically fertilised soil directly with more nutritive food. He regards the claim that organic food is more nutritious as debatable, reasoning that well-grown conventional produce can be just as nutritious as well-grown organic produce.[345]

Chemical free

Chemical free growing is what makes organic food better for human health, according to Anthony Sheldon.

> *The real winner with organics is that you are not using toxic inputs. That means it is safe for the people who produce the food and no one in the production line gets exposed to anything that could be harmful. And you are not putting anything out on your farm either.*[346]

Adopting chemical free agriculture was a big step in Anthony's conversion to organic methods. Ceasing reliance on agricultural chemicals such as chemical fertilisers, herbicides and pesticides caused him to radically change his farming practices. This was a major break with the farming methods used by the Sheldons prior to Huebie's death and by conventional farmers in the district. Huebie Sheldon, like most Mallee farmers, had used many artificial herbicides and fertilisers including nitrogenous fertilisers and superphosphate during the 1950s and 1960s. Anthony explained that during the 1960s, as wheat farms got bigger and debt increased, herbicides were labour saving, allowing farmers to cultivate more land. By the late 1960s Huebie Sheldon had completely embraced chemical farming.

> *From the end of the 1960s onwards he had this theory that the paddock was like a piece of blotting paper where you grew your crop and that you fed with nutrients and protected with chemicals.*[347]

In the late 1980s, Anthony experimented with 'chemical free' farming, sowing a small number of paddocks of wheat without using herbicides. While he got a few weeds he was pleased with the results. 'Actually I got some darn good crops.'[348] By the beginning of the 1990s Anthony felt he had 'gone as far as I could using artificial fertilisers and chemicals'.[349] He stopped using superphosphate in 1991 and herbicides and other agricultural chemicals in 1992. He controlled weeds by slashing and ploughing prior to sowing wheat when the soil was moist. He modified his seeding machinery so that he sows wheat densely to out-compete the weeds.

Although Anthony had not knowingly experienced any ill effects from using agricultural chemicals or consuming conventionally grown food, he has a precautionary approach to the use of chemicals. He felt that the use of poisonous substances for growing food could have a potentially detrimental effect on health and therefore it was better to avoid them.

> *I think organic food would have to be more healthy. Anything that goes into producing food that is a chemical, even if it is in minute amounts, well it is still present. If something that is toxic doesn't have to be used at all it has got to be better. If you had a half Chemical and Coke you'd probably get crook, you know,* he jokes. *Where there is a minute amount of stuff going on the food there has got to be some residual effect.*[350]

Sheldon was aware that there were dangers in handling chemicals for farmers.

> *I was careful the way I used chemicals. I always poured nice and slow and got out of the wind and when I was spraying a paddock before it was cropped I'd always spray so you'd turn from the wind, not sitting in the dust and drift following you. I never had side effects from using chemicals. I never got headaches or such like but I'd prefer not to use them. If a bloke can get away without using this stuff ... you hear things. There were certain products that people used in the 1950s that after 20 or 30 years it came out that you'd better stop using them. There was the issue with Agent Orange in the Vietnam War. That chemical was pretty similar to what we used for years to control turnip and broadleaf weeds.*

You start looking at things and asking yourself a few questions. I had some useful crops when I was still conventional but I'd never really liked spray. I didn't totally dislike it but it was something that if I didn't have to do it I'd be happier. I thought it was worth having a go at. Well it seemed to me that if you could still get as good results as what you were conventionally, well why not? [351]

When Anthony began farming organically he replaced the chemicals with other manufactured products that were not potentially harmful to human or animal health. Substituting natural or non-toxic products for chemicals became an integral part of his organic farming practice.[352] When Anthony was inspected prior to certification it was found one of the products he used for his sheep was not compatible with organic farming.

There was an animal care book that I'd read that recommended using linseed oil and kero for blowfly strike. This worked alright but they [the organic certification organisation] didn't like the idea of petroleum products being put on animals that are killed for human consumption. It turned out that when they said they'd prefer I didn't use that any more a new product came out through one of the chemical companies. It was a natural type product and worked brilliantly. There is also another issue with the sheep yards on the other block. I used those black treated pine posts years ago but, if you are going to do organic wool, they don't like the idea of the sheep rubbing against the treated pine posts. I've got a fairly major job there, pulling the yards down and replacing the posts with galvanized iron pipe. Once I'm confident I've got every angle covered with allowable inputs, I'll go the next step with the sheep.[353]

Ecological wellbeing: 'a long time and a good time'

For Anthony Sheldon, organic growing is not only about preventing erosion, improving soil fertility and chemical free farming; it is also about creating and maintaining a robust, well-functioning agricultural ecosystem to ensure both environmental and human wellbeing. His is both a short and a long-term view; ensuring a healthy environment is about safeguarding the future productivity of the farm and the wellbeing of the entire environment.

Anthony spoke of his desire to ensure the long-term productivity of his farm, 'I'm busy putting back as much as I can into the land so that a bloke has got a future on the land.'[354] Here he is expressing a version of the land ethic approach to environmental protection that was the mainstay of Australian organic growing; nature was a resource for humans and they damage or squander these resources to their own detriment.[355] A current version of this attitude is agricultural sustainability, whereby farming must ensure that the environment is robust enough to remain productive. As Anthony explains, 'If you rip the guts out of the land then retire to a villa in Queensland you haven't achieved anything. You have to give back to the land and nurture it.'[356] Like the organic farmers and gardeners discussed in 'Ecological wellbeing', Anthony Sheldon believes the organic grower has a responsibility not only to maintain a well-functioning agricultural environment, but to also improve that environment. 'An average farmer might farm the land for 30 to 40 years. You've got to be able to leave the land in better shape than when you started.'[357] For him, sustaining the farm environment so that it remains productive and using the agricultural resources wisely necessitates understanding and respecting the particularities and limitations of the local environment. 'If you farm within the limits of the land you can't miss out.'[358] Low rainfall, loose sandy soil and low fertility create limitations on farming in the Mallee which, if breached, can have disastrous results for both the soil and farmers' livelihoods, as was demonstrated in the inter-war years. For Anthony, organic farming must take account of these particular vagaries of the Mallee environment:

> *As far as it being too dry. People live in all parts of the world. You have to adapt your style to where you live. Number one is: don't make your landscape do something it can't or get it into a risky situation to try and get what you want out of it. If you work within the limits of what your landscape can do then basically your problems will disappear. That is the bottom line to the whole thing. The challenge we are facing, not only in Australia but everywhere, is to live within the limits of the landscape. If we do that we'll be here for a long time and a good time. I don't believe in short-term mentality. People who think like that will exhaust their resources and by the time they are 40 they'll be standing there on the bones of their arse looking at another 40 years. And then there won't be any good time, just a long time.*[359]

Improving the agricultural environment wellbeing of the whole ecosystem benefits everything, including humans. 'Not every single thing has to be measured in dollars and cents.'[360] Organic farming was about maintaining environmental wellbeing.

> *We've altered our landscape and weather patterns with no one to blame but ourselves. It is going to be a challenge, a big challenge. Down the track, well we only have one bloomin' planet to work on and if we mess up areas, then we are gone. The more natural you can work the whole set-up and work with nature the better it will be.*[361]

Anthony reiterates the importance of working with natural processes in agriculture, rather than against them. A fundamental aspect of ecological thinking is that nature has limits and to transcend these limits means to deplete finite natural stores. The majority of the energy expended in natural ecosystems contributes to the maintenance of these systems, and, correspondingly, a significant proportion of farm activity must be directed to maintain and conserve natural systems such as soil fertility and biodiversity. Neglecting the maintenance of these systems will lead to gradual degradation of agricultural land and more broadly of environmental systems.[362] Anthony Sheldon's organic farming method is a practical and intuitive response to these ecological concepts.

One of the principal ways in which Anthony, like members of the organic societies described in Chapter 3, enacts these ideas is to increase the indigenous biodiversity of his property. This does not, as he acknowledges, directly increase the productivity of the farm but, he believes will increase the overall wellbeing of the agricultural environment. When Huebie managed the property it was, according to Anthony, '1280 acres ploughed in one big chunk … a broadacre desert.'[363] To rectify this, Anthony planted vegetation belts of native and indigenous trees and shrubs along the perimeters of the paddocks. Species he planted included red gums, acacia and indigenous Mallee eucalypts. Although he hasn't yet finished planting, he estimates he has already planted over 25 000 trees and the total area covered is approximately 250 hectares, only slightly less than one-quarter of the total area of his farm (see Colour plate 4). He describes the internal conflict that planting for biodiversity initially engendered during his adoption of organic principles and the resolution of this conflict.

> *Here in the Mallee a certain amount of your fence lines are on drifty, unmanageable land which you don't mind fencing off and planting trees. But when your fence lines go across good country that will grow a ton to an acre of wheat every time it goes in, then you feel a bit crook in the guts planting trees, sacrificing good ground. I had a problem with that to start with but I don't any more.*[364]

Shelter, aesthetic value, and the introduction of greater floral and faunal diversity are, for Anthony, all part of organic farming. Three months after I visited his property Anthony was thrilled to tell me that a pair of wedge-tailed eagles was nesting in one of his wide shelter belts. He was protective of these birds, saying he was not going to tell any locals until the young birds had left the nest, for fear of egg collectors.

> *Biodiversity is something I understand a bit but probably don't understand as well as I should. Biodiversity is a thing that the ecosystem of the whole world is made of. If we have huge areas that have nothing, that can't be good either. If you look at a landscape anywhere in the world that is untampered with, animals and insects and plants are interacting with each other. You*

> *don't have all the trees and plants on one side, then a fence and all the animals on the other side of the fence. Things that are grown or produced naturally should be better than conventional stuff.*[365]

Through his intimate knowledge of his land and by experimenting and observing his farm environment, Anthony Sheldon moved away from the conventional farming techniques he grew up with and created a method of organic agriculture which was suited to his particular environment and which integrated the three main principles of organic growing: soil fertility and erosion control, chemical free farming and maintaining a robust ecosystem. His story of conversion to organic agriculture is an example of the application of organic growers' ideas about health and environment to a productive, commercial broadacre property in challenging environmental conditions.

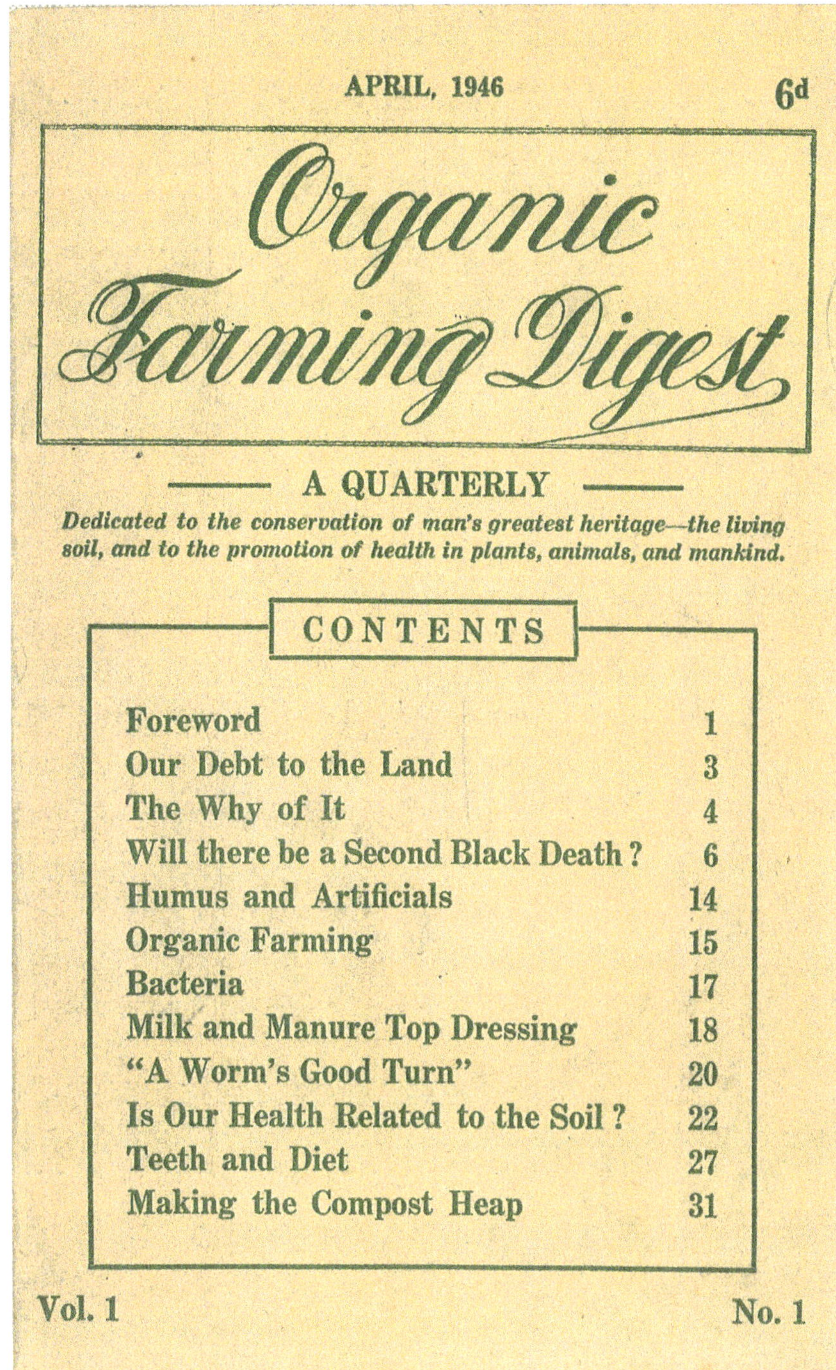

APRIL, 1946 6d

Organic Farming Digest

A QUARTERLY

Dedicated to the conservation of man's greatest heritage—the living soil, and to the promotion of health in plants, animals, and mankind.

CONTENTS

Vol. 1 No. 1

Plate 1: The cover of the first edition of the *Organic Farming Digest* produced by the Australian Organic Farming and Gardening Society in 1946. This was the first publication dedicated to organic growing in Australia.

(Source: Australian Organic Farming and Gardening Society, *Organic Farming Digest*, 1, no. 1, 1946)

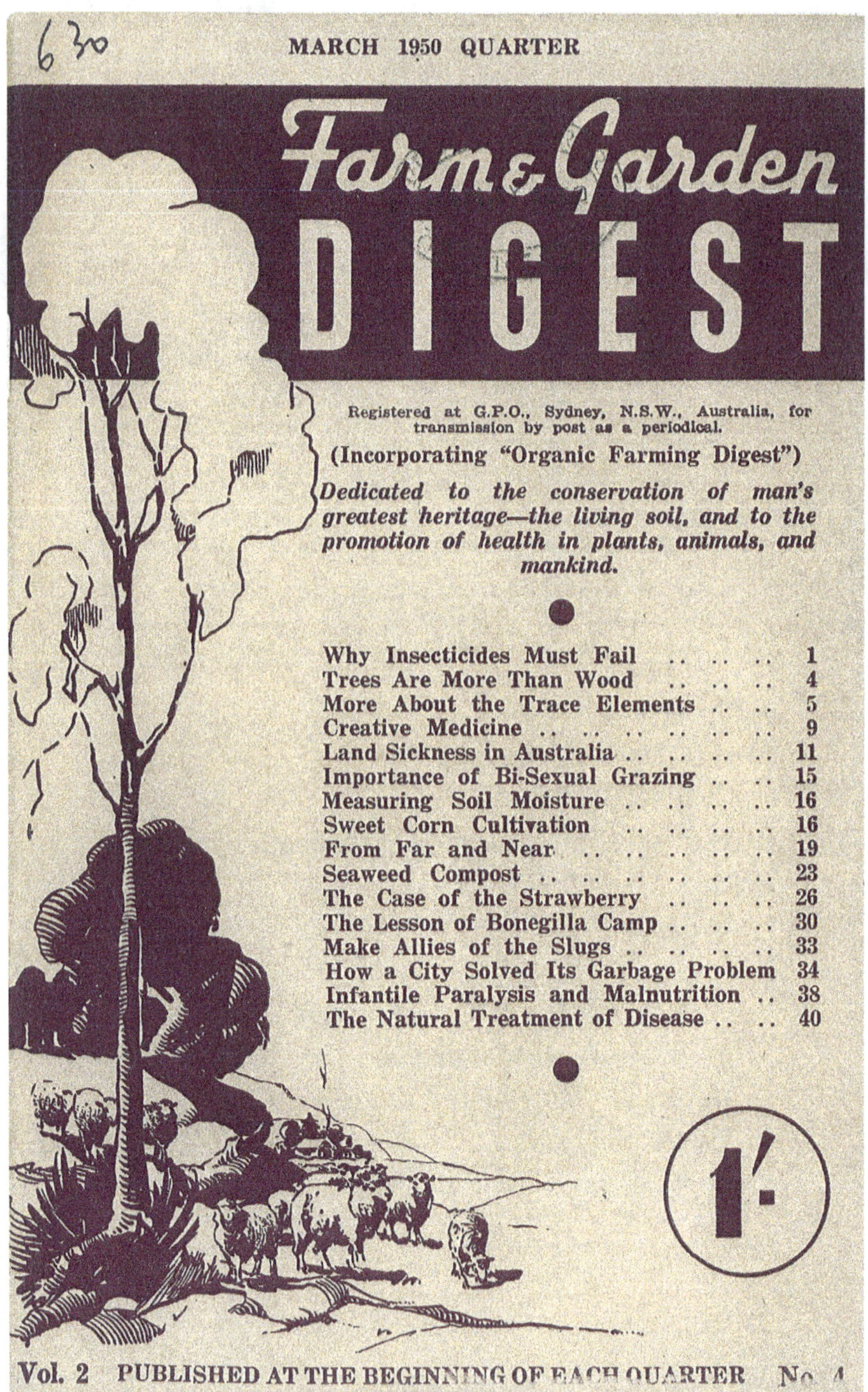

MARCH 1950 QUARTER

Farm & Garden DIGEST

Registered at G.P.O., Sydney, N.S.W., Australia, for transmission by post as a periodical.

(Incorporating "Organic Farming Digest")

Dedicated to the conservation of man's greatest heritage—the living soil, and to the promotion of health in plants, animals, and mankind.

1/-

Vol. 2 PUBLISHED AT THE BEGINNING OF EACH QUARTER No. 4

Plate 2: The cover of *Farm and Garden Digest* in 1950 depicts an iconic pastoral scene. The tree which dominates the cover has the unmistakable profile of the eucalypt.

(Source: Australian Organic Farming and Gardening Society, *Farm and Garden Digest* 2, no. 6, 1950)

Plate 3: Looking across Bald Blair in late autumn 2006.

(Source: Rebecca Jones)

Plate 4: A wide shelter belt of trees on Anthony Sheldon's mallee property in 2006.

(Source: Rebecca Jones)

Plate 5: The cover of a fertiliser promotion booklet issued by Nitrogen Fertilisers Pty Ltd in the 1920s illustrates an expert in a suit explaining the value of chemical fertilisers to the practical farmer (signified by the rolled shirt sleeves and spade). Farmers who did not adopt artificial fertilisers were condemned as backward.

(Source: Nitrogen Fertilisers Pty Ltd. 'Sulphate of Ammonia. Let's Introduce You ...' Melbourne: Nitrogen Fertilisers Pty Ltd, n.d.)

Plate 6: The cover of the first edition of *Earth Garden* magazine in 1972. The choice of the Adam and Eve woodcut displayed both the editors' commentary on 'the fall' of industrial society as well as their dreams of a return to the Garden of Eden.

(Source: *Earth Garden*, no. 1 (1972))

Plate 7: A compilation of articles from the first years of *Grass Roots* magazine published in 1979 shows three Back to the Landers tending their property.

(Source: Megg Miller and David Miller, eds. *Grass Roots, the Early Years*. Shepparton, Vic.: Night Owl Publishing, 1979)

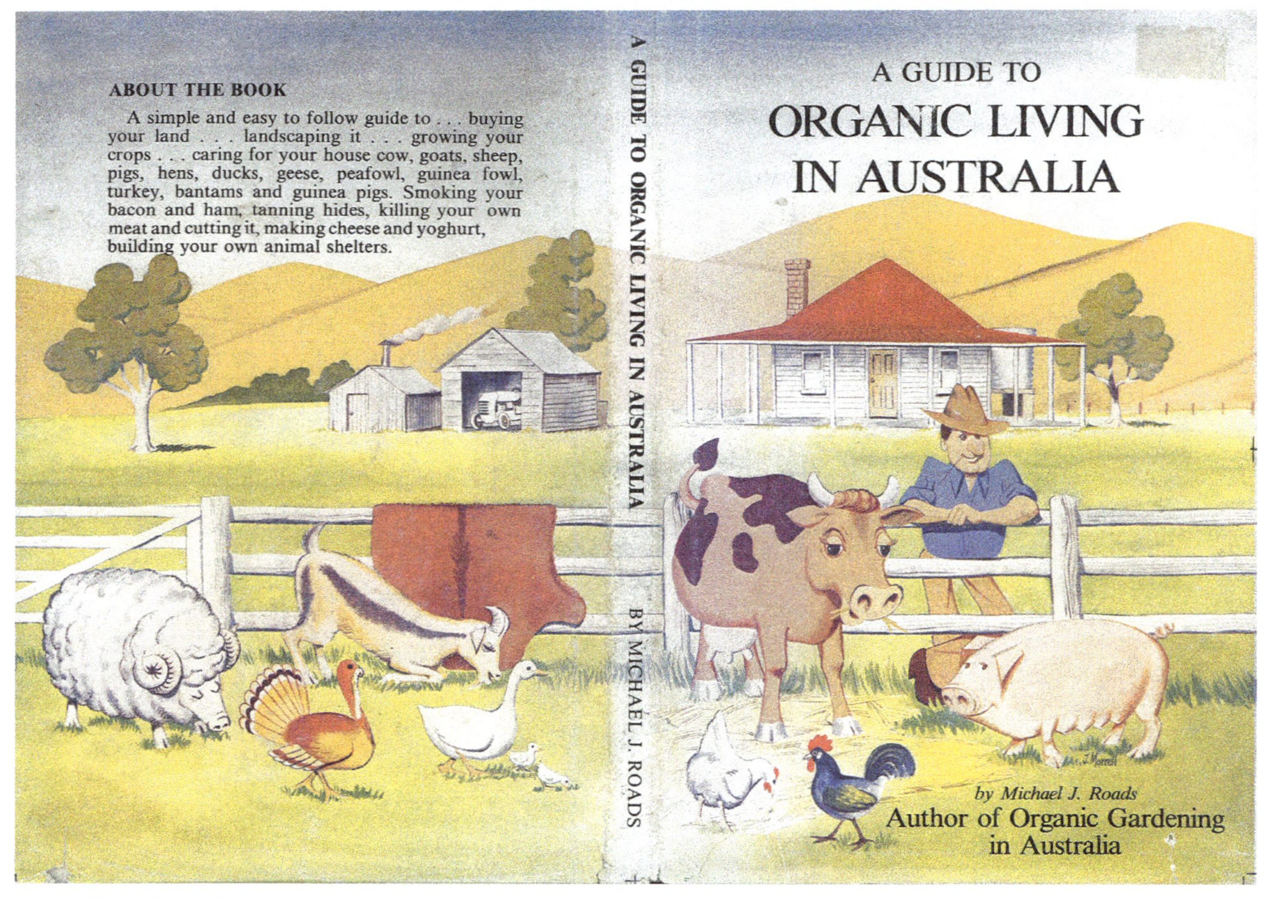

Plate 8: The cover of Michael Roads' organic self-sufficiency manual of 1977 depicts a childlike, idealised image of an organic smallholding.

(Source: Artist: Jim Morrell, Michael J. Roads, *A Guide to Organic Living in Australia*. Launceston, Tas.: Mary Fisher Bookshop, 1977)

The Organic Gardener and Farmer

ONE DOLLAR

REGISTERED FOR POSTING CATEGORY B

ISSN 0313 - 2242

Vol. 4 No. 1

AUTUMN EDITION 1979

Plate 9: The Tasmanian Organic Gardening and Farming Society's festival of 1979 adopted the flavour of the countercultural 'flower-power'.

(Source: Organic Gardening and Farming Society of Tasmania. *The Organic Gardener and Farmer* 4, no. 1, 1979)

4

Back to the Land

> *Down Home on the Farm: Where it's all at: There is a better life. It's away in the country with plenty of fresh air, sunshine, home-grown fruit and vegetables and home-baked bread. It's sitting by the open fire in winter eating the food you preserved in summer, eggs from your own chickens, milk from your own cows or goats.*[366]

This romanticised picture of the 'Back to the Land' life was promoted by the first edition of the magazine *Earth Garden* in 1972. 'Going Back to the Land' was the term adopted by people who, during the 1970s and 1980s, left Australian cities for small rural blocks to grow food organically for self-sufficiency and live what they described as an alternative existence. They were not commercial farmers or backyard gardeners but grew food for their own survival. Back to the Landers identified as organic growers and shared gardening methods with other organic growers of the period but the meanings they placed on organic growing differed markedly from other organic farmers and gardeners. Back to the Landers came from the countercultural movement of the late 1960s and 1970s and, for them, growing food organically for self-sufficiency was a means to rebel and achieve social change.[367] Reacting and rebelling against current societal values and ways of living meant creating – and recreating – a self-sufficient rural idyll of which the organic garden was the centrepiece. Back to the Landers were active and vocal among Australian organic growers in the 1970s and 1980s and their ideas about organic growing as social change became a key element of Australian organic growing at that time. However, equating self-sufficient organic food production with rebellion set Back to the Landers apart from their contemporaries in the

Australian organic farming and gardening societies. This resulted in a relationship that was at times cordial, at times uneasy and which created a distinct subgroup within Australian organic growing.

Australian Back to the Landers went back to the land armed with their own magazines and manuals. The most important of these were the magazines *Earth Garden* and *Grass Roots*, founded in 1972 and 1973 respectively. Within a short time both magazines came to define and focus the movement and readers described themselves as 'Earth Garden people', 'Grass Roots people', 'Grass rooters' and 'the Earth Garden society'. *Earth Garden* was edited by Keith and Irene Smith from New South Wales (see Colour plate 6).[368] *Grass Roots* (see Colour plate 7) was produced by Megg and David Miller who lived in Central Victoria and cooperated with others to publish the magazine and grow food self-sufficiently. Both magazines were aimed directly at people practising or aspiring to a Back to the Land lifestyle. *Grass Roots* was more deliberately non-expert and experiential than *Earth Garden.* Like *Victorian Compost News, Farm and Garden Digest* and the other organic growers' magazines discussed in previous chapters, *Grass Roots* and *Earth Garden* contained a mixture of theoretical discussion and practical advice. Unlike the organic societies' publications, the Back to the the Land magazines were written by a group of free-floating unaffiliated but like-minded individuals who shared values and ways of living but had no membership lists, organisational objectives or organised activities such as public speeches and field days. The magazines were augmented by self-sufficiency manuals written by individual Back to the Landers, such as *A Guide to Organic Living in Australia* published in 1977[369] by Tasmanian organic grower Michael Roads. This manual supplied gritty, practical advice and information to those seeking the Back to the Land existence. The aim of all these Back to the Land publications, unlike the newsletters produced by the organic organisations, was to provide the ideological and practical information a person needed to reject current societal values and change their way of life.[370]

Rebellion

'For those who wish to regain control of their lifestyle by exploring the alternative to modern mass consumption' was the by-line for the first edition of *Grass Roots.* The magazine explained this desire for change:

> *Today everyone is looking for an alternative to the life that big business forces on us. More people are concerned about the chemicals they consume with their food and the pollution all around them. You don't have to bow to the dragging monotony of set hours, set jobs, set transport and set wages.*[371]

Back to the Landers were rebelling against an amorphous, intangible enemy dubbed 'the system'. The system was the derisive name given to modern industrial living and all its perceived excesses: consumerism, materialism, complicated dehumanising technology, bureaucratic control, over-exploitation of resources, environmental destruction and alienation from nature.[372]

Back to the Landers' desire for rebellion did not evolve from earlier organic ideas of soil, chemical free and ecology. Interviews with Back to the Landers Jackie French and Megg Miller suggest that Back to the Landers in the 1970s and 1980s were largely unaware of their organic predecessors of the 1940s to the 1960s.[373] Their ideas were inspired by what has more recently become known as 'countercultural' thinking. Australian social scientist Denis Altman defines the counterculture as 'a social movement found in most Western societies since the mid-1960s and consisting mainly of young adults and teenagers acting out opposition to what they perceived as the dominant values of their society'.[374] The counterculture was a reaction against the conservatism and insularity of the 1950s, a decade still overshadowed by the fear and deprivation of war and depression. People of the counterculture were generally, although not exclusively young – in their late teens and twenties during the 1970s – middle-class and tertiary educated. Their middle-class, educated origins (Australians had unprecedented access to tertiary education during the 1960s and 1970s) gave them a sense of individualism and entitlement which, ironically, was at the heart of their rebellion against the system which bred them.[375] There was a restlessness and desire for broad social change which played out in various forms such as sexual freedom, political dissent, generational conflict, women's liberation, gay liberation, anti-war protests and environmental activism.[376]

Back to the Landers shared with other countercultural social movements a desire to overhaul individual and social values and the ways people lived their lives.[377] Unlike the organic farming and gardening societies who lobbied government, tried to change policy and practice and achieve bureaucratic and political influence, Back to the Landers strove for a change in personal values and ways of living, goals typical of the countercultural movements.[378] Their methods were to 'live it', 'talk it', raise consciousness and formulate new ways of living. Through the magazines *Earth Garden* and *Grass Roots* they hoped to raise consciousness and lead by example and the core of the magazines were the personal accounts of people who had gone back to the land. 'The crux of the counter-culture [was] the argument that one re-makes society by re-making the self,' explains Denis Altman.[379] Megg Miller remarks of that time:

> *You realised you could change your world and had the power to change your world. Even individuals knew they could change their world. ... I think we just wanted to upturn everything. I was ready for rebellion.*[380]

Back to the Landers were rebelling against 'the system' they equated with sickness and unhappiness. Industrial modernity and all its trappings was, they believed, leading to individual and societal sickness and alienation, a cancer in society which would bring about its own demise. The first issue of *Earth Garden* magazine in 1972 depicted Adam and Eve at The Fall: Eve eating the fruit of Satan which led to their eviction from the Garden of Eden (see Colour plate 6). In reproducing this image on the cover of *Earth Garden* the editors were depicting the destruction of paradise through the failings of humans as well as implying that the Back to the Land lifestyle was returning to paradise. The letter pages of *Grass Roots* and *Earth Garden* abounded with people's desire to shake off 'unhealthy' ways of living. Gerd and Ilse of Nambour, Queensland wrote in *Earth Garden*: 'Most people find that the civilized society type of existence is not conducive to peace of mind, and not conducive to perfect health, not conducive to … happiness I suppose.'[381]

Back to a yeoman idyll

Growing food organically provided a solution to disillusionment and ill health. For Back to the Landers, organic gardening represented an ideal and an alternative existence to the urban, wage-earning industrial life. The cover of Michael Roads' *A Guide to Organic Living in Australia*[382] paints an idyllic image of 'the organic lifestyle' (see Colour plate 8). A red-roofed house with a verandah stands amidst golden hills. A farmer (male), smiling, muscly, well fed, the hint of a pot belly, chewing a blade of grass, leans on a rustic timber fence surrounded by a mixed family of animals: sheep, goats, cow, chickens, pig, duck and turkey. The goat has half-closed eyes and a blissful expression on its face and all exude health and wellbeing, freedom and satisfaction; although does the cow hide draped on the fence hint at a touch of gritty realism? Smoke drifts from a chimney, a tractor waits comfortably in the shed and the grass is green and plentiful. *Grass Roots* editor Megg Miller had similar dreams of going Back to the Land in the Goulburn Valley in Victoria. 'We could have draught horses plodding nostalgically along farm lanes and happy sheep popping babies out and chooks sitting on their eggs reproducing.'[383] This was a very European ideal of rural fertility and abundance.

The yeoman idyll has been an enduring utopian myth in Britain and English-speaking Western countries such as the United States and Australia.[384] It was based on the figure of the yeoman farmer (usually male) who owned a small farm and through his own labour grew plants and raised animals for his own and his family's subsistence, selling excess for cash. He was neither owned by, nor accountable to, a master and was free to control his life and destiny. This idealised figure represented strength, independence, self-reliance, authenticity and industriousness and his property was abundant, intimate and human-scaled.

The yeoman, in his various guises, has been a model of Australian middle-class aspirations for freedom and independence, attracting both conservative and radical proponents.[385] Characterised by historian Graeme Davison as 'the dream of five acres and a cow', the yeoman idyll inspired the ideology behind rural settlement. This ideology has included the selection acts of the nineteenth century, closer and soldier settlements of the nineteenth and twentieth centuries and middle-class suburban expansion.[386] Ironically, a version of the rural idyll also inspired the political ideology of the conservative Country/National party, as exemplified by Harold White. Such political conservatives believed that rural pursuits were inherently virtuous and ennobling and bring out the best in people and, by contrast, city life is competitive, nasty and parasitical.[387] A small number of early Australian organic growers, prior to the 1970s, formed a precedent for organic self-sufficiency. In 1945, W.J. Caruthers in Ringwood (then a semi-rural area on the fringe of Melbourne) described his efforts to seek 'independence on five acres' in the *Victorian Compost News.* He advised that 'the average individual can … undoubtedly do much to liberate himself a little from the tightening vice of the present mass-producing economic system'.[388]

The 1970s Back to the Land version of the yeoman idyll was, like its predecessors, both a dream and a practical activity. Some Back to the Landers moved to 'the country' to grow food organically. Others found that the ideal was as important as the reality and they chose to remain in the city, poring over *Grass Roots* and *Earth Garden,* planning and dreaming. For both the dreamers and the doers, the yeoman idyll provided a rebellion against modern industrial society because it was believed to be close to nature and self-sufficient.

Close to nature

Jackie French left university in Brisbane in the early 1970s for a mango farm in southern Queensland. Hobart school teachers Jill and Tony Rayner bought an abandoned farm in the Huon Valley in southern Tasmania. Megg Miller left Melbourne and moved to the Goulburn Valley in central Victoria to grow fruit and vegetables, raise chickens and found *Grass Roots* magazine. A rural location was crucial to the Back to the Land organic dream. Popular rural locations were fringe or abandoned farming regions where land was cheap[389] such as Mullumbimby in northern New South Wales, the Yarra Valley east of Melbourne, the Huon Valley in southern Tasmania, Manjimup in southern Western Australia, Maleny in southern Queensland and the Atherton Tablelands in northern Queensland. These areas had good rainfall, acceptable levels of soil fertility and were conventionally attractive with all the major elements of the European rural picturesque: water in the form of lake, river or stream, hills or mountains, adequate rainfall and native vegetation interspersed with cleared land.

Back to the Landers were not literally 'going back' to rural areas because most were raised in the city or suburbs[390] but they were connecting metaphorically to a ideal of a rural area. Rural and urban, country and city have been enduring counterpoints used in English writing. Since at least the sixteenth century (and prior to that in classical Greece and Rome) it became possible to romanticise the rural once the urban existence became an established reality.[391] The 'moral cesspit' represented by the city contrasted with the fresh air, moral purity and good life of 'the country'. Eighteenth-century French philosopher Jean-Jacques Rousseau, inspired by antagonism towards the new scientific rationalism and emerging urban expansion, advocated that human fulfilment could not be found except by living among and depending upon trees, plants, animals. The 'countryside', the working environment of the yeoman, was romanticised as closer to nature therefore true, innocent, untrammelled and authentic.[392]

The archetypal exponent of this idyll was Henry Thoreau, an American writer who lived for two years, two months and two days (between 1845 and 1847) at Walden Pond in rural Massachusetts, in the northern United States. He deliberately withdrew from what he felt were the dehumanising effects of the Industrial Revolution and an urban existence where, he believed, happiness and fulfilment could not be obtained through wealth and material acquisition. Reacting against the industrial world, he sought closeness to nature by living in this rural location and rambling through the countryside, observing the plants, animals, climate and seasons. He had respect and nostalgia for the agrarian life exemplified by the community of Concord near where he lived, and made a virtue of self-reliance by living off his own labours, building a simple cabin, growing food, selling a small amount of surplus produce for cash and having few material needs. He described his experiences and reflected on rurality in *Walden, or Life in the Woods*, first published in 1854.[393]

Back to the Landers, following Rousseau and Thoreau, sought wellbeing of body and spirit by connecting with plants, animals, soil and seasons and by living in a rural area and growing food. When Jill and Tony Rayner described their arrival at their dream existence in the upper Huon Valley their reference points were the elements of the natural environment around them.

> *We finally arrived at the gate. Another half-mile through the property, all bush, and we came to a big solid, log bridge. Under the bridge flowed the most beautiful mountain river you have ever seen: giant boulders, manferns, waterfalls and pools. Around the corner and up the hill, the bush gave way to grass, buttercups, white daisies and Australian lavender. And right on the top of the hill sat a little house. We bought it. We didn't have to go another step. This was it. Over the next hour we just walked round the place in a dream ... We kept discovering more and more. Two swimming holes in the river, a mineral spring with wild watercress, five cleared paddocks, two giant pear trees, horse ploughs and sledge, broken fences and lookout points ... [We] just sat in the middle of it and grinned.*[394]

In only a couple of hours they had the farm populated, in their minds, with productive plants and animals:

> *And it's all ahead of us; the goats for milk, yoghurt and cheese, the chooks for meat and eggs, the garden for most of our food, bees for sweetness and a million sunflowers. We hope to use the plough again with a genuine, live Clydesdale, just for the fun of having a horse around ... By the way, we called it Green Valley Natural Farm.*[395]

A clearing in the bush provided Back to the Landers with connection to both the pastoral and wilderness ideal. Ted and Lusa of Tweed Heads enquired: 'Does anyone around here know of a small acreage for sale within 50 miles of Tweed Heads among mountains, the more isolated the better, preferably virgin land with creek?'[396] And John in New South Wales writes: 'We are moderately desperate to buy our own "piece of paradise" ... with natural bushland and some cleared grazing land.'[397] Back to the Landers desired enough cleared sunlit land to grow food but within view of, and proximity to, 'virgin' forest. This Back to the Land version of the yeoman idyll varied slightly from the ideal land sought by closer settlement and productive suburban gardeners who made little reference to 'wilderness' nature. However, it was akin to Thoreau's cabin in the woods, combining the agrarian ideal with the authentic natural experience of wilderness. Back to the Landers drew on a romantic tradition in which wilderness was revered as untrammelled by human destruction, untamed and therefore closer to a higher truth, akin to the Garden of Eden before the fall.[398] Creating a garden in the wilderness is another enduring metaphor for human achievement and ethical endeavour, particularly poignant in a settler society such as Australia.[399] Drawing on these myths, native bushland represented the authentic return to nature. Back to the Landers' desire to incorporate their farms into the native bushland was an exaggerated, romanticised version of organic growers' wish to incorporate native flora and fauna into their farms and gardens, a recognition that humans were dependent on the natural environment.

Living in a rural area, working with plants and animals, tilling the soil, getting your hands dirty, eating home-grown food; organic gardening provided Back to the Landers with a way to connect with nature. '[G]ardening puts you into the ecosystem, into nature. You became aware of clouds, frosts, the sun's heat and how many points of rain we had in that last downpour', remarks Megg Miller in *Grass Roots.*[400] Like Thoreau, Rousseau and other aspirants to a rural idyll, living in contact with nature was, for Back to the Landers, associated with health and vigour. Megg Miller explained this connection in a recent interview:

> *the core of what we did was ... touching base with Mother Earth ... It wasn't only healthy for the body but for the mind also. We both thought 'wow ... we*

could be freer in the country, free to express parts of our dreams'. We freed that child in us to go back and feel the pleasures of nature and observing nature and being in nature. ... Maybe we saw freedom in that old sense: freedom is nature, nature is untainted and untrammelled with worries and politics. I think nature was a symbol of our embracing a freer lifestyle.[401]

Similarly, Kay Earl from Edmonton in Queensland attributed her problem-free pregnancy to 'our earth-loving existence' and Marjorie Spear in the Atherton Tablelands found that: 'living and eating in harmony with nature has improved our health and increased our vigour'.[402]

Like the organic farmers and gardeners discussed in previous chapters, Back to the Landers believed that growing food using organic methods was inherently healthy. However, while they were interested in nutritious food, maintaining ecological wellbeing and chemical free growing, the primary attraction of self-sufficient organic gardening was that it brought them in close contact with the biophysical environment. Back to the Landers believed that a person's disposition, character and physical health were influenced by their environment and direct contact with a physical environment that was healthy, authentic and natural (as both the rural and the bush were believed to be) would bring health and wellbeing. This was another manifestation of the environmental determinism inherent in ecological versions of health in that it was the physical environment and people's relationship with that environment which delivered health and wellbeing.

Belief in the inherent healthfulness of the natural environment was a form of 'biophylia', a term coined by American biologist and entomologist E.O. Wilson.[403] Wilson explains that, because humans have evolved in close relationship to other forms of life, we have an innate affiliation with nature and depend on the natural world not only for our material wellbeing but also for our physiological, psychological, aesthetic, spiritual, cognitive and emotional wellbeing.[404] Living among trees, plants, soil, animals and insects was, in the yeoman idyll, an experience of returning to origins.

For some Back to the Landers human affinity with nature was described not just in terms of physical wellbeing but also in terms of spiritual health. Most Australian Back to the Landers, unlike their American peers,[405] did not embrace established religions but some did adopt an amorphous romantic spiritualism where the sacred was believed to reveal itself to humans through natural things.[406] For these organic growers, practical acts such as tending a garden became spiritual: 'you come to all sorts of transcendental states of mind in the garden. It automatically happens to you. If you just poke away with the discipline of a pick and shovel you become sanctified. The magic happens to you', explained a contributor to *Earth Garden*.[407] Biodynamic organic growing, based on Rudolf Steiner's Christian philosophy of anthroposophy, connected nature to cosmic forces of energy. Planting by the phases of the moon, harnessing cosmic energy by methods of stirring liquids and the creation of homeopathic remedies from plant materials offered organic growers another means to connect with spiritualism in nature. *Earth Garden* and *Grass Roots* published information about biodynamic methods and there was good attendance at biodynamic society meetings during the 1970s and 1980s.[408] Spiritualism in nature could also take a more pagan form. Marjorie Spear wrote to *Earth Garden* telling of the importance of fairies on her property, Harmony Farm:

> *The 'little people' (fairies) are a tremendous help. They like to live in organic gardens where humans acknowledge their existence and appreciate their work. ... They have guided my labours. I cannot see them but I am sure it has only been through their knowledge that I have been inspired to garden successfully in this difficult, though lovely, tropical climate.*[409]

Self-sufficiency

Megg and David Miller, as editors of *Grass Roots*, summed up the Back to the Land way of living as: 'self-sufficiency is growing', meaning self-sufficiency was about cultivating food; self-sufficiency was expanding; and self-sufficiency led to personal growth.[410] Being self-sufficient was a way that Back to the Landers could rebel by creating an alternative to urban living.

> *The first thing all of us did when we moved to the country was dig up our backyards and grow vegies. Milking a cow and carrying buckets of bathwater for a garden. It was just obligatory to have a garden. We were all committed to it.*[411]

The ideal was, through their own or communal labour, to produce enough food to live on. Excess could be bartered in exchange for produce they were unable to grow themselves. Home-grown vegetables and fruit became the symbol of the organic Back to the Lander. 'Think about it', exhorted a contributor to *Earth Garden* in 1972, 'get hold of Rodale's *Basic Book of Organic Gardening*. Read about mulch and compost, think about growing plants without DDT or chemicals.'[412] Many people also raised chickens, goats and other livestock. *A Guide to Organic Living in Australia* provided Back to the Landers with practical information essential to a self-sufficient existence: selecting land, growing vegetables, fruit and pasture, raising cows, goats, sheep, pigs, hens and other poultry, home butchering, smoking, tanning hide and yoghurt and cheese making.[413] Some Back to the Landers minimised their dependence on wider society by generating their own power using solar panels and a water wheel. Or they did as Jackie French did – building her house from local or salvaged material. Megg Miller remembers self-sufficiency in her own communal household in central Victoria:

> *We would spin, knit, make bread, and grow sprouts. There was a time when we thought you could have an entire lifestyle like that. There was a time when I even made my husband's jackets and I fired the buttons in the open fire; that is how all-embracing it was.*[414]

Rural self-sufficiency was about independence and control, independence from the society which Back to the Landers eschewed and control over daily activities. Writes Kate Matilda of Mt David, New South Wales, about growing food organically: 'I feel I am not just a passive piece of flotsam on the river, but am actively charting and pursuing my own destiny.'[415] Another Earth Garden contributor explains, 'For some it's the satisfaction of building their own life ... without having to rely on a boss, or pay a lot of money to tradesmen, farmers, fishermen, canning factories, butchers, clothing makers or bakeries.'[416]

Megg Miller's Back to the Land life was inspired by her grandmother's small self-sufficient farm with 200 chickens, pet sheep, working horses and acres of fruit trees producing sequentially. 'I just *loved* it and that has been my inspiration and that is what sent me on my path in life ... It was a way of life that I thought was fantastic.'[417] Self-sufficiency in food and reliance on the household's own land and labour avoided dependence on others for basic survival needs. American social researcher W.J. Belasco, who explored the United States' countercultural preoccupation with food, explains that in the 1970s growing food was a way that people could act immediately, in their own daily life rather than rely on governmental or bureaucratic change.[418] This was the era when 'personal is political' was a catchcry and many believed that the way you lived your life was a serious political act. Bypassing the anonymity and economic power of food-processing industries and agricultural chemical manufacturers was rebellion. Organic growing provided a way for Back to the Landers to create a viable alternative way of living which was a comment upon contemporary society. Reflecting on that time, Megg Miller recalls that growing food was 'so seditious, so anti the urban kind of thinking'.[419]

The Back to the Landers' rural ideal was just that – an ideal – and some found that the good life was also the hard life. Many who attempted organic self-sufficiency in the 1970s encountered a nature that was not always as benevolent as they had hoped. Rather than enabling self-fulfilment it sometimes encouraged disappointment. Marjorie Spear tackled a continual march of marauding predators in her tropical rainforest garden and in Kangaroo Ground, north-east of Melbourne, Neil Douglas's garden shrivelled before his eyes in drought and searing northerly winds.[420] Others found that beheading a lamb and breaking a chicken's neck was an experience that contrasted sharply with the naïve animal nursery on the cover of *A Guide to Organic Living*.[421] Home building, raising animals and growing food for self-sufficiency was hard physical labour. Just like generations of Australian selectors and closer settlers before them, Back to the Landers struggled with inadequate farming knowledge and poor land. Many organic Back to the Landers who had been raised in middle-class suburban households, often with little contact with rural life, didn't have the skills necessary for self-sufficiency. Jill Rayner, atop her hill in southern Tasmania, found her grins turned to grimaces:

> *Tony had never driven a nail, I had never so much as grown a radish and neither of us had any experience with animals except cats. The geese ate the cabbages, the cats chased the ducks, the beehive swarmed and we got not a pint of milk out of any of the goats. We did get a couple of dozen duck eggs but most of them were dropped in the pond.*[422]

But while some retreated to the city disappointed, many Back to the Landers incorporated adversity, deprivation and challenge into their lives, and learning about plants, animals and the land became part of going Back to the Land. Jill Rayner wove both challenge and adversity into her story of self-sufficiency, crediting them with creating a richer and fuller existence.

> *It was generally a very confusing time with much messing about and nothing getting done. But it was a very important time on reflection. We had to get to know ourselves thoroughly before we could hope to survive on the fundamentals of nature. It was the time of great adjustment!*[423]

Marjorie Spear wrote of the rewards of tackling a challenge head on.

> *We built up the impoverished soil here with all possible cheap and free organic materials ... It was hard work ... Work hard, build up your soil, and love your plants ... Thrift is the essential ingredient. ... I now get immense pleasure from working with my reasonably fertile soil which abounds in earthworms not there five years ago.*[424]

And in Violet Town, Victoria, Terry Frewin writes in *Grass Roots*:

> *... success to us is seeing the soil, mainly mudstone and ironstone gravel originally barren and eroded and growing little more than moss and meagre poor grass, slowly becoming more fertile and productive.*[425]

Thrift, hard work and overcoming adversity were integral to the image of the self-sufficient yeoman farmer, characterised by Australian historian Andrea Gaynor as 'respectable rather than rough, industrious rather than idle'.[426] Jill Rayner's, Marjorie Spear's and Terry Frewin's stories all conveyed the idea that growing food organically brought enrichment of body, land and soul which made the rewards of going Back to the Land even sweeter. As Jackie French sums up, 'It can make your life as rich and prolific as your garden.'[427]

Refuge

While being self-sufficient was a criticism of society, it was also about establishing a refuge. The sharp edge of sedition was blunted by a softer romantic glow of nostalgia – creating a form of rebellion that was escapist as well as radical. One of the escapist aspects of going Back to the Land was the desire to retreat from, rather than tackle, problems. *Earth Garden* recommended that readers withdraw to prepare for a better life.

> *The pollution won't go away, the water will continue to taste bad, the streets will remain dirty, the noise level high. But inside your private world, a house and a backyard in the suburbs ... you can ignore it while making plans to move out.*[428]

Going Back to the Land and growing food organically for self-sufficiency was partly about seeking a sanctuary.

> *... in this present materialistic world which often brings disappointment, dissatisfaction, boredom, hopelessness and disillusionment, the experience of eating your own fruit, fresh and ripe to perfection, will be the ultimate experience and available every day.*[429]

Back to the Landers' yeoman idyll drew upon the conservative element of the ideal which was about retreating from modern industrialism to a pre-industrial golden agrarian age. Historian Rennie Short explains that in times of change there is commonly a resurgence of interest in a rural idyll as an escape from social tension, providing 'the perfect past to the imperfect present and uncertain future'.[430] Back to the Land organic growers, much more than earlier organic farmers and gardeners, saw growing food organically as a retreat to an earlier, better time. Their dreams bore little resemblance to the reality of small-scale agriculture in Australia in the 1970s and 1980s, which had long been part of the industrial age and relied on manufactured pesticides and fertilisers, complicated agricultural technology, was subject to global commodity prices and was an integral part of Australia's capitalist economy. Back to the Landers' dreams did not lie in temporal reality but were located in a mythical ahistorical agricultural arcadia.[431] Marjorie Spear described herself as 'a peasant farmer'.[432] Illustrations in *Earth Garden* reinforced this nostalgia for an undetermined earlier time. Among readers' letters expressing their hopes, dreams and plans for going Back to the Land were placed undated, unattributed woodcuts: a long-skirted woman with small dog collects produce in a wicker basket in front of a picket fence; another long-skirted aproned and bonneted woman scatters grain for chickens against a backdrop of a cottage; and chickens peck beside a stream flowing past humble cottages, a stone wall and rustic timber

Figure 17: Reproductions of woodcuts from the 'land line' pages of *Earth Garden* magazine in the 1970s depict images of a romanticised European peasant arcadia.

(Source: *Earth Garden*, no. 14, 1976, p. 4; *Earth Garden*, no. 6, 1973, p. 4; and *Earth Garden*, no. 8, 1974, p. 54)

fence (Figure 17).[433] These images evoked a sense of the eighteenth, nineteenth or early twentieth centuries and suggested nostalgia for a pre-industrial, European, peasant-like existence but one that was romantic and wholesome rather than squalid and downtrodden.[434] The sketches almost certainly conveyed a British or European life rather than an Australian pioneering existence. There is nothing in these images to suggest an Australian past – no iconic references to eucalypts, wide horizons nor hint of native flora or fauna.

Some Back to the Landers hoped that the yeoman idyll would provide refuge from gender struggles, some of the strongest and bitterest battles of the 1970s. While many Back to the Landers attempted to redefine gender roles and traditional nuclear family structures by establishing communal and collective land ownership and household responsibilities, for others, the yeoman idyll continued to be experienced differently by men and women.[435] The vegetable garden was a site where both male and female Back to the Landers met but it was men who most often built houses, dug dams and created power sources while women tended children and prepared food. One (female) writer to *Earth Garden* asked bitterly in 1978:

Has the counterculture unthinkingly transferred the 'straight' dream of the rugged independent guy coming home to his 2.5 beautiful kids and dear little wifey busily baking bread in a sweet-smelling kitchen, from a red-brick monstrosity to a mud brick cottage?[436]

Back to the Landers' countercultural desire to rebel, whether by retreating or providing a deliberately alternative way of living set them apart from their contemporaries in the organic farming and gardening societies. Back to the Landers and members of the Australian farming and gardening societies all believed that human health was dependent on the biophysical environment and that organic growing constructed the right relationship with that environment. But unlike the organic farming and gardening societies, the goal of Back to the Landers was to retreat from and overturn the existing social order. Growing food organically for self-sufficiency was a way for them to do that. The different meanings that Back to the Landers and organic societies placed on organic growing created a fissure between the two groups.

'Grass Rooters' and 'Earth Garden people' frequently interacted with the organic growing societies. *Earth Garden* and *Grass Roots* regularly published information about organic groups and influential organic farmers such as Albert Howard, P.A. Yeomans and Eve Balfour. Megg Miller, as editor of *Grass Roots,* was invited to attend organic farming and gardening societies' events in Sydney and Melbourne and readers of *Grass Roots* and *Earth Garden* regularly sought information about organic growing from organic societies such as the Henry Doubleday Research Association in Sydney.[437] Back to the Lander Jackie French edited the newsletter of the Henry Doubleday Research Association and Michael Porcher, an active self-sufficiency advocate, was president of the Organic Farming and Gardening Society (Victoria) in the early 1980s. A Back to the Land countercultural flavour also influenced the organic farming and gardening societies in this period. For example, by the end of the 1970s the language of the counterculture was evident in organic farming and gardening societies' publications with the annual event of the Tasmanian Organic Gardening and Farming Society described as a 'festival', and advertised by cute, colourful, flowery imagery reminiscent of the 'flower power' of the counterculture (see Colour plate 9).

Despite interaction and mutual influence, Back to the Landers and the organic farming and gardening societies maintained parallel rather than integrated existences. Both Back to the Landers and members of the organic farming and gardening societies perceived the other to be a distinct and separate group. Back to the Lander Megg Miller, in a recent interview, described this relationship as 'our own groups alongside each other'.[438] From the other side of the fence, David Stephen, founder of the Tasmanian Organic Gardening and Farming Society recalls of the Back to the Landers: 'They were always seen as the fringe. They would even sit on the fringes at the meetings so they could get out quickly!'[439] Leicester Jones, another member of the Tasmanian Organic Society recognised Back to the Landers' radical aims and recalls: 'They wanted to offend, to be radical, to break down the established principles and traditional ideas and they did it rather successfully.'[440] With more contempt, organic garden writer Peter Bennett described them as 'fringe-mania types who would rather dig with a stick than a spade'.[441]

Occasionally the cordiality of relationships between the parallel groups deteriorated as a result of the different meanings they placed on organic growing. Organic gardener Leicester Jones and farmer Ray Mason recalled one festival of the Tasmanian Organic Gardening and Farming Society in the late 1970s when tensions bubbled to the surface. Back to the Landers were dancing and singing naked around a camp fire. Remembering this occasion, Leicester Jones remarked with annoyance, 'There was no need for that kind of thing. No need whatsoever.'[442] Ray Mason recalls, 'us old fellows were not going to put up with it … and we put them out the gates and they went their way'.[443] The fallout from this event for the Tasmanian Organic Gardening and Farming Society was considerable. The society lost 500 members – half its membership – on that weekend. Both groups were offended; the Back to the Landers by their eviction and the farmers and gardeners by the open display of contempt for social convention. 'Gee we were getting an awful bad image. It was the hippy image and it took a long time for us organic fellows to drop it', recalls Ray Mason.[444]

Back to the Land organic growers, like other organic growers, believed that human wellbeing depended on humans' relationship with the natural environment, although members of the organic societies were interested in nutrition, non-toxic food and environmental health whereas Back to the Landers emphasised personal wellbeing. Growing food organically for self-sufficiency was, Back to the Landers believed, a way of living which connected them to nature and allowed them to rely on the land, plants, animals and soil rather than industrial urban society. They were an energetic and vocal group within Australian organic growing in the 1970s and 1980s and their ideas and ways of living brought to Australian organic growing a belief in the inherent healthfulness of growing food organically for self-sufficiency. But despite their links with members of the organic farming and gardening societies, Back to the Landers were a parallel rather than integrated group, somewhat of an aberration among other Australian organic growers. Their use of organic gardening as a weapon of rebellion and broad social change set them in opposition to many other organic farmers and gardeners and their prominence was to diminish through the 1990s and 2000s. During these decades a new version of Back to the Land evolved which still valued personal wellbeing through living close to the natural environment and growing food organically, but moved away from the idea that this was political rebellion leading to broad social change. The Back to the Land goal of complete self-sufficiency mellowed, changing to partial self-sufficiency and with that the emphasis of going Back to the Land moved away from political action to personal enrichment. This modification is exemplified by organic gardener and writer Jackie French, whose story is told in the next case study.

Case Study 4: Jackie French

Jackie French perches on a rock in the shade of a fruit tree, microphone in hand, talking enthusiastically. Her audience of adults and children are here to view her large garden. They are attentive and knowledgeable, asking many questions about her growing techniques, plant species and food self-sufficiency. The garden is nestled in the upper reaches of the Araluen Valley, near Braidwood in the southern highlands of New South Wales (see Figure 18). Steep, rocky, bush-clad mountains rise on either side of the forested garden tucked in the base of the valley. A rock-strewn creek runs, when it has water, through the centre of the property. The house peers out from the tangled shade of trees and shrubs, and visitors push through ferns and palms flanking the stone steps to reach the front door. Around the house scramble 2 hectares of rocky, forested garden with vegetables, flowers, fruit trees and native plants intermingled. In the shade near the shed is a wire meshed chicken run and a wombat rustles and thumps in the shrubs behind the house. Jackie describes her garden as a wilderness.

> *Everything grows together. Pumpkins climb up the avocado trees, strawberries ramble under the kiwifruit and limes, chokos wander in the oranges, daisies poke through the lemon branches and there are wild parsnips, carrots and parsley coming up in the drive. ... Last year's corn stalks still take pride of place in the vegie garden. The birds eat the fruit and I get the rest. It's a mess. But it works.*[445]

I first visited Jackie French's home in winter 2006. Her warm sitting room, like her garden, exuded homely comfort rather than precise neatness and she directed me to the seat facing the window so I could watch the rosellas in the tree outside while we talked and munched homemade peanut biscuits. Later we strolled around

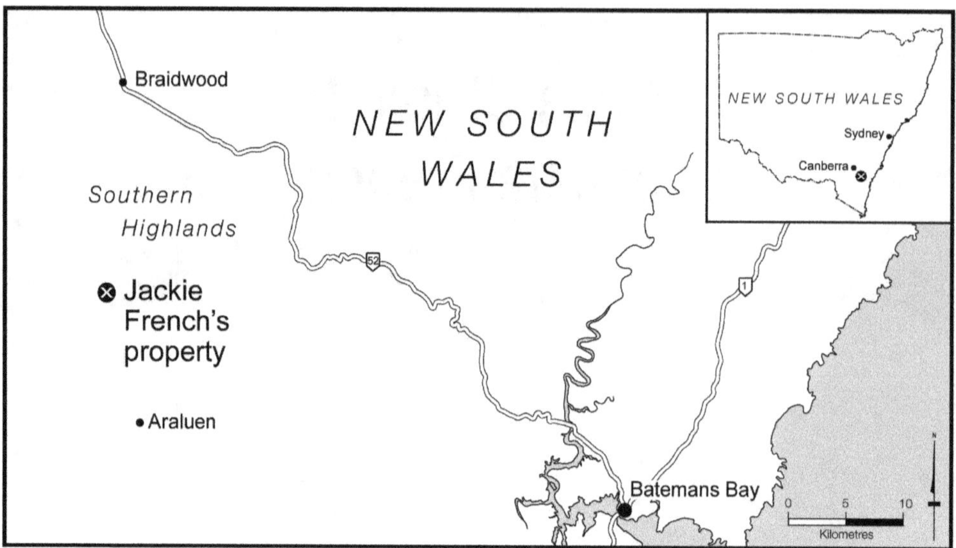

Figure 18: Map showing the location of Jackie French's property.

(Source: Arts Imaging Unit, School of Geography and Environmental Science, Monash University)

her orchard as the sun was shining and the air was sharp and cold. Although the deciduous fruit trees were long dormant there was still plenty to eat and she piled my arms with avocados, lemons and limes. When I joined an organised garden tour in spring later that year the forest garden was thick with life and vegetation, the trees providing cool shade from the sun which already hinted at the harsh summer heat to follow (Figure 19).

Jackie French is an example of a Back to the Land organic grower who 'returned' to live in a rural area and grow food organically for self-sufficiency. Her beliefs and way of life exemplified Back to the Land organic self-sufficiency of the 1970s and 1980s. Through the 1990s and 2000s she continued to garden organically but her ideas and her practice evolved. She created a contemporary version of organic self-sufficiency that had its ideological roots in Back to the Land but which was less idealistic and placed less emphasis on complete self-sufficiency. Through writing about her experiences of organic gardening and living self-sufficiently, Jackie French moved beyond the enclave of Back to the Landers and became a key figure in popularising organic growing and bringing it to the mainstream.

Going back to the land

Jackie French was a classic Back to the Lander. As a young woman in her early twenties she left university in Brisbane and dabbled with rural living on a Queensland mango farm before purchasing a neglected orchard in the upper

Figure 19: Jackie French in her 'wilderness' garden, November 2006.

(Source: Rebecca Jones)

reaches of the Araluen Valley. Applying the basic organic principles of chemical free cultivation and improving soil fertility, she set about developing her own Back to the Land self-sufficient garden. Growing food organically for self-sufficiency was for Jackie French, as for other Back to the Landers, about creating a different way of living. They believed they were the vanguard for change. Jackie French explains:

> *Society had changed so radically over such a short time. There really was a feeling that that accelerated rate of social change could continue and that within 10 or 20 years we could have a very different and a very good society.*

We assumed that if we found the ecological explanation, the management techniques and the solution then these things would be applied. If we found new ways to live then people would live that way.[446]

The new ways to live were about living and working closely with nature and being self-sufficient.

Living in a rural area, interacting closely with and depending upon plants and animals was, Jackie French believed, nurturing her physical and emotional wellbeing: 'I, like all humans, am part of the Earth. To work it, watch it, live within its rhythms – for me, that is the deepest satisfaction.'[447] She elaborates:

I have a feeling that anything that draws humans out of their houses into the natural world to observe the things around them and be part of the growing system is going to be a good thing. ... We do it because it is extraordinarily satisfying both intellectually and physically but also in a quite different way. Even with drought, bushfires, bad seasons, I love being part of it. It is not just physically and mentally rewarding. It is rewarding in a far deeper sense as well. I think life would be extraordinarily impoverished not living with the seasons and working with them.[448]

Living closely with nature meant observing and learning about her particular local environment in the Araluen Valley. This valley lies in mountainous country of the Great Dividing Range approximately 50 kilometres from the coast. Temperatures rise to the mid-forties in summer but fall below zero in winter. The official annual rainfall is 724 mm, but summers are dry and in winter, frost is frequent.[449] Jackie French began experimenting with the way plants grew in her environment, learning about the extraordinary complexity of native plants, animals and insects in her garden and adapting her gardening techniques to her local conditions. She grew trial plots of vegetables with as many as 30 experiments going at any one time and she studied the feeding habits of the native Polistes wasp (Paper wasp). As the wasps dropped their prey into her laundry tub she noted the different pest insects they were consuming at each season. She had little knowledge of the writings of her Australian organic predecessors from early organic farming and gardening societies, so was not able to benefit from their experience and, like them, she found that the British, American and European organic gardening techniques were not always appropriate for environmental conditions in the Araluen Valley.[450] Through observation and experimentation, Jackie French developed her own style of organic gardening which she called 'groves'. She planted circles or clumps of trees and shrubs, the rings increasing in size as each ring becomes established. With frosty winters and hot dry summers, reducing evaporation and increasing shelter from wind and frost was the key to gardening in the Araluen Valley. Fast-growing hardy trees provided shade and shelter for slower-growing and delicate plants. She planted closely and thickly and the interweaving branches of the trees created a microclimate of shade and shelter and provided mulch as the leaves fell.[451] Like permaculture and eco-gardening, methods of gardening developed in the same period as Jackie French's experiments, 'groves' mimic features of the forest: shelter, maximising productivity in a limited area, vertical layers of growth and integrating a diversity of plants in one area (Figure 20).[452] French's groves, like eco-gardening, incorporated native trees and shrubs into a productive garden. While Jackie French's techniques of using hardy, fast-growing trees as nursery plantings was not new,[453] combining annual and perennial food crops in the one space, maximising shelter and dispensing with designated beds was a deviation from traditional organic farming and gardening techniques.

Jackie French's organic gardening techniques were about creating a self-sufficient oasis. She built a garden that provided the food needs for herself and her son. She ate almost only what she grew, gathered or made on the property, including vegetables, fruit, eggs, chickens, nuts and milk. With the help of other Back to the Land people in the area she built her own house from stone, timber and scavenged building materials. She powered the house with solar panels poised on the roof and later with a water wheel built by her partner Bryan. She even made her own toothbrushes, soap, cosmetics and medicinal remedies. She speaks with pride

Figure 20: Jackie French's house nestled in the trees, November 2006.

(Source: Rebecca Jones)

about the resourcefulness that self-sufficiency engendered. Like other Back to the Landers, Jackie took pride in overcoming adversity on her property. She speaks with horrified glee of the desolation that was her property when she purchased it.

> *This place was desert and blackberry when we bought it. I hacked the first road through with a brush hook. There were a few trees left but they were pretty dead. The land was so worked out that in this area here not even grass would grow. It was pale orange hardpan. We had the soil tested and it had the highest salts and highest aluminium level they had ever come across ... It was appalling.*[454]

Transforming this desert into a productive wilderness garden was a source of pride and satisfaction.

Moving to partial self-sufficiency

While acknowledging the rewards of the Back to the Land life, during the late 1980s, after years of self-sufficiency Jackie French became more aware of its limitations and weary of its extremes: '[Total]' self-sufficiency 'is as insular as it is exhausting. You turn in on yourself. And there is little leeway for a crisis', she writes.[455] This realisation came as an epiphany:

> *I remember having pneumonia with a young baby and crawling in a storm to pick tomatoes and vegetables and thinking 'This is not good'. I remember a few years later realising that I was doing without because I wasn't going to buy anything that I couldn't grow. I realised this is in fact fairly silly. It was enough to make me realise that classic self-sufficiency was not a good idea.*[456]

Jackie modified her gardening practice, moving away from total to partial self-sufficiency and became strident in her criticism of the total approach.

> *Having gone through the experience myself, I have just this advice for those who want to be totally self-sufficient: don't do it. 'Almost self-sufficiency' though can make your life as rich and prolific as your garden. Which bits you choose is up to you ... There's a difference, between growing most of what you eat and growing everything. It is easy to grow most of your fruit and vegetables on a quarter acre – at least it's easy once you get into the swing of it ... But it is much, much harder to produce everything ...*[457]

Years of a Back to the Land life provided Jackie with fodder for her books as well as her body. She was able to turn her experience of organic self-sufficiency into an income, writing and speaking about gardening and self-sufficiency. Since the publication of her first gardening book in 1986, *Organic Gardening in Australia*,[458] she has published over 40 books about gardening (and at least as many children's books) as well as many magazine articles. She became a regular guest on the popular television gardening program *Burke's Backyard* and contributed to its associated magazine. She continued to produce what she described as a 'ridiculous abundance' of fruit and vegetables, and her garden still supported 800 fruit trees with over 270 varieties. But she grew only those fruit and vegetables she found satisfying, and which grew easily in the southern New South Wales highlands. Her solar panels were backed by a diesel generator (the water wheel stood idle due to drought) and she supplemented her gardening with shopping in town, now buys soap and cosmetics and never intends to build a house again.[459]

Popularising organic self-sufficiency

In the 1990s Jackie French became one of Australia's principal proponents of a modern style of pragmatic self-sufficiency.[460] She created, in her writings, a version of organic self-sufficiency which she called 'backyard self-sufficiency', modelled on her own practice and experience.[461] She evoked an image of the modern Jackie French-style garden in her book *Backyard Self-sufficiency,* first published in 1992:

> *I have two images of suburban life today. The first is of a neat house set in a mown lawn with trimmed shrubs and a sandpit; a clean kitchen with yesterday's take-away containers on the sink; and the latest videos to fill your life after dinner. The second is of a suburban jungle: a maze of tangled apple trees and grape vines, carpets of strawberries and kids with mulberry-stained faces who don't come inside till dark. You trip over a box of apples in the laundry and the kitchen smells of summer tomatoes and of the basil on the window sill. The kitchen shelves are full, and so are the lives of the inhabitants.*[462]

With backyard self-sufficiency she brought a modified version of the Back to the Land organic ideal to another generation and adapted partial self-sufficiency to urban living. The emphasis was on the personal rewards of growing edible produce rather than on total self-reliance. She exhorted gardeners to dispense with the obsession for neatness and grow only those things you enjoy growing. Close planting of mixed edible and ornamental plants and utilisation of spaces such as house walls, fences and beneath the washing line are methods she recommends.

The message is clear: a suburban backyard can be as abundant in fun as it is in food. She has borrowed from the Back to the Land ideal, the image of personal fulfilment in an abundant, productive paradise but backyard self-sufficiency has dispensed with the idea that gardening is about overcoming adversity; it is now all about pleasure. 'Gardens shouldn't be hard work – they should be fun', she writes; '"Home-made" really does make life richer'; and quite simply, 'I like growing food. It makes life richer.'[463]

Her skill as a garden writer in these backyard self-sufficiency books is to make gardening in general, and organic gardening in particular, attractive and accessible to a non-expert audience. Perhaps because she was writing children's books at the same time as she was writing about gardening, her writing is infused with fun and humour. When describing different methods to build a garden bed she writes:

> *The Dig-and-break-your-back-method. Dig deeply once; leave for three weeks for weeds to germinate; dig again, making sure you haul out all weed bits. Now visit your chiropractor for back restoration.*[464]

And when discussing pest control she remarks:

> *... most pests need to be controlled, not eradicated. If your impossible-to-live-with great-aunt Gladys planned to visit you, you wouldn't get out the arsenic. You'd find some way of discouraging her before she came.*[465]

While writing as an expert and providing a large amount of practical information about traditional organic subjects such as manure, compost and gardening without poisons, she cheerfully admits her mistakes. For example, she tells the story of partner Bryan mowing the grass and accidentally mowing all the asparagus too.[466] In doing so she emphasises that mistakes are part of the process and that organic gardening is an activity to muck in and try rather than an aloof and precise science.

There remains a hint of rebellion in Jackie's backyard organic self-sufficiency picture. Organic growing, it suggests, is about creating a different life with different priorities and leading a richer, and better life as a result. But unlike the Back to the Land ideal of the 1970s, backyard self-sufficiency was not about retreating from society and surviving outside the system. It suggested a way of life that could be combined with paid employment, and urban life that does not eschew comfort but combines growing fruit and vegetables with modern conveniences. It allows people to grow many types of fruit and vegetables while also being employed, travelling and owning modern consumer items.

In 1993 Jackie French became gardening editor and regular columnist for the *Australian* Women's Weekly. This gave her another means to introduce a wide readership to organic gardening. Through the *Women's Weekly* she was able to bring organics to the mainstream in a form acceptable to the popular press. When introducing Jackie French to *Women's Weekly* readers in May 1993, the editor writes: 'Enjoy her humour, wisdom and common sense.'[467] She is promoted for her 'down to earth' homely qualities, and the photograph of a rather dishevelled, childlike Jackie French contrasts with the sophisticated, urbane image of the previous gardening editor Valerie Swain. Through her columns of practical gardening advice and tips, Jackie French gently introduces her readers to gardening without dependence on manufactured pesticides, herbicides and fungicides. She describes mulching and interspersing ornamental and edible plants. She is flexible about the occasional use of chemicals but also shares with readers recipes for her homemade organic preparations, using substances such as sodium bicarbonate, oil and milk for fungus control and physical methods of pest control such as squashing and hosing.[468] She introduces readers to growing edible plants with articles such as 'orchard on the windowsill' and 'living off your land'.[469] Organic gardening, she implies, is comfortable, not challenging. The word 'organic' is rarely mentioned and the methods are described to readers not as radical and subversive, as they were in *Earth Garden* and *Grass Roots*, but as traditional and 'tried and true'.

The version of organic gardening presented by Jackie French in her publications today is a long way from the radical rethinking of values and ways of living proposed by Back to the Landers in the 1970s and 1980s. Her version also differs from the polite but forceful diatribes written by members of the organic farming and gardening societies of the 1940s, 1950s and 1960s campaigning for soil fertility, chemical free and nature conservation. Jackie French has created a version of organic gardening that is palatable to the mainstream, and therefore continues to be published. It introduces readers to organic techniques in a way which only covertly challenges them to consider the relationship of growing, the physical environment and human health, a contrast to the 1970s Back to the Landers' overt rebellion and also to the organic farming and gardening societies' earnest advocacy of earlier decades. But Back to the Landers' beliefs about the inherent individual healthfulness of living with nature and growing food organically resonate with today's organic gardeners, albeit in a modified form. Jackie French's version of organic gardening and her publications echo earlier Back to the Land beliefs but provide a voice and a model for a new generation of organic gardeners in the 1990s and 2000s.

5

Australian organic farming and gardening in the 2000s

Organic farming is today described as an industry and its growers as 'producers', the food they grow is now 'an agricultural sector'[470] and organic farmers take out certification with government-regulated organic organisations. Among gardeners, organic methods have become an orthodoxy: television gardening programs regularly feature organic information,[471] the ABC publishes the magazine *Organic Gardening* and organic gardeners face an arsenal of manufactured organic products. These products range from certified organic pest control remedies to conveniently packaged bags of mulch and pelletised chicken manure. Industrialisation and government regulated certification of organic farming and gardening have transformed the face of Australian organic growing. Despite these obvious changes, do the key principles, central to organic growers of the past, still resonate within Australian organic farmers and gardeners today? Are the original principles of organic growing – the necessity of soil rich in humus and organic matter; the importance of growing food without the use of manufactured chemical fertilisers or pesticides; the necessity of preserving the functioning of natural ecosystems on the farm and beyond; and among some 'Back to the Land' organic growers, the desirability of growing food for self-sufficiency – still relevant in the 2000s? Drawing, again, upon interviews and the writings of organic farmers and gardeners,[472] I will explore whether the beliefs underpinning organic farming and gardening through its first 40 years remain relevant to Australian organic growers today or alternately, as some researchers claim, whether changes in the economics of organic farming and gardening have eroded the defining beliefs of organic growing.

Certification and industrialisation in Australian organic farming

The largest change to transform Australian organic growing in the last 20 years has been the introduction of government-regulated certification schemes of organic farmers. The development of standards for commercial organic farming in the late 1980s, and their revision during the next 20 years, was an attempt to assure consistent, verifiable standards of food production. Adherence to these standards is seen to guarantee the healthiness of the produce and the healthiness of the agricultural land upon which it is grown. Certification of growers against these standards also allowed organic growers for the first time to profit commercially from what they believed to be healthier food production.

There had been a series of hesitant moves towards agreed standards for organic production in Australia since the mid-twentieth century, encouraged by the development of organic standards in Britain, Europe and, later, California. The internationally recognised 'Demeter' trademark, developed in Europe in the 1920s, had been used to denote some biodynamic produce in Australia since the 1950s. In 1967 the Bio-Dynamic Research Institute, led by Alex Podolinsky (who influenced Ray Mason's farming methods discussed in the second case study) began to certify produce using this trademark.[473] Some guidelines for other organic growers were developed in different parts of Australia in the late 1970s and 1980s but they were not widely applied, adherence was not enforceable and nor were they verified by inspections but relied on the integrity and goodwill of farmers.[474]

A coalition of approximately 30 Australian organic growers groups formed in 1986 to provide a coordinated approach to develop common standards among organic growers and to lobby government. This group became the National Association for Sustainable Agriculture Australia (NASAA). The first farm certified according to NASAA standards was Dick and Dot McNeill's orchard, poultry and vegetable farm at Kurrajong North near Sydney. Inspectors examined the farm, soil, animals and tested for pollutants.[475] This process replaced the purely honour-based system previously adhered to by members of organic organisations. As trade in organic food became more globalised there was a perceived need for guarantees of organic production standards and Australian organic farmers' agitation for organic production guidelines became more urgent when the European Union demanded that imported organic produce have a legally enforceable standard of production. NASAA, with the involvement of the Commonwealth Government Australian Quarantine and Inspection Service (AQIS) and other organic growers developed a national standard for certifying organic and biodynamic farms and produce in 1992.[476] During the 1990s and 2000s various non-government certification organisations developed their own standards based on the AQIS minimum standards. Although these standards were developed to verify the quality of exported produce they were also used to certify produce for domestic consumption. In late 2009 the Commonwealth Government peak standards organisation, Standards Australia, released new Australian standards for organic and biodynamic production. These standards were based on the AQIS guidelines but provided common standards for domestic production rather than for export production.[477]

In the mid-2000s there were seven Australian organic organisations certifying Australian organic farms, the largest of these being NASAA and Australian Certified Organic (ACO), the certification arm of the organic growers' association Biological Farmers of Australia. These two organisations now certify the majority of the estimated 2300 Australian certified organic farms. These farms are located in all states and territories and manage approximately eight to 12 million hectares of land between them, the largest area of organically managed land in the world. The vastness is due largely to huge beef stations and cereal farms in northern and central Australia.[478]

Certification formed the foundations of what has become known as the 'organic industry'. While organic growers of the past such as Ray and Elma Mason and Harold White sold their produce on the general market, certification of standards of production enabled organic produce to be distinguished from non-organic produce. This allowed farmers to sell their products as identifiably and verifiably 'organic' and charge a premium for this. Certified organic cereal, livestock, fruit and vegetables sold in Australia in 2006 commanded a price premium of between 50 and 75 per cent more than the equivalent conventionally grown item.[479] The value of organic produce grown in Australia is now estimated to be more than $100 million, with fruit, vegetables, cereals and milk important domestic products and cereals and beef the most important export products, sent to Europe, Japan, North America and increasingly, other parts of Asia.[480]

The development of government-regulated, commercially oriented organic certification schemes has caused some commentators of organic farming to question the degree to which the traditional values and practices of organic growing have remained relevant or been eroded. Some academic sociological researchers in North America and Western Europe[481] and more recently in Australia[482] have argued that core organic values and practices have been compromised as government bureaucracies and large food-processing industries have become involved in regulating organic farming methods. They argue that organic farmers are motivated by commercial rather than ideological principles. However, other researchers of organic farming in Europe, New Zealand, Canada[483] and Australia[484] have countered that while there is *some* evidence that the structure of organic farming has changed, the core organic principles have not been compromised. For example, in Australia export-oriented organic beef and wheat properties operate on a very large scale and international food-processing companies have become involved in the processing of organic food.[485]

This change in the structural organisation of some types of organic farms has not, however, had a profound impact on the underlying beliefs of organic growers themselves nor on the principles upon which their organic methods are based.[486] Some European researchers argue that core organic principles have actually been reinforced rather than eroded by government regulated certification.[487] To understand whether core organic values have been compromised by certification and industrialisation, I will return to each of the four key elements discussed in previous chapters – soil, chemical free, ecological wellbeing and Back to the Land – and explore their resonance with Australian organic farmers and gardeners today.

Soil

Fertile, humus-rich soil, the founding principle of Australian organic growing in the 1940s, continues to be the first principle of organic farming and gardening. Increasing soil humus as a means of encouraging sound growth of plants and animals continues to be attended to with the same energy by organic farmers and gardeners today as it was in the decade immediately after the Second World War. 'It all comes back to the health of the soil, a matter of first things first', writes organic gardener Brenda Little in 2000 in the introduction to *The Australian Organic Gardening Handbook*.[488] Fertile, humus-rich soil features prominently in the certification standards of ACO, NASAA and the 2009 Australian Standards. Echoing Albert Howard's writings 70 years earlier, the NASAA standards explain:

> *Healthy soil is the prerequisite for healthy plants, animals and products. The maintenance of soil health by ecologically sound means is at the heart of organic production systems ... NASAA places great emphasis on the levels of organic matter and humus maintained in soils as an indicator of sustainability and of organic status ... Optimum soil fertility, soil structure and biological activity are fundamental aims of organic farming.*[489]

South Australian beef farmer Brice Douglas, interviewed on his farm at the edge of the Adelaide Hills in 2006, explained that his first action as an organic grower was to test the mineral and organic content of the soil on his farm. Following these tests he applied dolomite to reduce the acidity of the soil and then added calcium and magnesium, the same method used by Ray Mason to improve his soil in the early 1970s. 'By the next year you could see the difference in the pasture. Just in one year', Brice remarked.[490] Like the organic growers of the 1940s and 1950s, Victorian dairy farmers Ron and Bev Smith describe bringing life to their soil through organic methods. When they began farming organically in

Gippsland in 1980 'the soil smelt lifeless', they recall. By 2005, after 25 years of organic practices, 'there was abundant soil, life, bacteria and fungi ... The soil smells rich and sweet.'[491]

Compost, animal manure and green cover crops remain the stalwarts of organic farming and gardening. Queensland sugar-cane farmers Anthony and Debbie Skopp, also interviewed in 2006, practise sheet composting where they spread organic matter directly onto the soil to decompose. As the organic matter breaks down it increases the humus content in the soil.[492] Australian organic standards recommend animal manure as fertiliser and soil conditioner just as the organic societies did in the 1940s and 1950s. However, organic farmers and gardeners are now advised to compost manure prior to application to food crops to reduce danger of contamination from micro-organisms.[493] To fertilise his farm, Queensland banana farmer Desmond Chappel applies composted chicken manure ('one large Milo can per plant') rather than the artificial fertilisers used by conventional banana growers and Anthony Sheldon rotates grazing animals and crops so the animal manure will fertilise the paddocks prior to sowing.[494] Green cover crops are also used to increase the organic content of the soil. Just as Harold White ploughed in grass and legumes to increase soil organic matter and raise nitrogen levels, Desmond Chappel now sows a legume crop of peas or beans prior to planting the bananas.

Composting, manuring and green cover crops remain essential organic methods but the use of human sewage as fertiliser, so enthusiastically promoted by organic societies in the 1940s and 1950s, has not regained popularity since its fall from favour in the 1960s. Australian organic standards prohibit the use of human sewage on land used for the production of human or animal feed.[495] Preoccupation with hygiene, concern about the heavy metal content of municipal sewage as well as fear of a negative public image of organics have all contributed to the rejection of human sewage as a fertility source by commercial organic farmers. When the United States government proposed the use of sewage sludge in its national organic standards there was strong dissent from organic groups.[496] Some organic gardening publications make reference to the high nitrogen content of human urine and advocate the use of composting toilets[497] but the use of human sewage is no longer seen as core organic practice as it was, briefly, in the 1940s and 1950s.[498]

Organic farmer Brice Douglas, formerly a naturopath and osteopath, explains the connection between fertile soil and the health of plants, animals and humans:

> *You can go out into the paddock anywhere [on my farm] now and dig and there are earthworms everywhere. The dung beetles have come back and here in the pond in front of our house and in our four dams there are frogs everywhere. It is just the same as the human body which is what I did for 38 years [as a naturopath and osteopath]. You find out what is the problem, the*

base cause, the deficiency. You give them the minerals and vitamins to restore their health. That is exactly what you are doing with the soil. The end result is healthy animals that you have no problems with.[499]

However, organic growers today are more equivocal about making a direct link between humus-rich soil and absence of human disease, assertions that were central to organic growing in the 1940s. NASAA states that one of the aims of organic farming is: 'to produce food of high nutritional value'.[500] But the organisation does not then go on to assert that the production of nutrient-rich food is *dependent* on soil enriched with organic matter. Similarly, Anthony Sheldon remarks of the nutritional superiority of organic food for human consumption: 'well, the jury is still out on that one'.[501]

There is scant scientific evidence to either prove or disprove the nutritional superiority of organic food compared to conventionally grown produce. There are still few large-scale studies of the nutritional content of organic food and there are inconsistencies between the methodologies and findings of smaller-scale studies.[502] However, some reliable evidence is now emerging that organically grown food may have more concentrated levels of some vitamins and antioxidants and micronutrients and this knowledge is beginning to enter organic growers' discussions.[503]

Apparently contradicting the centrality of humus-rich soil to organic production is the recent certification of non-soil-based organic marine and fresh water aquaculture production.[504] For example, two mussel farms at Portarlington on Port Phillip Bay in Victoria have been certified by ACO. These aquaculture operations are considered organic because they cooperate with natural processes; they work within and do not disrupt nor pollute the bay ecology and are chemical free. But aquaculture is clearly not soil-based, which has created an anomaly for standards which continue to define organic systems as soil-based systems. This anomaly reflects the history of organic farming and gardening in Australia and the continued importance of Australian organic growing societies' belief in the importance of soil humus being the foundation of human health.

Chemical free

Raising plants and animals without the use of synthesised chemical fertilisers, pesticides, herbicides and fungicides continues to be a significant means by which today's organic growers assert the healthfulness of their produce. For many people today 'chemical free' is synonymous with organic. For example, the introduction to a generalist Australian organic vegetable gardening book published by the Australian Broadcasting Corporation states: 'Growing organically by definition is growing without the use of chemical pesticides and fertilisers.'[505]

Many of the pesticides and fertilisers available to farmers and gardeners today are different from those used in previous decades, but organic growers' aversion to chemicals has changed little since the campaigns against DDT and superphosphate in the 1950s, 1960s and 1970s. Organic standards prevent the use of all synthesised chemicals. Prohibition also extends to naturally occurring substances which are known to be toxic (such as nicotine).[506] Organic farmers and gardeners continue to reject artificially synthesised chemicals as unhealthy. Organic beef farmer Brice Douglas explains his disapproval of agricultural pesticides and fertilisers:

> *It is logical. The residues left from the chemicals and the sprays, they have to affect you. If you are eating an animal that has been reared using chemicals – treating for worms, eating grass that has been grown with fertilisers and sprayed with pesticides to kill the bugs and beetles – the end result is that you are doing exactly the same thing as drinking the chemical.*[507]

The desire to farm without the use of artificial chemicals is still a significant motivation for growers to adopt organic practices. Organic turkey and macadamia farmer Matthew Jamieson grew up on a conventional beef property in central Queensland and tells of his experiences of illness due, he believes, to contact with agricultural chemicals.

> *All my family have died of cancers. By the time I was 34 I was the oldest of my descent line. I grew up at the stage when everyone was spraying 245T and everyone in our rural community had stillborn babies which I can only put down to all the volatile chemicals ... We used to spray the cattle with some organophosphate. My father would be on one side and I would be on the other, spraying it on the cattle but also on each other. We put barrier cream on our hands and were wearing overalls but we'd be soaking wet.*[508]

Other organic farmers echo Matthew's belief in the harmful effects of working with chemicals. Gippsland dairy farmers Ron and Bev Smith believe that Ron's chronic asthma was caused by superphosphate and after converting to organic farming Ron's asthma left him.[509] Surveys of organic farmers in the last 20 years confirm that organic farmers' concerns about the health of their families, consumers, animals and themselves motivated them to convert to organic farming.[510] Stories abound among organic growers of rashes, itches, flaky skin, cancer and respiratory ailments, even death – all of which they attribute to agricultural chemicals.[511] Telling and retelling stories about chemical poisoning affirms organic growers' collective aversion to chemicals and the belief in the comparative healthfulness of organic produce.

Aversion to the unnaturalness of chemical fertilisers and pesticides also underpins current organic growers' rejection of genetically modified (or GM) plants and animals. The process of genetic modification results in synthetically constructed entities achieved by joining fragments of DNA from different organisms, including organisms of different species (such as rice with daffodils or fish with tomatoes). It results in combinations of genetic material which could not occur through normal reproduction and hybridisation. Therefore, organic growers are opposed to genetically modified organisms as 'unnatural' products which 'have no place in organic production systems' – the same argument they have used against chemical fertilisers and pesticides for 60 years.[512] Australian organic standards prohibit genetically modified or genetically engineered products and processes from any aspect of organic production, including the use of genetically modified seeds and plants and contamination of a crop by genetically modified organisms will result in decertification.[513]

Just as organic growers of the 1950s, 1960s and 1970s viewed all synthesised products with suspicion, and distrusted government and scientific claims of their 'safety', so genetically modified organisms are opposed by organic growers on precautionary grounds as well as on principle. There is currently no firm evidence confirming the presence or absence of health and environmental effects of genetically modified organisms.[514] Therefore organic standards take a position which echoes the precautionary principle, reasoning that actions should be avoided if there is a possible threat of serious or irreversible environmental damage.[515] For example, this approach is built into the Australian organic standards[516] and *Botanica's Pocket Organic Gardening* remarks:

> *Going on previous scientific experience we know that changing one part of an ecosystem will always result in some kind of knock-on effect, resulting in unforeseen changes in other directions that lead to environmental problems.*[517]

Organic growers today, unlike their counterparts in earlier decades have access to a plethora of manufactured products which are 'chemical free' and considered to be organically acceptable. Increased use of products which conform to organic principles began in the late 1970s and early 1980s with the small-scale domestic concoction of plant and mineral-based organic remedies for pests and diseases. During the 1990s and 2000s these organic remedies began to be manufactured commercially on an industrial scale and organic farmers and gardeners now have access to manufactured remedies such as concentrated seaweed fertiliser, organic fruit fly bait and garlic spray. Brice Douglas sprinkles powdered sulphur on his cattle to control lice.[518] Similarly, many organic gardeners now use solutions of *Bacillus thuringiensis,* a naturally occurring commercially available bacteria sold as 'Dipel', which is a stomach poison to caterpillars but is not poisonous to humans, animals or non-target insects. Organic farmer Anthony Sheldon sees the substitution of 'unsafe' manufactured products with 'safe' manufactured products as an important part of the future of organics. He sees large chemical industries as having a role in Australian organic farming, manufacturing non-toxic agricultural products.

> *If more of these products can work their way into the market to replace stuff that is toxic it can only do good. They are not putting themselves out of business because they are still making a product that does the job but is safe. Hopefully that type of thing is the way of the future. The big companies that supply chemicals now, they have the expertise and, in time, could make natural products. They could still be in business but selling stuff that is non-toxic and it has got to be a good thing.*[519]

Relying on manufactured products to control pests and diseases, maintain fertility and contain weeds has come to be known, among organic growers, as 'input substitution'; replacing poisonous, synthesised 'conventional' chemicals with non-toxic, non-polluting 'organic' substances. Australian organic standards incorporate both an input substitution and systemic approach to organic farming. The standards prohibit synthetically compounded chemicals which have been created or changed chemically[520] and encourage farmers to use systemic preventative measures. Products which are not toxic to humans, animals and non-target species, not polluting and not synthesised are allowed but only as a 'last resort', an uncharacteristic response to unusual events. The standards encourage farmers to work towards less reliance on external inputs and develop strategies to ensure that 'the use of substances shall not take the place of management practices that aim at prevention for the control of pests and diseases'.[521]

The input substitution approach to organic farming has been criticised by some organic growers, for example, in Australia by Jackie French and internationally by Hardy Vogtmann, honorary president of the International Federation of Organic Agricultural Movements (IFOAM).[522] Both insist that organic farming and gardening should be about creating systems of production that prevent pests and diseases through fertile soil, encouraging beneficial fauna and working with natural processes rather than replacing one remedy with another. This argument echoes the original soil fertility approach of organic growers in the 1940s. Although manufactured organic inputs are made of plant and rock extracts and other naturally occurring products they are manufactured using industrial processes and stretch the definition of 'natural'. The toxicity of a product such as Dipel or powdered sulphur is limited to the target species, but their use challenges the definition of 'poison'. The concept of relative toxicity which emerged in the 1970s, whereby pest control remedies were viewed as 'relatively safe' therefore 'relatively organic', has become more pronounced with the use of these products by organic farmers and gardeners. The debate surrounding this approach to organic farming and gardening has revealed conflicting philosophies between an emphasis on systemic or ecological preventions and remedy-based solutions similar to a biomedical approach. The importance of input substitution to organic growing today suggests that many organic farmers and gardeners are accommodating of a biomedical approach to health and farming which sits, sometimes uncomfortably, within the broader ecological philosophy of organic growing.

Ecological wellbeing

Matthew Jamieson, northern New South Wales organic turkey and macadamia farmer interviewed for this study in 2006 describes himself as 'Farmer Giles of Ham'. *Farmer Giles of Ham* is a short story written by J.R.R. Tolkien about a genial farmer who battles dragons.[523] After studying science and entomology, Matthew worked at the Environment Centre in Darwin and became involved in campaigning against forest clearance, the destruction of rivers and the rights of West Timorese people in Indonesia. For Matthew, organic farming is an extension of environmental activism – another way for him to slay dragons.

> *I feel that the world needs to change. I always felt that producing food with sustainable farming was the right thing to be doing. I wanted to produce something sound that doesn't have a negative effect on the planet.*[524]

The importance of ecological wellbeing to human health and the interdependence of human wellbeing upon the wellbeing of the whole environment remain core principles of Australian organic farming and gardening today. The maintenance of ecological systems through organic agriculture is identified by IFOAM, the international peak body for organic grower organisations, as one of the key principles of organic farming: 'Organic agriculture should be based on living ecological systems and cycles, work with them, emulate them and help sustain them.'[525] The preface to the general organic farming text, *Botanica's Pocket Organic Gardening* also, more poetically, situates organic growing as part of the wider natural world.

> *Organic gardening ... is about living in trust with Nature and respecting all life on the planet. This book will take you on the gentle path to recognising that we are part of the living world, not separate from it.*[526]

Ecological principles have been enshrined in Australian standards for organic production. The NASAA national standards state that:

> *... ecosystem principles of relevance to organic production include respect for inter-connectivity. Organic farmers harness the capacity of the ecosystem to produce economic services, but must do so in ways that enhance the provision of other ecosystem services for others and for future generations to enjoy. The farm is a functional part of the wider landscape in which it is*

located and actively contributes to the long-term ability of the landscape to provide ... ecological ... services.[527]

Similarly, Australian Standards state that:

> ... *the aim is to enhance biodiversity on farm enabling 'eco-system services' to enhance the productivity and sustainability of organic farming operations and the surrounding environment.*[528]

Organic farming and gardening societies of the 1950s, 1960s and 1970s encouraged organic growers to protect and enhance on-farm native flora, fauna and habitats as a way of cooperating with native ecosystems. Today the national standards make it mandatory for certified organic farmers to protect primary native ecosystems on their properties such as forest, scrub, wetlands and native pastures. They are required to maintain and increase these ecosystems by setting aside at least 5 per cent of their property as refuges for indigenous flora and fauna and native habitat ecosystems and maintaining refuge planting.[529] On his 40-hectare property, Matthew Jamieson has reserved 3 hectares of indigenous subtropical rainforest which is approximately 8 per cent of the total farm area.

As drought, climate change and resource conservation have become poignant issues in Australia during the 2000s, organic growers have promoted organic methods of food production as part of broader environmental solutions to ecological damage. In this context human health is defined in the broadest sense; not so much in terms of particular diseases but as a matter of human and planetary survival. *Organic Gardener* magazine links organic practice to conservation and sustainable living through its regular 'green living segments', which profile issues such as green power, ethical investment, minimal consumption, eco-tourism, water and energy efficiency. For example, an article in *Organic Gardener* profiles a number of households who are cutting their household energy use and another discusses ways of reducing the environmental impact of the office environment through the use of sustainable and non-polluting building materials and furnishings, ecological building design and reduction in energy and water use.[530] *The Australian Organic Gardening Handbook* reiterates organic growing as a solution to environmental destruction:

> *The evidence of the way we have polluted the planet on which we all depend for existence has become frightening. The hole in the ozone layer, the death of rivers, the salinisation of land ... but there is something that can be done, and more and more people are doing it ... Organic gardening ... has become the obvious and sensible method to employ.*[531]

One of the best-known Australian organic gardeners, Peter Cundall, former presenter of ABC television's *Gardening Australia* and regular contributor to the

ABC's gardening magazines, is also a strong advocate for environmental causes such as the campaign against the pulp mill in the Tasmanian Tamar Valley and efforts to ameliorate climate change.[532]

Australian organic growers and their societies have, in the last 20 years, been enthusiastic and sympathetic supporters rather than chief players in campaigns for conservation issues beyond the agricultural perimeter. However, during the 2000s, organic growers have begun to see themselves as having a central role in mitigating global warming. Organic organisations such the Biological Farmers of Australia, the Rodale Institute in the United States and IFOAM, as well as Australian scientists such as Tim Flannery now speak about organic farming as a strategy for combating climate change. Organic farming is discussed as a strategy for reducing the amount of carbon dioxide, one of the most problematic greenhouse gases contributing to global warming.[533] Carbon is one of the natural constituents of soil, being contained in the organic matter component of the soil. The absorption of carbon by the soil is part of the continual cycling of carbon between air, vegetation and animals in the process of growth and decay. Soil naturally contains more carbon than both vegetation and the atmosphere.[534] Organic practices such as composting, mulching, cover crops, manuring and recycling crop wastes such as stubble all increase the organic matter in the soil and therefore can also raise carbon levels in soil, creating a long-lived secure store of carbon. By increasing soil carbon which comes largely from carbon dioxide gas, atmospheric carbon is reduced. The amount of carbon sequestered in this way varies according to soil type. Soils in arid agricultural areas, such as inland Australia, are able to store up to 150 kilograms of carbon per hectare while soils in moist cool or humid areas such as temperate, coastal southern Australia and tropical northern Australia are able to store up to 1000 kilograms per hectare. Therefore, regular organic agricultural food production methods have the potential to offset global carbon dioxide emissions by between 5 and 15 per cent.[535]

Organic organisations also argue that organic methods are a solution to high energy consumption which also contributes to climate change. Organic growing techniques are more energy efficient methods of food production. They require fewer fossil fuels and contribute less to global warming and resource depletion.[536] Large amounts of energy are required to manufacture artificial fertilisers, therefore organic farming techniques, which do not use manufactured fertilisers, are a less fossil fuel intensive method of agriculture. Organic farming systems also create fewer greenhouse gases such as nitrous oxide, produced by the soluble nitrogenous fertilisers used in conventional farming.[537]

The importance of humus-rich soil to human health is now as much a question of ecological wellbeing as it is to the production of nutritious food. Although some organic growers today appear less certain of the nutritional superiority of food grown in humus-rich soil compared to conventional produce, organic soil's role in improving human health remains secure through its contribution to ecological wellbeing by assisting to combat environmental damage through global warming.

Back to the Land

In the 2000s going Back to the Land has endured as a stereotype of organic growing, although today it is a caricature rather than an accurate representation of Australian organic farmers and gardeners. Back to the Land ideas are still evident among some organic growers but they no longer focus on total self-sufficiency, rebellion and separation but emphasise partial self-sufficiency, life enrichment and ecological responsibility. During the 1970s and 1980s Back to the Landers were a subgroup within the wider organic movement, as discussed in Chapter 4. Certification and regulation of organic agriculture have further marginalised Back to the Land ideas from the key organic farming and gardening principles.

Australian organic standards established organic beliefs about soil, chemical free and ecological wellbeing as integral aspects of organic growing. However, Back to the Land values were not incorporated into the standards which has made these values even less integral to organic principles. The development of verifiable standards for organic growing and certification of organic farms allowed organic farmers, for the first time, to prove to consumers that their produce was grown according to particular criteria which enabled them to demand, and receive, higher prices for their produce. Now that farming organically could be commercially advantageous, some organic growers were keen to present organic farming as an industry rather than a social movement. Back to the Landers' rejection of modern industrialism was seen to be incompatible with the regulatory commercial spirit of certification and some organic farmers tried to dissociate themselves from the Back to the Land image of the 1970s and 1980s. A writer to the magazine *Australian Organic News* in 1992, the year the National Organic Standards were launched, complained:

> *With the change from 'movement' to 'industry' the place for the well-meaning but impractical enthusiast has shifted from the orchard to the home garden ... to put it bluntly, those who refuse to recognise the change of organics from movement to industry are getting in the way of the development of that industry and the potential it holds for significant benefits for individuals and the nation alike in terms of healthy food and the spin-off advantages of organic production.*[538]

The cost of certification further reinforces the separation of Back to the Land organic growers from commercial organic farmers. When NASAA certification schemes commenced in the late 1980s, certification cost farmers $75 per year which covered the cost of administration and inspections.[539] This fee was prohibitive for Back to the Landers, such as Jackie French, who led a financially marginal, semi-self-sufficient existence selling surplus organic produce locally. Most of these organic growers did not seek certification and were therefore not able to sell their produce as certified organic.[540]

Although Back to the Land values have been marginalised from Australian organic standards, Back to the Land beliefs continue as a niche within organic gardening. The Back to the Land magazines *Grass Roots* and *Earth Garden* continue to be published[541] and provide information about growing food, alternative energy production and home building. Permaculture, with its emphasis on small-scale food production, minimising environmental impact and critiquing industrial food production provides a subgroup within the organic movement which is most oriented towards Back to the Land beliefs. At least eight permaculture organisations now exist in metropolitan and regional Australia[542] and permaculture is discussed at length within many organic publications.[543] Tasmanian organic gardener Linda Cockburn, with her partner and son, are pursuing a Back to the Land style dream, similar to that sought by Back to the Landers in the 1970s and 1980s. Their goal is to reduce their energy consumption by organically growing as much of their own food as possible, generating power through solar panels, collecting rainwater and using only foot and bicycle transport. They have recently begun to build their own home in southern Tasmania with sustainably sourced material. Linda sums up her lifestyle as 'healthier, fitter, wealthier and happier'.[544]

Although the Cockburn family's way of life differs little from the Back to the Land organic growers of the 1970s and 1980s, the political focus of going Back to the Land has receded. Going Back to the Land is now more a way of life than an act of political rebellion. Organic gardeners continue to be drawn to the wellbeing they associate with working with and living among nature. For example, *Botanica's Pocket Organic Gardening* states that:

> *Organic gardening gives us the opportunity to regain control over one of the basic needs in life – food ... We co-evolved with our food plants grown by natural means and it seems that the lesson, repeated in so many areas, is that our bodies are best served by working with the pattern long evolved by Nature.*[545]

However, this is now translated not as separating oneself from the 'urban' or 'industrial' world but as incorporating nature into everyday life through gardening, growing food and living in a less resource intensive way. It is no longer considered a form of radical rebellion. Linda Cockburn's primary goal is to change how she lives in a less resource intensive way, rather than to overhaul societal values as was the aim of the Back to the Land movement of the 1970s and 1980s. Cockburn's articles nestle alongside descriptions of ethical investments, home retrofitting for energy and water efficiency, eco-travel and commercial organic products. Self-sufficiency is now one option of many to reduce our environmental impact and enrich lives.

Grass Roots editor, Megg Miller, believes that fewer organic gardeners today are interested in complete self-sufficiency. 'That total outlook has been recognised as leading you to an early grave. It is too hard ... some of us like music and good books and culture and that is just as important.'[546] Today, emphasis has shifted from total to partial self-sufficiency. Most organic growers interested in self-sufficiency practise a Jackie French style of partial self-sufficiency which combines food production with other forms of income. Jackie French lives in southern New South Wales, has a large fruit orchard and vegetable garden and raises chickens, but earns her primary income from writing and public speaking. Megg Miller still lives in central Victoria and grows many fruit and vegetables, keeps chickens and pet sheep, but earns an income editing *Grass Roots* and other specialist magazines. Many of Megg Miller's and Jackie French's Back to the Land contemporaries live on their properties and continue to grow food, but very few now live self-sufficiently and most have an alternative source of income.[547]

Returning to the question posed at the beginning of this chapter: do the key principles of Australian organic growing still resonate with organic farmers and gardeners today? Researchers of current organic farming, who return only to the recent past of the 1970s and 1980s as the source of organic principles, would inevitably conclude that the ideological basis for organic growing today has deviated from its original principles. Australian organic farmers and gardeners today grapple with issues such as genetic modification, climate change, a plethora of commercially manufactured organic products, national standards and the certification of aquaculture – issues which organic growers of the past would not have recognised. Commercial organic growers are now controlled by regulations and guidelines and, as a result, can command a premium for their produce. Commercial organic growing can now be profitable as well as ideological. Back to the Land values of self-sufficiency, living close to nature and radical rebellion have been further marginalised from core organic ideas.

However, it is not possible to understand organic farming and gardening in Australia today without understanding its history and the emergence and establishment of its defining ideas over the 70 years since the founding of Australia's first organic growers' societies in the 1940s. Comparing the defining principles of organic growing which emerged in the 1940s and 1950s with Australian organic growing today reveals that the core principles have been reinforced rather than eroded by certification and industrialisation.

Despite its increasingly industrialised and regulated appearance, Australian organic farming and gardening continues to be characterised by three of the key principles of organic growing that defined Australian organic growing from the 1940s through to the 1980s: humus-rich soil, chemical free and ecological wellbeing. The explanation of the term 'organic agriculture' in NASAA's constitution illustrates the integration and endurance of these three principles into the definition of organic:

> *Organic agriculture means a system of agriculture able to balance productivity with low vulnerability to problems such as pest infestation and environmental degradation while maintaining the quality of land for future generations. In practice this involves a system which avoids or largely excludes the use of synthetically compounded fertilisers, pesticides, growth regulators, livestock feed additives and other harmful or potentially harmful substances. It includes the use of technologies such as crop rotations, mechanical cultivation and biological pest control; and such material as legumes, crop residues, animal manures, green manures, other organic wastes and mineral bearing rocks. The intention is to encourage natural biological systems.*[548]

Would a member of the Victorian Compost Society or the Living Soil Association of Tasmania, Harold White, the Back to the Landers of the 1970s, a reader of *Farm and Garden Digest* or any of the other Australian organic farmers and gardeners described in this history recognise Australian organic farming and gardening today? Undoubtedly. They may be bemused by changes to Australian organic growing during the 1990s and 2000s, but would note that there remains a continuity of values and practices from 1940s through to the present. Organic growing continues to rest on the same belief that human health and wellbeing depend on the health and wellbeing of the biophysical environment, an idea which remains as relevant in the 2000s as it did at the founding of Australia's first organic growers' societies in the 1940s.

The wheel of life

From the beginning, Australian organic growers saw the biophysical environment as a system of which humans were a part. The picture they had of this relationship between humans and non-humans increased in complexity over time. Initially it was a cyclical interaction illustrated by a mandala – a cycle between soil, growth and decay. Organic growers' understanding broadened to include an appreciation of the effects of artificial chemicals on human, plant and animal health. The complexity of this wheel increased still further as understanding of the farm and garden's place in broader biological systems emphasised humans' dependence upon the wellbeing of all forms of life. For some organic growers, such as the Back to the Landers, this entailed being self-sufficient by living and working closely with nature. The integration of these ideas into Australian organic growing created a vision of a rich, complex wheel of life in which humans were but one element of an interdependent system.

The interaction of humans with this system in the farm and garden created domesticated ecologies[549] – to again borrow Donald Worster's phrase discussed at the beginning of this history – but they were ecologies in which humans worked as a member rather than as the centrepiece. Organic farms and gardens were both 'natural' and 'human-constructed' environments moulded, changed and adapted to human food production. Although anthropocentric in their endeavour, organic growers approached food production with humility, recognising that even as farmers and gardeners shaped their environments, they too were shaped by it. They learnt to change their practices to suit variations in rainfall, soil, topography, vegetation and climate and were able to adapt their imported methods to local conditions. The domesticated ecologies and the native environments from which they were carved, in turn, had helped to shape Australian organic growing principles and practices.

These principles were underpinned by the ecological view that human wellbeing depended upon environmental wellbeing. Belief in the healthfulness of growing food in humus-rich soil; the avoidance of chemicals potentially toxic to insects, plants, animals and humans; the importance of well-functioning native ecosystems to human food production; and the healthfulness of living and working among nature all illustrate Australian organic growers' belief in the dependence of human health, wellbeing and survival upon the non-human world and its systems. They argued that Earth's ecosystems provide services – climatic, hydrological, biological and ecological – which must be protected to create the conditions for human health.[550] Working with and within biological systems provides the best chance of ongoing human health, wellbeing and survival and, according to organic beliefs, organic farming and gardening provides the means for achieving this.

This ecological perspective on health contrasted with the emphasis of the biomedical model which was the dominant framework for understanding health throughout the twentieth century. Organic growers saw the biomedical model as placing too much emphasis on cure of disease rather than prevention, on individuals rather than environments and on vectors of disease rather than systemic contributors. Embracing the ecological perspective, organic growers developed a system for food production, farming, gardening and maintaining human health that emphasised soundly functioning natural systems, rather than individual solutions, and focused on the interrelationship of humans with the natural environment rather than the dominance of people over it. These ideas set organic growers apart from dominant ideas, establishing organic farming and gardening as an 'alternative' to conventional practices.

The consistency of the organic message over 70 years and the practicality of its application to food production and land management provide a set of principles and practices which at times challenge dominant ideas about agriculture and more broadly about humans' ways of interacting with the environment around them. Throughout 70 years of organic growing in Australia, organic farmers and gardeners have grappled with environmental challenges such as soil erosion, chemical toxicity, loss of habitat and genetic modification. Faced with current uncertainties about global warming, loss of biodiversity, water shortage and food security many people are considering the need to renegotiate the way we interact with the land. Organic farming and gardening provides an example for conceptualising and interacting with nature. Listening to the voices of organic farmers and gardeners themselves can reveal alternative ways of thinking. As permaculturalist David Holmgren noted, some of the most interesting and innovative things happen on the margins[551] and those who choose to walk out of step with the mainstream can suggest new and surprising answers.

Endnotes

Introduction

1 Willer Yussefi, Helga Yussefi, and Minou Yussefi, *The World of Organic Agriculture: Statistics and Emerging Trends 2006* (Frick, Switzerland: Research Institute of Organic Agriculture, 2006), p. 24.

2 Donald Worster, 'Transformations of the Earth: Toward an Agroecological Perspective in History,' *Journal of American History* 76, no. 4 (1990): p. 1093.

3 The biophysical environment is the physical environment which supports life. Therefore it includes plants, animals, microscopic life, insects, soil, and other living organisms as well as the atmosphere, climate and geological features. It includes both human managed parts of the 'natural' environment, such as farms and gardens as well as bushland and wilderness.

4 The word 'ecology' was created by German biologist Ernst Haeckel in 1866 from the Greek words '*oikos*' (household, place) and '*logos*' (study of), emphasising things within their context rather than as isolated elements. Donald Worster, *Nature's Economy: A History of Ecological Ideas* (Melbourne: Cambridge University Press, 1992).

5 Donald Worster, *Nature's Economy: A History of Ecological Ideas* (Melbourne: Cambridge University Press, 1992). These points are also made in Martin Mulligan and Stuart Hill, *Ecological Pioneers: A Social History of Australian Ecological Thought and Action* (Cambridge University Press, 2001), Deborah Bird Rose, 'The Ecological Humanities in Action: An Invitation,' *Australian Humanities Review*, no. 31–32 (2004). Andrea Gaynor, *Harvest of the Suburbs: An Environmental History of Growing Food in Australian Cities* (Perth: University of Western Australia Press, 2006), p. 4.

6 A.J. McMichael, 'Health and Disease: An Ecological Perspective,' in *Human Frontiers, Environments and Disease: Past Patterns, Uncertain Futures* (Cambridge University Press, 2001); A.J. McMichael, 'Population,

Environment, Disease, and Survival: Past Patterns, Uncertain Futures,' *Lancet* 359 (2002).

7 Mildred Blaxter, *Health* (Cambridge, UK; Malden, USA: Polity Press, 2004), pp. 7–8, 32. The Greek physician Hippocrates, wrote *Airs, Waters and Places* in about 400BC in which he described his beliefs about health and medicine. So called 'Hippocratic medicine' was probably a combination of ancient beliefs which was consolidated and adapted to Greek culture by many people, including Hippocrates.

8 Mildred Blaxter, *Health* (Cambridge, UK; Malden, USA: Polity Press, 2004), pp. 7–8.

9 Mildred Blaxter, *ibid.*, pp. 10–12; A.J. McMichael, *Human Frontiers, Environments and Disease: Past Patterns, Uncertain Futures* (Cambridge University Press, 2001), pp. 157–8, 322.

10 Warwick Anderson, *The Cultivation of Whiteness* (Melbourne: Melbourne University Press, 2002), p. 42–45.

11 A.J. McMichael, *Human Frontiers, Environments and Disease: Past Patterns, Uncertain Futures* (Cambridge University Press, 2001), p. 163.

12 A.J. McMichael, *ibid.*, pp. 80–1.

13 These statements paraphrase explanations of environmental history provided in: William Cronon, 'A Place for Stories: Nature, History and Narrative,' *Journal of American History* 78, no. 4 (1992); J.R. McNeill, 'Observations on the Nature and Culture of Environmental History,' *History and Theory, Theme Issue* 42 (2003); Donald Worster, 'Transformations of the Earth: Toward an Agroecological Perspective in History,' *Journal of American History* 76, no. 4 (1990).

14 Ann Curthoys and John Docker, *Is History Fiction?* (Sydney: UNSW Press, 2005).

15 Rudolf Steiner is better known in Australia for his educational theories. In Australia, biodynamics has a history which is at times parallel to other organic growers and at times convergent. Biodynamic practices are discussed in more detail in the second case study. Permaculture is discussed in more detail in Chapter 3.

16 The proliferation of organic societies and publications in the 1970s is discussed in Chapters 3 and 4.

17 The post-1970 magazines and newsletters I have used as sources are periodical publications of the Soil Association of South Australia, Brisbane Organic Growers Group, Tasmanian Organic Gardening and Farming Society, Henry Doubleday Research Association of New South Wales and Western Australian Organic Growers Association.

18 The name of this magazine was changed to *Organic Growing* in 1980.

19 These magazines are discussed in more detail in Chapter 5.

20 The only major publication by an Australian organic grower, prior to the 1970s is discussed in the first case study. Examples of post-1970s books by individual organic growers include: Peter Bennett, *Australia and New Zealand Organic Gardening*, 1st ed. (French's Forest, NSW: Child and Associates, 1979); Jackie French, *Backyard Self-Sufficiency* (Melbourne: Aird Books, 1992); Jackie French, *Organic Gardening in Australia* (French's Forest: Reed, 1986); Michael J. Roads, *A Guide to Organic Living in Australia* (Launceston: Mary Fisher Bookshop, 1977). These and other monologues are discussed in Chapters 2, 3, 4 and 5.
21 *Grass Roots* and *Earth Garden* are discussed in more detail in Chapter 4, 'Back to the Land'.
22 *Transcript of Evidence of the Royal Commission on the Bread Industry before Judge Stretton*, 8 June, 1949.
23 Kate Darian-Smith and Paula Hamilton, *Memory and History in Twentieth-Century Australia* (Melbourne: Oxford University Press, 1994), pp. 1–6; Janet McCalman, 'The Uses and Abuses of Oral History,' *Canberra Historical Journal*, no. 21 (1988).
24 R. Samuel and P. Thompson, 'Introduction,' in *The Myths We Live By*, eds R. Samuel and Paul Thompson (London: Routledge, 1990), p. 21.
25 R. Samuel and P. Thompson, *ibid.*, p. 21; Alistair Thomson, 'A Past You Can Live With: Digger Memories and the Anzac Legend,' *Oral History Association of Australia Journal*, no. 13 (1991): pp. 16–17.
26 R. Samuel and P. Thompson, 'Introduction,' in *The Myths We Live By*, ed. R. Samuel and Paul Thompson (London: Routledge, 1990), p. 21; Lucy Taksa, 'The Masked Disease: Oral History, Memory and the Influenza Pandemic 1918–1919,' in *Memory and History in Twentieth-Century Australia*, eds K. Darian-Smith and P. Hamilton (Melbourne: Oxford University Press, 1994), p. 77; Alistair Thomson, 'A Past You Can Live With: Digger Memories and the Anzac Legend,' *Oral History Association of Australia Journal*, no. 13 (1991): pp. 16–17.
27 Janet McCalman, *Struggletown: Public and Private Life in Richmond* (Carlton, Vic: Melbourne University Press, 1985), p. 182.
28 The absence of interviews with organic growers in outback South Australia, Northern Territory, north Queensland and Western Australia indicates finite resources for this project rather than their absence from the history of organic farming and gardening. Documentary accounts from growers in remote Australia have been included where relevant.
29 Rachel Carson, *Silent Spring* (London: Hamish Hamilton, 1963).
30 For example, D. Buck, C. Getz, and J. Guthman, 'From Farm to Table: The Organic Vegetable Commodity Chain of Northern California,' *Sociologia Ruralis* 37, no. 3–20 (1997); J. Guthman, 'Regulating Meaning, Appropriating Nature: The Codification of Californian Organic Agriculture,' *Antipode* 30

(1998); S. Jordan, H. Shuji, and R. Izawa, 'Conventionalization in the Australian Organic Industry: A Case Study of the Darling Downs Region,' in *Sociological Perspectives of Organic Agriculture: From Pioneer to Policy*, eds G. Holt and M. Reed (Wallingford, UK and Cambridge, USA: CABI, 2006); H. Tovey, 'Food, Environmentalism and Rural Sociology: On the Organic Farming Movement in Ireland,' *Sociologia Ruralis* 37 (1997).

31 Philip Conford, author of *Origins of the Organic Movement* – a history of British organic agriculture, writes that while organic methods have existed for centuries, identification as an organic grower only began once an alternative existed. Philip Conford, *The Origins of the Organic Movement* (Edinburgh, UK: Floris Books, 2001), p. 17. A.M. Scofield claims that probably the first use of the word 'organic' to define a particular set of ideas and practices was by British agriculturalist Lord Walter Northbourne as a chapter heading in his book *Look to the Land.* This was mentioned in A.M. Scofield, 'Organic Farming: The Origin of the Name', *Biological Agriculture and Horticulture* 4 (1986).

Chapter 1: Soil

32 The principal sources used for this chapter are the newsletters of the first three Australian organic farming and gardening societies. These are: *Victorian Compost News,* the newsletter of the Victorian Compost Society; *Organic Farming Digest* renamed *Farm and Garden Digest,* published by the Australian Organic Farming and Gardening Society of New South Wales and the newsletter of the Living Soil Association of Tasmania. I have drawn upon the *Victorian Compost News* from its inception in 1947 to the mid-1960s, the entire range of the *Organic Farming Digest* and *Farm and Garden Digest* from 1946 to 1954 and the intermittent publications of the Living Soil Association of Tasmania through the 1950s.

33 George Seddon, 'Words and Weeds: Some Notes on Language and Landscape', in *Landprints: Reflections on Place and Landscape* (Melbourne: Cambridge University Press, 1997), p. 18.

34 G.W. Leeper and N.C. Uren, *Soil Science: An Introduction*, 5th ed. (Melbourne: Melbourne University Press, 1993), p. 215.

35 G.W. Leeper and N.C. Uren, *ibid.*, p. 232.

36 Ann Young and Robert Young, *Soils in the Australian Landscape* (Melbourne: Oxford University Press, 2001), pp. 49–52.

37 Paul Carter, *Lie of the Land* (London & Boston: Faber and Faber, 1996), pp. 1, 15.

38 N. Barr and J. Cary, *Greening a Brown Land. The Australian Search for Sustainable Land Use* (Melbourne: Macmillan, 1992), pp. 30–2, 118–45.

39 Peter E. Charman and Brian W. Murphy, *Soils: Their Properties and Management*, 2nd ed. (Melbourne: Oxford University Press, 2000), pp. 265–6.
40 Jenny Keating, *The Drought Walked Through: A History of Water Shortage in Victoria* (Melbourne: Department of Water Resources Victoria, 1992), pp. 123–51.
41 N. Barr and J. Cary, *Greening a Brown Land. The Australian Search for Sustainable Land Use* (Melbourne: Macmillan, 1992), pp. 56–60, 133.
42 Gabrielle Howard was a partner in Albert Howard's research during the 1920s but died suddenly in 1930.
43 Philip Conford, *The Origins of the Organic Movement* (Edinburgh, UK: Floris Books, 2001), pp. 50–9; Suzanne Peters, 'The Land in Trust: A Social History of the Organic Farming Movement' (PhD, McGill University, 1979), pp. 34–49.
44 'County Palatine of Chester Local Medical and Panel Committee Medical Testament,' in *British Medical Journal Supplement* (1939), pp. 1, 6. *The Medical Testament* was described by Phillip Conford, historian of the British organic movement as the single most important document for the development of British organic agriculture. It was first published in the *New English Weekly* in April 1939 then reiterated and resigned in 1957 in *The Lancet* and the *British Medical Journal.* Philip Conford, *The Origins of the Organic Movement* (Edinburgh, UK: Floris Books, 2001), p. 247.
45 Albert Howard, *An Agricultural Testament* (Oxford, UK: Oxford University Press, 1940).
46 Albert Howard, *Farming and Gardening for Health or Disease* (UK: Faber & Faber, 1945).
47 A.J. McMichael, *Human Frontiers, Environments and Disease: Past Patterns, Uncertain Futures* (Cambridge: Cambridge University Press, 2001), p. 319.
48 Warwick Anderson, *The Cultivation of Whiteness* (Melbourne: Melbourne University Press, 2002), p. 40.
49 Warwick Anderson, *ibid.*, pp. 11–13.
50 A.J. McMichael, *Human Frontiers, Environments and Disease: Past Patterns, Uncertain Futures* (Cambridge: Cambridge University Press, 2001), p. 319.
51 Among the first organic societies was the Humic Compost Club founded in New Zealand in 1941. According to Philip Conford, the first meeting of the British Soil Association was held in 1947. Philip Conford, *The Origins of the Organic Movement* (Edinburgh, UK: Floris Books, 2001), p. 252. This was a year after the establishment of the Australian Organic Farming and Gardening Society and the same year as the founding of the Victorian Compost Society. An organisation called Arbeitsgemeinshaft Natürlicher Landbau und Siedlung (Natural Farming and Back to the Land Association) was founded in 1927 in Germany which shared with British and Australian organic growers an

emphasis on soil fertilised with organic matter. The German society differed from its Australian and British counterparts in that it also emphasised vegetarianism, agriculture without animals and minimal use of technology. G. Vogt, 'The Origins of Organic Farming,' in *Organic Farming: An International History*, ed. W. Lockeretz (UK: CAB International, 2007), pp. 14–15.

52 The most active Australian biodynamic practitioners during this period were Alex Podolinsky in Victoria and Bob and Louise Williams in New South Wales.

53 Alberto Melucci, *Nomads of the Present: Social Movements and Individual Needs in Contemporary Society* (Philadelphia: Temple University Press, 1989).

54 Victorian Compost Society, *Victorian Compost News* 12, no. 4 (1958): annual report supplement.

55 Australian Organic Farming and Gardening Society, *Organic Farming Digest* 1, no. 1 (1946): p. 1; Living Soil Association of Tasmania, *Compost, Why and How* (Sydney: 1946), p. 1; Victorian Compost Society, *Victorian Compost News* 7, no. 12 (1953): pp. 137–51.

56 Victorian Compost Society, *Victorian Compost News* 14, no. 3 (1960): p. 49.

57 After Albert Howard's death, Louise Howard, Albert's second wife became patron of the Victorian Compost Society.

58 Victorian Compost Society, *Victorian Compost News* 1, no. 1 (1947): p. 1.

59 Australian Organic Farming and Gardening Society, *Organic Farming Digest* 2, no. 1 (1949): p. 4.

60 The newsletter was quoting the physician G.T. Wrench. Australian Organic Farming and Gardening Society, *Organic Farming Digest* 2, no. 1 (1949): p. 4.

61 Australian Organic Farming and Gardening Society, *Farm and Garden Digest* 2, no. 8 (1951): p. 36.

62 Australian Organic Farming and Gardening Society, *Organic Farming Digest* 1, no. 1 (1946): p. 3.

63 Victorian Compost Society, *Healthy Soil Is the Key to Good Health* (Victorian Compost Society, n.d.).

64 Living Soil Association of Tasmania, *Newsletter*, no. 1 (1950): p. 1.

65 European agricultural biological research which provided the scientific context for organic beliefs is described in G. Vogt, 'The Origins of Organic Farming,' in *Organic Farming: An International History*, ed. W. Lockeretz (UK: CAB International, 2007), pp. 11–12.

66 J.R. McNeill and V. Winiwarter, 'Breaking the Sod: Humankind, History and Soil,' *Science* 304, no. 5677 (2004); A.M. Scofield, 'Organic Farming: The Origin of the Name,' *Biological Agriculture and Horticulture* 4 (1986).

67 Albert Howard, *An Agricultural Testament* (Oxford, U.K.: Oxford University Press, 1940); Albert Howard, *Farming and Gardening for Health or Disease* (UK: Faber & Faber, 1945); Albert Howard and Yeshwant Wad, *The Waste*

Products of Agriculture: Their Utilization as Humus (UK: Oxford University Press, 1931).

68 Australian Organic Farming and Gardening Society, *Farm and Garden Digest* 2, no. 10 (1951): p. 3; Living Soil Association of Tasmania, *Compost, Why and How* (Sydney: 1946), p. 3.

69 Philip Conford, *The Origins of the Organic Movement* (Edinburgh, UK: Floris Books, 2001), p. 17.

70 Australian Organic Farming and Gardening Society, *Organic Farming Digest* 1, no. 7 (1947): p. 20.

71 Victorian Compost Society, *The Compost Heap: The Principles and Practice of Making Compost by the 'Indore' Method as Originated by the Late Sir Alfred Howard* (Melbourne: Victorian Compost Society, 1951).

72 Philip Conford, *The Origins of the Organic Movement* (Edinburgh, UK: Floris Books, 2001), p. 64.

73 For example in William Adamson and William Elliot, *Adamson's Australian Gardener: An Epitome of Horticulture for the Colony of Victoria*, 10th ed. (Melbourne: George Robertson, 1879), p. 155.

74 Margaret Simons, *Resurrection in a Bucket: The Rich and Fertile Story of Compost* (Allen and Unwin, 2004), pp. 74–5.

75 Living Soil Association of Tasmania, *Compost, Why and How* (Sydney: 1946); Victorian Compost Society, *The Compost Heap: The Principles and Practice of Making Compost by the 'Indore' Method as Originated by the Late Sir Alfred Howard* (Melbourne: Victorian Compost Society, 1951).

76 Organic Farming and Gardening Society (Aust.), *Good Earth* 26, no. 3 (1973): pp. 38–9; Victorian Compost Society, *Victorian Compost News* 2, no. 3 (1948): pp. 17–18.

77 Marjorie Hutton Neve, *This Mad Folly: A History of Australian Pioneer Women Doctors* (Sydney: Library of Australian History, 1980), pp. 127–30; Kerreen Reiger, *The Disenchantment of the Home: Modernizing the Australian Family 1880–1940* (Melbourne: Oxford University Press, 1985), p. 131; Geoffrey Serle, ed., *Australian Dictionary of Biography, vol. 2, 1891–1939* (Melbourne: Melbourne University Press, 1988), pp. 456–7.

78 *Transcript of Evidence of the Royal Commission on the Bread Industry before Judge Stretton*, 8 June, 1949, p. 402–3.

79 Victorian Compost Society, *Victorian Compost News* 5, no. 9 (1951): pp. 107–9.

80 Andrea Gaynor, *Harvest of the Suburbs: An Environmental History of Growing Food in Australian Cities* (Perth: University of Western Australia Press, 2006), pp. 23–4; Rebecca Jones and Janice Chesters, 'Muck, Bugs and Decay: The Preoccupations of Early Australian Organic Gardening', *Studies in Australian Garden History* 2 (2006).

81 F.H. Brunning, *The Australian Gardener*, 19th ed. (Melbourne: F.H. Brunning, 1920), p. 20.
82 Australian Organic Farming and Gardening Society, *Organic Farming Digest* 1, no. 7 (1947): p. 12.
83 This term to describe human sewage was coined by Margaret Simons and used as a chapter title in: Margaret Simons, *Resurrection in a Bucket: The Rich and Fertile Story of Compost* (Allen & Unwin, 2004), p. 111.
84 Philip Conford, *The Origins of the Organic Movement* (Edinburgh, UK: Floris Books, 2001), pp. 58, 86.
85 For example, Brisbane Organic Growers Inc., 'Newsletter,' (1993), pp. 4–5; Jackie French, interviewed by the author, 8 July 2006; Leicester Jones, interviewed by the author, 28 June 2006.
86 Barry McGowan, 'Chinese Market Gardens in Southern and Western New South Wales,' *Australian Humanities Review* (2005).
87 Victorian Compost Society, *Victorian Compost News* 8, no. 11 (1954).
88 Victorian Compost Society, *Victorian Compost News* 2, no. 3 (1948): p. 21; Victorian Compost Society, *Victorian Compost News* 7, no. 1 (1953): p. 8.
89 Victorian Compost Society, *Victorian Compost News* 2, no. 3 (1948): p. 21; Victorian Compost Society, *Victorian Compost News* 2, no. 6 (1948): p. 50; Victorian Compost Society, *Victorian Compost News* 10, no. 9 (1956): p. 132; Victorian Compost Society, *Victorian Compost News* 7, no. 3 (1953): p. 49.
90 Victorian Compost Society, *Victorian Compost News* 7, no. 8 (1953): p. 96.
91 Organic Farming and Gardening Society (Aust.), *Good Earth* 26, no. 3 (1973): p. 38; Victorian Compost Society, *Victorian Compost News* 2, no. 3 (1948): p. 18.
92 A.J. McMichael, *Human Frontiers, Environments and Disease: Past Patterns, Uncertain Futures* (Cambridge: Cambridge University Press, 2001).
93 Drew Hutton and Libby Connors, *A History of the Australian Environment Movement* (Cambridge: Cambridge University Press, 1999), pp. 79–80, 82, 86; Kerreen Reiger, *The Disenchantment of the Home: Modernizing the Australian Family 1880–1940* (Melbourne: Oxford University Press, 1985).
94 Warwick Anderson, *The Cultivation of Whiteness* (Melbourne: Melbourne University Press, 2002), p. 51.
95 Kerreen Reiger, *The Disenchantment of the Home: Modernizing the Australian Family 1880–1940* (Melbourne: Oxford University Press, 1985), pp. 43–4.
96 Examples of gardeners being discouraged from disposing of nightsoil in gardens are cited by: Victorian Compost Society, *Victorian Compost News* 10, no. 9 (1956): p. 130, as well as F.H. Brunning, *The Australian Gardener*, 19th ed. (Melbourne: F.H. Brunning, 1920), p. 14.
97 Victorian Compost Society, *Victorian Compost News* 2, no. 3 (1948): p. 21.
98 Victorian Compost Society, *Victorian Compost News* 14, no. 3 (1960): p. 50; Victorian Compost Society, *Victorian Compost News* 7, no. 5 (1953): p. 49.

99 Victorian Compost Society, *Victorian Compost News* 11, no. 3 (1957): p. 35.
100 Victorian Compost Society, *Victorian Compost News* 6, no. 11 (1952): pp. 1–2.
101 Victorian Compost Society, *Victorian Compost News* 2, no. 10 (1948): p. 93.
102 Philip Conford, *The Origins of the Organic Movement* (Edinburgh, UK: Floris Books, 2001), pp. 58–9.
103 Australian organic growers discussed the disadvantages of Indore composting in Australian conditions and the relative lack of availability of animal manure in the following: Australian Organic Farming and Gardening Society, *Organic Farming Digest* 1, no. 1 (1946): p. 2; Victorian Compost Society, *Victorian Compost News* 12, no. 4 (1958): p. 63; Victorian Compost Society, *Victorian Compost News* 2, no. 8 (1948): p. 70. Brunning's gardening books note the increasing shortage of manure in urban areas: F.H. Brunning, *The Australian Gardener*, 19th ed. (Melbourne: F.H. Brunning, 1920), p. 20.
104 Organic Farming and Gardening Society (Aust.), *Good Earth* 20, no. 3 (1966): p. 42.
105 Victorian Compost Society, *Victorian Compost News* 4, no. 8 (1950): p. 87.
106 Victorian Compost Society, *Victorian Compost News* 6, no. 7 (1952): p. 81. These methods followed the recommendations of Maye Bruce, an Englishwoman, who created a method of composting called 'Quick Return' or 'QR'. A description of the use of herbs as compost accelerators is described by Bio-Dynamic Agriculture Australia on their website: Biodynamic Agriculture Australia, *What Is Biodynamics* (2004 [cited 24 July 2006]); available from www.biodynamics.net.au.
107 Victorian Compost Society, *Victorian Compost News* 7, no. 12 (1953): pp. 149–50.
108 Victorian Compost Society, *Victorian Compost News* 5, no. 5 (1951): p. 49.
109 Growing leguminous plants such as members of the pea and bean family is an ancient agricultural practice, not one invented by Australian organic growers. J.R. McNeill and V. Winiwarter, 'Breaking the Sod: Humankind, History and Soil,' *Science* 304, no. 5677 (2004).
110 Living Soil Association of Tasmania, *Newsletter*, no. 1 (1950).
111 Victorian Compost Society, *Victorian Compost News* 4, no. 9 (1950): p. 105.
112 Keyline farming techniques are discussed by: Martin Mulligan and Stuart Hill, *Ecological Pioneers: A Social History of Australian Ecological Thought and Action* (Cambridge: Cambridge University Press, 2001), pp. 193–202; as well as P.A. Yeomans' son Allan: P.A. Yeomans, *The Challenge of the Landscape: The Development and Practices of Keyline* (Sydney: Keyline Publishing, 1958).
113 Martin Mulligan and Stuart Hill, *Ecological Pioneers: A Social History of Australian Ecological Thought and Action* (Cambridge: Cambridge University Press, 2001), pp. 198–9; P.A. Yeomans, *The Challenge of the Landscape: The Development and Practices of Keyline* (Sydney: Keyline Publishing, 1958), p.

139. In 1974 P.A. Yeomans won the Prince Phillip Prize for Australian Design for the reconstructed chisel plough which was then called the 'Bunyip Slipper Imp with Shakerator', the 'shakerator' being a vibrator which assisted in breaking heavy soil clods. The chisel plough is now a ubiquitous part of conventional as well as organic Australian agriculture.

114 The relevance of his techniques to organic farming is discussed by: Victorian Compost Society, *Victorian Compost News* 15, no. 4 (1961): p. 73. It is also discussed by the Organic Farming and Gardening Society (as the Victorian Compost Society was known in 1983): Organic Farming and Gardening Society (Aust.), *Good Earth* 36, no. 4 (1983): p. 55. P.A. Yeomans' son Ken explained that Yeomans' chief interest was in influencing mainstream agriculture rather than organic farmers. Ken Yeomans, interviewed by the author, 24 May 2006.

115 Martin Mulligan and Stuart Hill, *Ecological Pioneers: A Social History of Australian Ecological Thought and Action* (Cambridge University Press, 2001), p. 194.

Case Study 1: Harold White

116 Guyra's average annual rainfall is comparable to Perth's average annual rainfall of approximately 850 mm, is less than the average annual rainfall of Sydney (1212 mm), Brisbane (1149 mm) and Darwin (1500 mm) but is higher than the average rainfall of Melbourne (656 mm), Hobart (628 mm) and Adelaide (530 mm).

117 Sam White and Elizabeth White, interviewed by the author, 26 May 2006.

118 Sam White, like his grandfather, grazes cattle and sheep and has an Angus cattle stud at Bald Blair. However, Sam does not practise organic techniques, seeing them as impractical in today's agricultural economic climate. Sam also questions the viability of organic beef farming in New England given the prevalence of worm and fluke parasites.

119 H.F. White and C.S. Hicks, *Life from the Soil* (Melbourne: Longmans, Green and Co., 1953).

120 Stanton Hicks was adviser to both the New South Wales and Victorian organic societies and his writings regularly featured in the organic newsletters.

121 H.F. White, *After 50 Years: Human Life and the Food Chain* (Guyra: H.F. White, 1959); Harold F. White, *The Why and the Wherefore of Cultivation* (South Melbourne: The Pastoral Review, 1957).

122 H.F. White and C.S. Hicks, *Life from the Soil* (Melbourne: Longmans, Green and Co., 1953), p. 32.

123 H.F. White and C.S. Hicks, *ibid.*, p. 32.

124 Ian Lunt, *Effects of Stock Grazing on Biodiversity Values in Temperate Native Grasslands and Grassy Woodlands in South Eastern Australia: A Literature Review* (Canberra: Environment ACT, 2005); R.M. Tremont, 'Life-History Attributes of Plants in Grazed and Ungrazed Grasslands on the Northern Tablelands of New South Wales,' *Australian Journal of Botany* 42, no. 5 (1994).

125 'Red Leg' is *Bothriochloa macra*, a perennial native grass. Spear Grass is used to describe a variety of species of *Austrostipa* grasses and Tussocky Poa may be *Poa sieberiana* but is also a term used to describe other Poa species. 'Wild Sorghum' is *Sorghum leiocladum*. 'Pastures on New England Wool Properties', in *Land, Water and Wool, Northern Tablelands Project Fact Sheet* (Canberra: Commonwealth Government Land and Water Australia, 2007); H.F. White and C.S. Hicks, *Life from the Soil* (Melbourne: Longmans, Green and Co., 1953).

126 H.F. White and C.S. Hicks, *Life from the Soil* (Melbourne: Longmans, Green and Co., 1953), pp. 28–32.

127 H.F. White and C.S. Hicks, *ibid.*, p. 39.

128 Graham White and Mary White, interviewed by the author, 26 May 2006.

129 Graham White and Mary White, interviewed by the author, 26 May 2006; Sam White and Elizabeth White, interviewed by the author, 26 May 2006.

130 During the First World War, Harold White fought at the Somme, Armentières and Mont St Quentin in France and at Messines in Belgium.

131 Graham White and Mary White, interviewed by the author, 26 May 2006.

132 H.F. White and C.S. Hicks, *Life from the Soil* (Melbourne: Longmans, Green and Co., 1953), p. 39.

133 H.F. White and C.S. Hicks, *ibid.*, pp. 39, 60, 99.

134 Harold White was awarded the Distinguished Service Order (DSO) in 1917 and the Croix de Guerre in 1918.

135 *Phalaris tuberosa* is now more commonly known as *Phalaris aquatica*. It was probably first introduced to Australia by the Toowoomba Botanic Gardens from New York in the 1880s. *Phalaris tuberosa* has been found by some farmers to be toxic to sheep in some parts of Australia but this was not experienced by the Whites at Bald Blair. CSIRO, Register of Australian Herbage Plant Cultivars: Phalaris (CSIRO, 1972 [cited 28/11/07 2007]); available from www.pi.csiro.au/ahpc/grasses/pdf/australian.pdf, Sorting Phalaris Names (University of Melbourne, 2000 [cited 28/11/07 2007]); available from www.plantnames.unimelb.edu.au/Sorting/Phalaris.

136 Graham White and Mary White, interviewed by the author, 26 May 2006.

137 Graham White and Mary White, interviewed by the author, 26 May 2006.

138 The replacement of native grasses with exotic species was strongly promoted by the Department of Agriculture during the first half of the twentieth century and a combination of grass and legumes (usually clover) was the

recommended standard pasture mix. N. Barr and J. Cary, *Greening a Brown Land. The Australian Search for Sustainable Land Use* (Melbourne: Macmillan, 1992), pp. 29–41; H.F. White and C.S. Hicks, *Life from the Soil* (Melbourne: Longmans, Green and Co., 1953), pp. 45–52.

139 J.R. McNeill and V. Winiwarter, 'Breaking the Sod: Humankind, History and Soil', *Science* 304, no. 5677 (2004).

140 N. Barr and J. Cary, *Greening a Brown Land. The Australian Search for Sustainable Land Use* (Melbourne: Macmillan, 1992), pp. 30–5.

141 H.F. White and C.S. Hicks, *Life from the Soil* (Melbourne: Longmans, Green and Co., 1953), p. 56.

142 H.F. White and C.S. Hicks, *ibid.*, p. 57.

143 H.F. White and C.S. Hicks, *ibid.*, pp. 63–4.

144 H.F. White, *After 50 Years: Human Life and the Food Chain* (Guyra: H.F. White, 1959), p. 3.

145 Australian Organic Farming and Gardening Society, *Organic Farming Digest* 1, no. 1 (1946): p. 4.

146 Graham White and Mary White, interviewed by the author, 26 May 2006. The best-known example of Balfour's writing is E.B. Balfour, *The Living Soil* (London: Faber & Faber, 1944).

147 The work of George Stapleton and Robert Elliot is described in Philip Conford, *The Origins of the Organic Movement* (Edinburgh, UK: Floris Books, 2001).

148 H.F. White and C.S. Hicks, *Life from the Soil* (Melbourne: Longmans, Green and Co., 1953), p. 32.

149 Sam White and Elizabeth White, interviewed by the author, 26 May 2006.

150 H.F. White and C.S. Hicks, *ibid.*, p. 42.

151 H.F. White, *After 50 Years: Human Life and the Food Chain* (Guyra: H.F. White, 1959), p. 44; H.F. White and C.S. Hicks, *Life from the Soil* (Melbourne: Longmans, Green and Co., 1953), p. 48.

152 Graham White and Mary White, interviewed by the author, 26 May 2006.

153 Graham White and Mary White, interviewed by the author, 26 May 2006.

154 H.F. White, *After 50 Years: Human Life and the Food Chain* (Guyra: H.F. White, 1959), p. 54.

155 The phrase 'directing classes' was coined by Alfred Davidson and discussed in Andrew Moore, *The Secret Army and the Premier* (Sydney: University of New South Wales Press, 1989), p. 75. Harold White's community appointments included, among others, executive member of the Graziers Association, the New England and North-West Producers Company, the Armidale School, the Armidale Newspaper and the New England University College.

156 Australian Organic Farming and Gardening Society, *Organic Farming Digest* 1, no. 1 (1946): p. 6.

157 Australian Organic Farming and Gardening Society, *Organic Farming Digest* 1, no. 7 (1947): pp. 21–3.
158 H.F. White and C.S. Hicks, *Life from the Soil* (Melbourne: Longmans, Green and Co., 1953), pp. 117–19.
159 Harold F. White, *The Why and the Wherefore of Cultivation* (South Melbourne: The Pastoral Review, 1957), p. 20.
160 Harold White did not write about his political or social beliefs, except indirectly when discussing his organic methods and White family members interviewed were unable to readily discuss his class values in relation to his organic ideas. Therefore this discussion is speculative, informed by circumstantial rather than definitive evidence.
161 Australian Organic Farming and Gardening Society, *Organic Farming Digest* 1, no. 7 (1947): p. 21–3.
162 The 'Old Guard' and the 'New Guard' were both conservative, anti-communist organisations. The New Guard was more open, outspoken and publicly visible than the Old Guard which Andrew Moore describes as secretive, reclusive and 'defensively rather than offensively oriented'. Andrew Moore provides a detailed discussion of the Old Guard in Andrew Moore, *The Secret Army and the Premier* (Sydney: University of New South Wales Press, 1989); Geoffrey Serle, ed., *Australian Dictionary of Biography, vol. 2, 1891–1939* (Melbourne: Melbourne University Press, 1988), p. 467.
163 Andrew Moore, *The Secret Army and the Premier* (Sydney: University of New South Wales Press, 1989), pp. 6–7, 74–107.
164 Harold White's membership of the New States Movement is noted in Andrew Moore, *The Secret Army and the Premier* (Sydney: University of New South Wales Press, 1989), p. 467; Geoffrey Serle, ed., *Australian Dictionary of Biography, vol. 2, 1891–1939* (Melbourne: Melbourne University Press, 1988). Agitation for an autonomous state in northern New South Wales finally subsided in the late 1960s after defeat in a referendum. The New States Movement is described in more detail by Andrew Moore, *The Secret Army and the Premier* (Sydney: University of New South Wales Press, 1989), pp. 103–7.

Chapter 2: Chemical free

165 A chemical fertiliser containing 10 parts nitrogen, 6 parts phosphorus and 10 parts potassium.
166 *Pentachlorophenate* is a chemical herbicide.
167 This is an edited version of a letter published in Australian Organic Farming and Gardening Society, *Farm and Garden Digest* 2, no. 12 (1952): pp. 6–7.
168 Rachel Carson, *Silent Spring* (London: Hamish Hamilton, 1963), p. 6.

169 The primary sources for this chapter, like the first thematic chapter 'Soil', are the newsletters of the first three Australian organic farming and gardening societies: *Victorian Compost News,* the newsletter of the Victorian Compost Society; *Organic Farming Digest* renamed *Farm and Garden Digest,* published by the Australian Organic Farming and Gardening Society of New South Wales; and the newsletter of the Living Soil Association of Tasmania. I have drawn upon the entire range of the *Organic Farming Digest* and *Farm and Garden Digest* from 1946 to 1954, the intermittent publications of the Living Soil Association of Tasmania through the 1950s, and the *Victorian Compost News/Good Earth* from its inception in 1947 to the early 1980s. I have also drawn upon publications of the later organic societies in Western Australia, Brisbane, South Australia and Tasmania as well as oral history interviews with past organic farmers and gardeners.

170 Victorian Compost Society, *Victorian Compost News* 2, no. 8 (1948): p. 70.

171 Rebecca Jones and Janice Chesters, 'Muck, Bugs and Decay: The Preoccupations of Early Australian Organic Gardening', *Studies in Australian Garden History* 2 (2006).

172 R.F. Korcak, 'Early Roots of the Organic Movement: A Plant Nutrition Perspective', *Hort Technology* 2 (1992). The title of Justus von Liebig's research paper was *Organic Chemistry in its Application to Agriculture and Physiology.* Confusingly, Liebig uses the word 'organic' in a different context to the way it is used in the term 'organic farming'. For Liebig, as for most chemists, 'organic' denoted the presence of elemental carbon in a chemical compound.

173 Philip Conford, *The Origins of the Organic Movement* (Edinburgh, UK: Floris Books, 2001), pp. 38–9; R.F. Korcak, 'Early Roots of the Organic Movement: A Plant Nutrition Perspective', *Hort Technology* 2 (1992).

174 F.H. Brunning, *The Australian Gardener,* 19th ed. (Melbourne: F.H. Brunning, 1920), p. 20.

175 Nitrogen Fertilisers Pty Ltd, 'Sulphate of Ammonia. Let's Introduce You …' (Melbourne: Nitrogen Fertilisers Pty Ltd, n.d.), pp. 5–7, 15.

176 The use of artificial fertilisers increased steadily between 1931 and 1971 except for brief setbacks during the two World Wars when raw materials were difficult to source. Commonwealth of Australia, *Official Yearbooks of the Commonwealth of Australia* (Canberra: Commonwealth Bureau of Census and Statistics, 1951–1971).

177 G.W. Leeper and N.C. Uren, *Soil Science: An Introduction*, 5th ed. (Melbourne: Melbourne University Press, 1993), p. 215.

178 Commonwealth of Australia, *Official Yearbooks of the Commonwealth of Australia* (Canberra: Commonwealth Bureau of Census and Statistics, 1961), p. 939. The Gilbert and Ellice Islands are part of the Pacific islands now known as Kiribati.

179 An early form of superphosphate was manufactured in Britain by combining sulphuric acid with pulverised animal bones, bones being a rich source of phosphorus. According to a gruesome rumour, in Britain, human bones sourced from battlefields were also used; Jenny Uglow, *A Little History of British Gardening* (London: Pimlico, 2005), p. 236. Superphosphate made from bone dust was first manufactured in Australia at Yarraville in Melbourne in 1878; J.E. Kolm, 'Fertilisers,' in *Technology in Australia 1788–1988* (Australian Science and Technology Heritage Centre, 2000).

180 Victorian Compost Society, *Victorian Compost News* 2, no. 9 (1948): p. 89.

181 Australian Organic Farming and Gardening Society, *Farm and Garden Digest* 2, no. 10 (1951): p 3; Australian Organic Farming and Gardening Society, *Organic Farming Digest* 1, no. 5 (1947): p. 23.

182 Leicester Jones, interviewed by the author, 28 June 2006.

183 Peter Bennett, interviewed by the author, 22 February 2006.

184 Leicester Jones, interviewed by the author, 28 June 2006.

185 Peter Bennett, interviewed by the author, 22 February 2006.

186 Victorian Compost Society, *Victorian Compost News* 6, no. 1 (1952): p. 8.

187 Australian Organic Farming and Gardening Society, *Farm and Garden Digest* 2, no. 4 (1950): p. 4.

188 Henk Verhoog *et al.*, 'The Role of the Concept of the Natural (Naturalness) in Organic Farming,' *Journal of Agricultural and Environmental Ethics* 16 (2003).

189 Organic Gardening and Farming Society of Tasmania, *The Organic Gardener and Farmer* 3, no. 2 (1978): p. 24.

190 Australian Organic Farming and Gardening Society, *Farm and Garden Digest* 2, no. 10 (1951): p. 3.

191 Australian Organic Farming and Gardening Society, *Organic Farming Digest* 1, no. 1 (1946): p. 4.

192 Peter Bennett, *Australia and New Zealand Organic Gardening*, 1st ed. (Frenchs Forest, NSW: Child and Associates, 1979), p. 7.

193 Living Soil Association of Tasmania, *Compost, Why and How* (Sydney: 1946), p. 6.

194 Australian Organic Farming and Gardening Society, *Farm and Garden Digest* 2, no. 5 (1950): p. 30.

195 'The NPK mentality' was a phrase attributed to Albert Howard and used by many people, for example, Peter Bennett, interviewed by the author, 22 February 2006. It was also mentioned in the Organic Gardening and Farming Society of Tasmania's, *The Organic Gardener and Farmer* 3, no. 2 (1978): p. 24.

196 Organic Gardening and Farming Society of Tasmania, *The Organic Gardener and Farmer* 3, no. 2 (1978): p. 24.

197 Soil Association of South Australia, *Newsletter*, Nov. 1980.

198 Philip Conford, *The Origins of the Organic Movement* (Edinburgh, UK: Floris Books, 2001), pp. 81–97.

199 Rebecca Jones and Janice Chesters, 'Muck, Bugs and Decay: The Preoccupations of Early Australian Organic Gardening', *Studies in Australian Garden History* 2 (2006).
200 *The Australian Gardener: A Monthly Journal of Floriculture and Horticulture* May (1910): p. 23.
201 Organochlorides are also known as chlorinated hydrocarbons. Another version of the chemical name for DDT is: 1,1-bis(4-chlorophenyl)-2,2,2-trichloroethane).
202 Rachel Carson, *Silent Spring* (London: Hamish Hamilton, 1963), p. 18.
203 Richard Aitken and Michael Looker, eds, *Oxford Companion to Australian Gardens* (Melbourne: Oxford University Press, 2002), p. 136. Australian Academy of Science, *The Use of DDT in Australia* (Canberra: Australian Academy of Science, 1972), p. 9, by contrast, states that the first use of DDT was by the Australian military in 1942 and the first civilian use in Australia was 1946.
204 Leslie Brunning and Harold Alston, *The Australian Gardener: A Complete and Practical Guide Dealing with the Growing of Fruit, Flowers and Vegetables*, 30th ed. (Melbourne: Robertson and Mullens, 1949), p. 382.
205 Australian Academy of Science, *The Use of DDT in Australia* (Canberra: Australian Academy of Science, 1972), pp. 12–13, 52–9; N. Barr and J. Cary, *Greening a Brown Land. The Australian Search for Sustainable Land Use* (Melbourne: Macmillan, 1992), pp. 188–93.
206 Ray Mason and Elma Mason, interviewed by the author, 27 June 2006.
207 Australian Academy of Science, *The Use of DDT in Australia* (Canberra: Australian Academy of Science, 1972), p. 11.
208 Australian Organic Farming and Gardening Society, *Organic Farming Digest* 1, no. 6 (1947): p. 23.
209 Australian Organic Farming and Gardening Society, *Organic Farming Digest* 1, no. 9 (1948): p. 13; Australian Organic Farming and Gardening Society, *Organic Farming Digest* 1, no. 11 (1948): p. 3.
210 Victorian Compost Society, *Victorian Compost News* 2, no. 4 (1948): p. 32.
211 Australian Organic Farming and Gardening Society, *Farm and Garden Digest* 2, no. 4 (1950): p. 3.
212 Australian Organic Farming and Gardening Society, *Farm and Garden Digest* 2, no. 4 (1950): p. 1. The reporting of this event by the Australian Organic Farming and Gardening Association was a prophecy of widely reported and damaging incidents in the 1960s and late 1980s when organochloride residues were found in dairy products and beef exported to the USA, events which were to threaten one of Australia's most important export markets. N. Barr and J. Cary, *Greening a Brown Land. The Australian Search for Sustainable Land Use* (Melbourne: Macmillan, 1992), p. 179.

213 Australian Organic Farming and Gardening Society, *Farm and Garden Digest* 2, no. 10 (1951): pp. 30–1.
214 Victorian Compost Society, *Victorian Compost News* 11, no. 5 (1957): p. 77.
215 Leicester Jones, interviewed by the author, 28 June 2006.
216 Victorian Compost Society, *Victorian Compost News* 7, no. 3 (1953): p. 16.
217 Australian Organic Farming and Gardening Society, *Farm and Garden Digest* 3, no. 1 (1952): p. 39.
218 That nature was normally in a balanced state was an idea championed by ecological sciences for much of the first half of the twentieth century. One of the chief proponents of these ideas was the ecologist Eugene Odum. He argued that particular natural communities and nature as a whole was self-regulating and evolving towards a stable state of equilibrium and that normality was equilibrium or evolving towards equilibrium. Others, such as United States ecologist Frederic Clements argued that environments were dynamic and evolved towards a climax or stable state. These ideas are explored in depth by Donald Worster, *Nature's Economy: A History of Ecological Ideas* (Melbourne: Cambridge University Press, 1992).
219 Australian Organic Farming and Gardening Society, *Farm and Garden Digest* 2, no. 4 (1950): p. 1.
220 Victorian Compost Society, *Victorian Compost News* 15, no. 1 (1961): p. 14.
221 Victorian Compost Society, *Victorian Compost News* 6, no. 1 (1952): p. 3; Victorian Compost Society, *Victorian Compost News* 5, no. 10 (1951): p. 121.
222 Rachel Carson, *Edge of the Sea* (Boston: Houghton Mifflin, 1955); Rachel Carson, *The Sea Around Us* (London: Panther, 1951).
223 Linda Lear, *Rachel Carson: Witness for Nature* (New York: Henry Holt, 1997), pp. 312–33; Craig Waddell, *And No Birds Sing: Rhetorical Analyses of Rachel Carson's Silent Spring* (Carbondale: Southern Illinois University Press, 2000), pp. 6–7. The Long Island spray program resulted in the compulsory spraying of an organic farm against the wishes of its owners. These owners had contact with Rachel Carson.
224 Rachel Carson, *Silent Spring* (London: Hamish Hamilton, 1963), pp. 183–8; G. Solomon and T. Schettler, 'Environmental Endocrine Disruption', in *Life Support: The Environment and Human Health*, ed. Michael McCally (Massachusetts: MIT Press, 2002).
225 Drew Hutton and Libby Connors, *A History of the Australian Environment Movement* (Cambridge: Cambridge University Press, 1999), p. 90.
226 Linda Lear, *Rachel Carson: Witness for Nature* (New York: Henry Holt, 1997), pp. 411–41.
227 Rebecca Jones and Janice Chesters, 'Muck, Bugs and Decay: The Preoccupations of Early Australian Organic Gardening', *Studies in Australian Garden History* 2 (2006).

228 *Yates Garden Guide*, 29th ed. (Melbourne: Angus and Robertson, 1965), p. 252.

229 Australian Academy of Science, *The Use of DDT in Australia* (Canberra: Australian Academy of Science, 1972), p. 60. DDT was deregistered for most uses in Australia in the mid-1980s.

230 Rachel Carson, *Silent Spring* (London: Hamish Hamilton, 1963), p. xvii; Linda Lear, *Rachel Carson: Witness for Nature* (New York: Henry Holt, 1997), p. 434.

231 For example, Victorian Compost Society, *Victorian Compost News* 17, no. 4 (1963): pp. 49–56.

232 Organic Farming and Gardening Society (Aust.), *Good Earth* 23, no. 1 (1970): p. 13.

233 Organic Farming and Gardening Society (Aust.), *Good Earth* 22, no. 2 (1968): p. 23.

234 David Stephen, interviewed by the author, 26 June 2006.

235 Financial membership of the society was reported to be at an all-time low of 200 members in 1962–1963. Victorian Compost Society, *Victorian Compost News* 17, no. 3 (1963): p. 39. By 1967, membership was increasing rapidly, possibly as a result of the controversy in the years following the publication of *Silent Spring* and the increased activity of the organic society in this area. Organic Farming and Gardening Society (Aust.), *Good Earth* 21, no. 2 (1967): p. 18. Membership numbers for the society ceased to be published in 1968 when the format of the magazine changed.

236 Henry Doubleday Research Association, 'Newsletter,' no. 1 (1970). The first Henry Doubleday Research Association was founded by Lawrence Hills in Britain in the 1950s. The Association was named after an innovative farmer who in the 1870s imported Russian comfrey to Britain and experimented with its use as medicine, fodder and green manure. Hills was impressed by Doubleday and continued his research with comfrey. Hills was also influenced by Albert Howard and Rudolf Steiner and the Association's research focus broadened to include methods of organic farming and gardening. A branch of the Henry Doubleday Research Association was established in Sydney with affiliated groups in Western Australia and Queensland. From these affiliates emerged the Western Australian Organic Growers Association and the Brisbane Organic Gardeners Group.

237 A. Conacher and J. Conacher, *Organic Farming in Australia* (Nedlands, WA: University of WA, 1982).

238 Brisbane Organic Growers Group, *Pesticides and Alternatives: A Guide to Safer Pest Control for Gardeners and Householders* (Toowong, Queensland: Brisbane Organic Growers Group, 1978).

239 Jeanette Conacher, *Pests, Predators and Pesticides: Some Alternatives to Synthetic Pesticides* (Wembley, WA: Organic Growers Association WA, 1980).

240 Peter Bennett, *Australia and New Zealand Organic Gardening*, 1st ed. (Frenchs Forest, NSW: Child and Associates, 1979).

241 Bordeaux and Burgundy mixtures are fungicides that had been used in Australia since the 1880s. Bordeaux mixture is made from copper sulphate mixed with builders' lime (calcium hydroxide). Burgundy mixture is made from copper sulphate and washing soda (sodium carbonate).

242 Peter Bennett, *Australia and New Zealand Organic Gardening*, 1st ed. (Frenchs Forest, NSW: Child and Associates, 1979), p. 72; Jeanette Conacher, *Pests, Predators and Pesticides: Some Alternatives to Synthetic Pesticides* (Wembley, WA: Organic Growers Association WA, 1980), p. 71.

243 Judy McMaugh, *What Garden Pest or Disease is That?* (Sydney: New Holland Publishers, 2000), p. 45.

244 This issue will be discussed in more detail in Chapter 5.

Cast Study 2: Ray and Elma Mason

245 Penguin has higher rainfall than Perth (850 mm), Melbourne (656 mm), Hobart (628 mm) and Adelaide (530 mm) but less than the average annual rainfall of Sydney (1212 mm), Brisbane (1149 mm) and Darwin (1500 mm). Due to the colder climate, evaporation of rainfall would be less than the mainland capitals.

246 Ray Mason and Elma Mason, interviewed by the author, 27 June 2006. Grass tetany is caused by deficiency of magnesium in pasture. Dairy cows are susceptible to this condition when nitrogen and potassium fertilisers have been used to promote grass growth in spring. Pat Coleby, *Healthy Cattle Naturally* (Melbourne: Landlinks Press, 2002), pp. 152, 43.

247 Ray Mason and Elma Mason, interviewed by the author, 27 June 2006.

248 Peter Bennett, interviewed by the author, 22 February 2006.

249 Ray Mason and Elma Mason, interviewed by the author, 27 June 2006; David Stephen, interviewed by the author, 26 June 2006.

250 Ray Mason and Elma Mason, interviewed by the author, 27 June 2006.

251 Ray Mason and Elma Mason, *ibid.*

252 Ray Mason and Elma Mason, *ibid.*

253 Ray Mason and Elma Mason, *ibid.* Blackleg and pulpy kidney are bacterial diseases which can affect cows when they are in poor health.

254 Ray Mason and Elma Mason, *ibid.* Mycorrhiza are soil fungi that have a symbiotic relationship with plant roots and help to convert soil nutrients to a form usable by the plant.

255 Ray Mason and Elma Mason, *ibid.*

256 Ray Mason and Elma Mason, *ibid.*

257 Ray Mason and Elma Mason, *ibid.*

258 Leicester Jones, interviewed by the author, 28 June 2006.

259 Ray Mason and Elma Mason, interviewed by the author, 27 June 2006.
260 Ray Mason and Elma Mason, *ibid.*
261 David Stephen, interviewed by the author, 26 June 2006.
262 David Stephen, *ibid.*
263 Ray Mason and Elma Mason, interviewed by the author, 27 June 2006.
264 Ray Mason and Elma Mason, *ibid.*
265 Ray Mason and Elma Mason, *ibid.*
266 Bio-Dynamic Research Institute, *Demeter Bio-Dynamic Agriculture in Australia* (Bio-Dynamic Research Institute, 2005 [cited 6 November 2006]); available from www.demeter.org.au, G. Vogt, 'The Origins of Organic Farming,' in *Organic Farming: An International History*, ed. W Lockeretz (UK: CAB International, 2007), pp. 19–21.
267 Biodynamic Agriculture Australia, *What Is Biodynamics* (2004 [cited 24 July 2006]); available from www.biodynamics.net.au.
268 Biodynamic Agriculture Australia, *ibid.; Good Earth* 27, no. 1 (1974): p. 9.
269 Ray Mason and Elma Mason, interviewed by the author, 27 June 2006.
270 Ray Mason and Elma Mason, *ibid.*
271 Ray Mason and Elma Mason, *ibid.*

Chapter 3: Ecological wellbeing

272 Australian Organic Farming and Gardening Society, *Farm and Garden Digest* 2, no. 4 (1950): p. 2.
273 The primary sources which have informed this chapter are the newsletters of Australia's first three organic farming and gardening societies: *Victorian Compost News,* the newsletter of the Victorian Compost Society which changed its name to the Organic Farming and Gardening Society (Aust.) and the name of its newsletter to *Good Earth* in the mid-1960s; *Organic Farming Digest, Farm and Garden Digest,* published by the Australian Organic Farming and Gardening Society of New South Wales and the newsletter of the Living Soil Association of Tasmania. I have also consulted publications from the post-1970s organic societies, particularly the newsletters of the Brisbane Organic Growers, the Soil Association of South Australia, the Organic Gardening and Farming Society of Tasmania and *Permaculture*, the newsletter of the permaculture association.
274 Australian Organic Farming and Gardening Society, *Farm and Garden Digest* 2, no. 7 (1950): pp. 1–3.
275 Australian Organic Farming and Gardening Society, *Farm and Garden Digest* 3, no. 1 (1952): p. 39.
276 Australian Organic Farming and Gardening Society, *Organic Farming Digest* 2, no. 1 (1949): p. 26. Other examples of revegetation projects by organic farmers are described in Victorian Compost Society, *Victorian Compost News*

3, no. 10 (1949): p. 130; Victorian Compost Society, *Victorian Compost News* 8, no. 1 (1954): p. 1; Victorian Compost Society, *Victorian Compost News* 12, no. 4 (1958): pp. 60–1.

277 Martin Mulligan and Stuart Hill, *Ecological Pioneers: A Social History of Australian Ecological Thought and Action* (Cambridge University Press, 2001), p. 199. See Chapter 1 for a more comprehensive discussion of P.A. Yeomans.

278 Australian Organic Farming and Gardening Society, *Organic Farming Digest* 1, no. 9 (1948): p. 32.

279 Australian Organic Farming and Gardening Society, *Farm and Garden Digest* 2, no. 7 (1950): p. 1.

280 Victorian Compost Society, *Victorian Compost News* 16, no. 2 (1962): p. 34.

281 Forests and trees have had a dual role in European, and by inheritance, Australian mythology, both reviled and revered. Forests were symbols of the untamed wild areas beyond the fringe of agricultural domination, admirable as well as dangerous. They were 'untouched' but also home to evils, both faunal and spiritual. The evil spirits beyond the light of the home fires in *Beowulf*, the wolf in Little Red Riding Hood and the stoats and weasels of the Wild Wood in *The Wind in the Willows*, are three of many examples of the dangers of forest wilderness in European folklore. This idea is discussed in detail by Michael Bunce, *The Countryside Ideal: Anglo-American Images of Landscape* (London and New York: Routledge, 1994).

282 N. Barr and J. Cary, *Greening a Brown Land. The Australian Search for Sustainable Land Use* (Melbourne: Macmillan, 1992), p. 80.

283 N. Barr and J. Cary, *ibid*., pp. 80–1.

284 Victorian Compost Society, *Victorian Compost News* 13, no. 4 (1959): p. 82.

285 *Yates Garden Guide*, 29th ed. (Melbourne: Angus and Robertson, 1965). Although the popular fashion for native gardens in Australia was in the 1970s, notable garden designers such as Edna Walling were using a mixture of native and exotic species in gardens during the 1950s.

286 Australian Organic Farming and Gardening Society, *Farm and Garden Digest* 3, no. 1 (1952): p. 39.

287 Victorian Compost Society, *Victorian Compost News* 19, no. 1 (1965): pp. 1–2.

288 Victorian Compost Society, *Victorian Compost News* 6, no. 3 (1952): pp. 29–30.

289 For example: Organic Farming and Gardening Society (Aust.), *Good Earth* 22, no. 1 (1968): p. 18.

290 A. Leopold, *A Sand County Almanac* (Oxford University Press, 1987), pp. 239–51.

291 Victorian Compost Society, *Victorian Compost News* 11, no. 5 (1957): p. 70.

292 Victorian Compost Society, *Victorian Compost News* 7, no. 2 (1953): p. 16.

293 Victorian Compost Society, *Victorian Compost News* 16, no. 2 (1962): p. 53. Recognising laws and limits within nature is a crucial aspect of ecological

thinking. Martin Mulligan and Stuart Hill, *Ecological Pioneers: A Social History of Australian Ecological Thought and Action* (Melbourne: Cambridge University Press, 2001), pp. 1–15.

294 Australian Organic Farming and Gardening Society, *Farm and Garden Digest* 3, no. 1 (1952): p. 39.

295 Victorian Compost Society, *Victorian Compost News* 7, no. 2 (1953): pp. 16–17.

296 A.J. McMichael, *Human Frontiers, Environments and Disease: Past Patterns, Uncertain Futures* (Cambridge: Cambridge University Press, 2001), p. 332.

297 Australian Organic Farming and Gardening Society, *Organic Farming Digest* 1, no. 11 (1948): p. 3; Victorian Compost Society, *Victorian Compost News* 6, no. 8 (1952): p. 94; Victorian Compost Society, *Victorian Compost News* 8, no. 8 (1954): p. 121.

298 Victorian Compost Society, *Victorian Compost News* 8, no. 8 (1954): p. 121.

299 Victorian Compost Society, *Victorian Compost News* 14, no. 3 (1960): pp. 50–1; Victorian Compost Society, *Victorian Compost News* 7, no. 6 (1953): p. 70; Victorian Compost Society, *Victorian Compost News* 3, no. 11 (1949): p. 130.

300 For example, Victorian Compost Society, *Victorian Compost News* 6, no. 8 (1952): p. 94; Victorian Compost Society, *Victorian Compost News* 7, no. 9 (1953): p. 110.

301 Australian Organic Farming and Gardening Society, *Farm and Garden Digest* 3, no. 5 (1954): pp. 2, 41. The journal ceased to be printed due to the cost of printing and production.

302 The Organic Farming and Gardening Society (Aust.), formerly the Victorian Compost Society, was the only one of the original three Australian organic growers groups still active by the beginning of the 1970s.

303 Organic Farming and Gardening Society (Aust.), *Good Earth* 32, no. 2 (1979): p. 32; Organic Farming and Gardening Society (Aust.), *Good Earth* 29, no. 1 (1976): p. 42.

304 Organic Farming and Gardening Society (Aust.), *Good Earth* 24, no. 1 (1971): p. 6; Organic Farming and Gardening Society (Aust.), *Good Earth* 23, no. 3 (1970): p. 52.

305 Brisbane Organic Growers Group, 'Newsletter,' Aug. 1981, p. 3.

306 Soil Association of South Australia, *Newsletter*, Nov. 1977.

307 For example Organic Gardening and Farming Society of Tasmania, *The Organic Gardener and Farmer* 1, no. 1 (1976).

308 By the mid-1970s there were organic societies in all the capital cities except Darwin and in many regional areas. Some of the most active of these societies were the Brisbane Organic Growers Group, the Organic Growers Association of Western Australia, the Henry Doubleday Research Association in New

South Wales, the Tasmanian Organic Gardening and Farming Society and the Soil Association of South Australia.

309 Libby Robin, *Defending the Little Desert: The Rise of Ecological Consciousness in Australia* (Melbourne: Melbourne University Press, 1998), pp. 139–40.

310 Libby Robin, *Defending the Little Desert: The Rise of Ecological Consciousness in Australia* (Melbourne: Melbourne University Press, 1998), p. 140.

311 Drew Hutton and Libby Connors, *A History of the Australian Environment Movement* (Cambridge: Cambridge University Press, 1999), pp. 125–6.

312 Mauricio Schoijet, '*Limits to Growth* and the Rise of Catastrophism,' *Environmental History* 4, no. 4 (1999).

313 Donald Worster, *Nature's Economy: A History of Ecological Ideas* (Melbourne: Cambridge University Press, 1992), p. 341.

314 Donald Worster, *Nature's Economy: A History of Ecological Ideas* (Melbourne: Cambridge University Press, 1992), pp. 30–1, 339–40.

315 Donald Worster, *Nature's Economy: A History of Ecological Ideas* (Melbourne: Cambridge University Press, 1992), p. 30–1, 105.

316 Libby Robin, *Defending the Little Desert: The Rise of Ecological Consciousness in Australia* (Melbourne: Melbourne University Press, 1998), p. 144.

317 Peter Bennett, *Australia and New Zealand Organic Gardening*, 1st ed. (Frenchs Forest, NSW: Child and Associates, 1979). The most recent edition of this book was published under the title *Organic Gardening* in 2006.

318 Peter Bennett, interviewed by the author, 22 February 2006.

319 Stuart Hill outlines the main precepts of ecological thinking in the introduction to: Martin Mulligan and Stuart Hill, *Ecological Pioneers: A Social History of Australian Ecological Thought and Action* (Melbourne: Cambridge University Press, 2001), pp. 8–11. That diversity and complexity confer stability is one important component of ecological thinking.

320 Peter Bennett, interviewed by the author, 22 February 2006; Peter Bennett, *Australia and New Zealand Organic Gardening*, 1st ed. (Frenchs Forest, NSW: Child and Associates, 1979), p. 7.

321 Bill Mollison and David Holmgren, *Permaculture One: A Perennial Agricultural System for Human Settlements* (Melbourne: Transworld Publishers, 1978).

322 Martin Mulligan and Stuart Hill, *Ecological Pioneers: A Social History of Australian Ecological Thought and Action* (Melbourne: Cambridge University Press, 2001), pp. 202–6, David Holmgren, *Hepburn Permaculture Gardens: 10 Years of Sustainable Living* (Hepburn: Holmgren Design Services, 1996).

323 *Permaculture*, spring 1978, p. 2.

324 Organic Farming and Gardening Society (Aust.), *Good Earth* 28, no. 3 (1975): p. 42.

325 Coralie Whitby, *Eco-Gardening* (Adelaide: Rigby, 1981). The Organic Farming and Gardening Society (Aust.) was a continuation of the Victorian Compost Society.

326 Organic Farming and Gardening Society (Aust.), *Good Earth* 35, no. 1 (1982): p. 11.

327 Organic Farming and Gardening Society (Aust.), *Good Earth* 36, no. 4 (1983): p. 50.

328 Informal conversations with past members of the Organic Farming and Gardening Society suggest that an ageing membership and inability to get members to assume executive positions, as well as personality and ideological clashes between particular members, contributed to the end of the society. The society continued to be listed as an organic contact in the magazine *Earth Garden* until 1986 although it was no longer active.

Case Study 3: Anthony Sheldon

329 Deb Anderson, 'Drought, Risk and Rural Endurance: Ways of Thinking the Australian Climate' (paper presented at the Museum Victoria History and Meaning of Things, Melbourne, 11 May 2005).

330 The Mallee is very dry compared to most populated areas in Australia. The average annual rainfall of 250–310 mm is considerably lower than all of Australia's capital cities, the nearest being Adelaide's average annual rainfall of 530 mm.

331 Anthony Sheldon, interviewed by the author, 6 April 2006.

332 Peter E. Charman and Brian W. Murphy, *Soils: Their Properties and Management*, 2nd ed. (Melbourne: Oxford University Press, 2000), pp. 265–6.

333 N. Barr and J. Cary, *Greening a Brown Land. The Australian Search for Sustainable Land Use* (Melbourne: Macmillan, 1992), pp. 132–3.

334 Droughts were recorded in the Mallee in 1914, the 1920s, 1937–39, 1943–45. Jenny Keating, *The Drought Walked Through: A History of Water Shortage in Victoria* (Melbourne: Department of Water Resources Victoria, 1992).

335 Anthony Sheldon, interviewed by the author, 6 April 2006.

336 Jenny Keating, *The Drought Walked Through: A History of Water Shortage in Victoria* (Melbourne: Department of Water Resources Victoria, 1992), p. 136.

337 Francis Ratcliffe, *Flying Fox and Drifting Sand: The Adventures of a Biologist in Australia* (Sydney: Angus and Robertson, 1947).

338 Anthony Sheldon, interviewed by the author, 6 April 2006.

339 N. Barr and J. Cary, *Greening a Brown Land. The Australian Search for Sustainable Land Use* (Melbourne: Macmillan, 1992), p. 35.

340 Anthony Sheldon, interviewed by the author, 6 April 2006.

341 G.W. Leeper and N.C. Uren, *Soil Science: An Introduction*, 5th ed. (Melbourne: Melbourne University Press, 1993), pp. 179–80.
342 Anthony Sheldon, interviewed by the author, 6 April 2006.
343 Anthony Sheldon, *ibid.*
344 Anthony Sheldon, *ibid.*
345 Anthony Sheldon, *ibid.*
346 Anthony Sheldon, *ibid.*
347 Anthony Sheldon, *ibid.*
348 Anthony Sheldon, *ibid.*
349 Anthony Sheldon, *ibid.*
350 Anthony Sheldon, *ibid.*
351 Anthony Sheldon, *ibid.*
352 This issue is discussed in more detail in Chapter 5.
353 Anthony Sheldon, interviewed by the author, 6 April 2006.
354 Anthony Sheldon, *Future Harvest Exhibition* (Melbourne: Museum Victoria, 1997). Anthony Sheldon formed a case study in the exhibition *Future Harvest* co-curated by the author at Museum Victoria in 1997–98.
355 A. Leopold, *A Sand County Almanac* (Oxford University Press, 1987), pp. 201–26. These sentiments have also been expressed by many Australian conservationists including Drew Hutton and Libby Connors, *A History of the Australian Environment Movement* (Cambridge: Cambridge University Press, 1999).
356 Anthony Sheldon, interviewed by the author, 6 April 2006.
357 Anthony Sheldon, *Future Harvest Exhibition* (Melbourne: Museum Victoria, 1997).
358 Anthony Sheldon, *ibid.*
359 Anthony Sheldon, interviewed by the author, 6 April 2006.
360 Anthony Sheldon, *ibid.*
361 Anthony Sheldon, *ibid.*
362 A.J. McMichael, *Human Frontiers, Environments and Disease: Past Patterns, Uncertain Futures* (Cambridge University Press, 2001), pp. 283–317; Martin Mulligan and Stuart Hill, *Ecological Pioneers: A Social History of Australian Ecological Thought and Action* (Cambridge University Press, 2001), pp. 9–11.
363 Anthony Sheldon, interviewed by the author, 6 April 2006.
364 Anthony Sheldon, *ibid.*
365 Anthony Sheldon, *ibid.*

Chapter 4: Back to the Land

366 *Earth Garden*, no. 1 (1972): p. 4.

367 Dennis Altman, 'The Counter-Culture: Nostalgia or Prophecy?,' in *Australian Society: A Sociological Introduction*, eds A.F. Davies, S. Encel, and M.J. Barry (Melbourne: Longman Cheshire, 1977); Jan Pakulski, *Social Movements: The Politics of Moral Protest* (Melbourne: Longman Cheshire, 1991).

368 Editorship of *Earth Garden* passed to Alan and Camille Thomas in 1986. Megg Miller is still the editor of *Grass Roots.*

369 Michael J. Roads, *A Guide to Organic Living in Australia* (Launceston: Mary Fisher Bookshop, 1977).

370 Jan Pakulski, *Social Movements: The Politics of Moral Protest* (Melbourne: Longman Cheshire, 1991).

371 *Grass Roots*, no. 6 (1973): p. 1.

372 Dennis Altman, 'The Counter-Culture: Nostalgia or Prophecy?,' in *Australian Society: A Sociological Introduction*, eds A.F. Davies, S. Encel, and M.J. Barry (Melbourne: Longman Cheshire, 1977).

373 Jackie French, interviewed by the author, 8 July 2006; Megg Miller, interviewed by the author, 30 March 2006.

374 Dennis Altman, 'The Counter-Culture: Nostalgia or Prophecy?,' in *Australian Society: A Sociological Introduction*, eds A.F. Davies, S. Encel, and M.J. Barry (Melbourne: Longman Cheshire, 1977), p. 450.

375 Dennis Altman, *ibid.*, p. 452; Peter Cock, *Alternative Australia: Communities of the Future?* (Melbourne: Quartet Books, 1979), p. 228.

376 Peter Cock, *Alternative Australia: Communities of the Future?* (Melbourne: Quartet Books, 1979); Seamus O'Hanlon and Tanja Luckins, eds, *Go Melbourne! Melbourne in the Sixties* (Melbourne: Circa, 2005), pp. viii, x.

377 Peter Cock, in his study of the Australian counterculture, makes the point that these 'alternative lifestylers' or 'counterculturalists' were diverse in their motivations. He distinguishes between those people who adopted the lifestyle for political and ideological reasons and those who were looking for a cheap, labour-free existence. Peter Cock, *Alternative Australia: Communities of the Future?* (Melbourne: Quartet Books, 1979). While the 'chilled out hippy drop-out' is the popular stereotype of the counterculture, as Peter Cock reveals, and as I discuss in this chapter, the Back to the Landers, as well as many other groups within the counterculture, did not conform to this stereotype but were active and ideological in their motivations.

378 Jan Pakulski, *Social Movements: The Politics of Moral Protest* (Melbourne: Longman Cheshire, 1991), p. xiv; Alain Touraine, *The Voice and the Eye: An Analysis of Social Movements* (Cambridge: Cambridge University Press, 1981), pp. 6–7.

379 Dennis Altman, 'The Counter-Culture: Nostalgia or Prophecy?,' in *Australian Society: A Sociological Introduction*, eds A.F. Davies, S. Encel, and M.J. Barry (Melbourne: Longman Cheshire, 1977), p. 464.

380 Megg Miller, interviewed by the author, 30 March 2006.

381 Keith Smith and Irene Smith, eds, *The Earth Garden Book: Self-Sufficiency in Australia*, 1st ed. (West Melbourne: Nelson (Australia), 1975), p. 48.

382 Michael J. Roads, *A Guide to Organic Living in Australia* (Launceston: Mary Fisher Bookshop, 1977).

383 Megg Miller, interviewed by the author, 30 March 2006.

384 Michael Bunce, *The Countryside Ideal: Anglo-American Images of Landscape* (London and New York: Routledge, 1994), pp. 5–36; Raymond Williams, *The Country and the City* (Oxford: Oxford University Press, 1973).

385 Andrea Gaynor, *Harvest of the Suburbs: An Environmental History of Growing Food in Australian Cities* (Perth: University of Western Australia Press, 2006), pp. 54–7; Rennie John Short, *Imagined Country: Environment, Culture and Society* (London: Routledge, 1991), pp. 30–3. A version of the yeoman idyll existed in Germany in the late nineteenth and early twentieth centuries in the 'Land Reform' and 'Food Reform' movements which were anti-industrial, anti-urban and anti-technology. Proponents were vegetarian and believed in preserving rural ways of living, nature and animals. They grew food for self-sufficiency without the use of technology or animals. They were the precursors for one of Germany's earliest groups of organic growers, the Arbeitsgemeinshaft Natürlicher Landbau und Siedlung (Natural Farming and Back to the Land Association) in the 1920s. G. Vogt, 'The Origins of Organic Farming,' in *Organic Farming: An International History*, ed. W. Lockeretz (UK: CAB International, 2007), pp. 12–13, 15.

386 Graeme Davison, *The Rise and Fall of Marvellous Melbourne* (Carlton: Melbourne University Press, 1978), p. 185; Andrea Gaynor, *Harvest of the Suburbs: An Environmental History of Growing Food in Australian Cities* (Perth: University of Western Australia Press, 2006), pp. 48–66; J.M. Powell, *Mirrors of the New World: Images and Image-Makers in the Settlement Process* (Canberra: Australian National University Press, 1977), p. 48.

387 Don Aitken, '"Countrymindedness": The Spread of an Idea', *Australian Cultural History* 4 (1985).

388 Victorian Compost Society, *Victorian Compost News* 3, no. 10 (1950): pp. 111–13.

389 Peter Cock, *Alternative Australia: Communities of the Future?* (Melbourne: Quartet Books, 1979), p. 94.

390 Peter Cock, *ibid.*, p. 212.

391 Rennie John Short, *Imagined Country: Environment, Culture and Society* (London: Routledge, 1991), pp. 30–3; Raymond Williams, *The Country and the City* (Oxford: Oxford University Press, 1973), pp. 9–17.

392 Michael Bunce, *The Countryside Ideal: Anglo-American Images of Landscape* (London and New York: Routledge, 1994), p. 26; Rennie John Short, *Imagined*

Country: Environment, Culture and Society (London: Routledge, 1991), pp. 6, 31; Raymond Williams, *The Country and the City* (Oxford: Oxford University Press, 1973), pp. 23–47.

393 Henry David Thoreau, *Walden* (Princeton, USA: Princeton University Press, 1971).

394 Jill Rayner, 'Back to the Land,' in *The Earth Garden Book: Self-Sufficiency in Australia*, eds Irene Smith and Keith Smith (West Melbourne: Nelson (Australia), 1975), pp. 39–40.

395 Jill Rayner, *ibid.*, p. 39–40.

396 *Earth Garden*, no. 11 (1975): p. 29.

397 *Earth Garden*, no. 21 (1978): p. 26.

398 Rennie John Short, *Imagined Country: Environment, Culture and Society* (London: Routledge, 1991), p. 10.

399 Rennie John Short, *ibid.*

400 Megg Miller and David Miller, eds, *Grass Roots, the Early Years* (Shepparton: Night Owl Publishing, 1979), p. 34.

401 Megg Miller, interviewed by the author, 30 March 2006.

402 Keith Smith and Irene Smith, eds, *The Earth Garden Book: Self-Sufficiency in Australia*, 1st ed. (West Melbourne: Nelson (Australia), 1975), pp. 9, 38.

403 E.O. Wilson, 'Biophilia and the Conservation Ethic,' in *The Biophilia Hypothesis*, eds S.R. Kellert and E.O. Wilson (Washington DC: Island Press, 1993).

404 Stephen R. Kellert, 'The Biological Basis for Human Values of Nature,' in *Biophilia Hypothesis*, eds E.O. Wilson and S.R. Kellert (Island Press, 1993); E.O. Wilson, 'Biophilia and the Conservation Ethic,' in *The Biophilia Hypothesis*, eds S.R. Kellert and E.O. Wilson (Washington DC: Island Press, 1993).

405 Suzanne Peters, 'The Land in Trust: A Social History of the Organic Farming Movement' (PhD, McGill University, 1979), pp. 180–1.

406 Rennie John Short, *Imagined Country: Environment, Culture and Society* (London: Routledge, 1991), p. 10.

407 Keith Smith and Irene Smith, eds, *The Earth Garden Book: Self-Sufficiency in Australia*, 1st ed. (West Melbourne: Nelson (Australia), 1975), p. 19.

408 David Stephen, interviewed by the author, 26 June 2006.

409 Keith Smith and Irene Smith, eds, *The Earth Garden Book: Self-Sufficiency in Australia*, 1st ed. (West Melbourne: Nelson (Australia), 1975), p. 8.

410 Megg Miller and David Miller, eds, *Grass Roots, the Early Years* (Shepparton: Night Owl Publishing, 1979), p. 4.

411 Megg Miller, interviewed by the author, 30 March 2006.

412 *Earth Garden*, no. 1 (1972): p. 4; Robert Rodale, ed., *The Basic Book of Organic Gardening* (USA: Ballentine, 1971). This book was a collection of articles from

the United States magazine *Organic Gardening.* It was published before Australians had begun to publish their own organic gardening books. The Rodale Society in the United States was a copious producer of information about organic gardening and farming.

413 Michael J. Roads, *A Guide to Organic Living in Australia* (Launceston: Mary Fisher Bookshop, 1977).

414 Megg Miller, interviewed by the author, 30 March 2006.

415 *Earth Garden*, no. 45 (1985): p. 6.

416 *Earth Garden*, no. 1 (1972): p. 4.

417 Megg Miller, interviewed by the author, 30 March 2006.

418 W.J. Belasco, *Appetite for Change: How the Counter-Culture Took on the Food Industry* (New York: Cornell University Press, 1993).

419 Megg Miller, interviewed by the author, 30 March 2006.

420 Keith Smith and Irene Smith, eds, *The Earth Garden Book: Self-Sufficiency in Australia*, 1st ed. (West Melbourne: Nelson (Australia), 1975), pp. 8, 20.

421 Michael J. Roads, *A Guide to Organic Living in Australia* (Launceston: Mary Fisher Bookshop, 1977).

422 Jill Rayner, 'Getting It Straight,' in *The Earth Garden Book: Self-Sufficiency in Australia*, eds Irene Smith and Keith Smith (West Melbourne: Nelson (Australia), 1975), pp. 40–1.

423 Jill Rayner, 'Getting It Straight,' in *The Earth Garden Book: Self-Sufficiency in Australia*, eds Irene Smith and Keith Smith (West Melbourne: Nelson (Australia), 1975), pp. 40–1.

424 Keith Smith and Irene Smith, eds, *The Earth Garden Book: Self-Sufficiency in Australia*, 1st ed. (West Melbourne: Nelson (Australia), 1975), pp. 8–9.

425 *Grass Roots*, no. 15 (1975): p. 14.

426 Andrea Gaynor, *Harvest of the Suburbs: An Environmental History of Growing Food in Australian Cities* (Perth: University of Western Australia Press, 2006), p. 54.

427 Jackie French, interviewed by the author, 8 July 2006.

428 *Earth Garden*, no. 1 (1972): p. 4.

429 *Earth Garden*, no. 56 (1987): p. 19.

430 Rennie John Short, *Imagined Country: Environment, Culture and Society* (London: Routledge, 1991), p. 31.

431 Raymond Williams, 'Literature and Rural Society,' in *The Raymond Williams Reader*, ed. John Higgins (Oxford: Blackwell, 2001).

432 Keith Smith and Irene Smith, eds, *The Earth Garden Book: Self-Sufficiency in Australia*, 1st ed. (West Melbourne: Nelson (Australia), 1975), p. 9.

433 Another image of men raking hay was too poor a quality to be reproduced here but can be located in the original at *Earth Garden*, no. 11 (1975): p. 28.

434 The cover of Philip Conford, *The Origins of the Organic Movement* (Edinburgh, UK: Floris Books, 2001) depicts the silhouette of two Clydesdale horses pulling a light jinker upon which a man in a peaked cap sits. This evokes a romantic image that tends to suggest organic farming is about eschewing technology, rather than part of modern agriculture. This idea is only part of the story of organic growing conveyed in his text.
435 Peter Cock, *Alternative Australia: Communities of the Future?* (Melbourne: Quartet Books, 1979), pp. 216–17. That the yeoman idyll is different for both men and women is noted by Andrea Gaynor in discussing suburban Australian gardeners. Andrea Gaynor, *Harvest of the Suburbs: An Environmental History of Growing Food in Australian Cities* (Perth: University of Western Australia Press, 2006).
436 *Earth Garden*, no. 21 (1978): p. 21.
437 Henry Doubleday Research Association, 'Newsletter,' no. 45 (1981); Megg Miller, interviewed by the author, 30 March 2006.
438 Megg Miller, interviewed by the author, 30 March 2006.
439 David Stephen, interviewed by the author, 26 June 2006.
440 Leicester Jones, interviewed by the author, 28 June 2006.
441 Henry Doubleday Research Association, 'Newsletter,' no. 45 (1981).
442 Leicester Jones, interviewed by the author, 28 June 2006.
443 Ray Mason and Elma Mason, interviewed by the author, 27 June 2006.
444 Ray Mason and Elma Mason, *ibid.*

Case Study 4: Jackie French

445 This quote comes from the online introduction to Jackie French's book *Wilderness Garden* which is available on her personal website at www.jackiefrench.com. Similar sentiments are expressed by Jackie French in the introduction to her book: Jackie French, *The Wilderness Garden: Beyond Organic Gardening* (Melbourne: Aird Books, 1992), p. 1.
446 Jackie French, interviewed by the author, 8 July 2006.
447 Jackie French, *Earth Gardener's Companion: A Month by Month Guide to Organic Planting, Gardening and Harvesting* (Trentham, Vic.: Earth Garden Magazine, 1990), p. 4.
448 Jackie French, interviewed by the author, 8 July 2006.
449 The average annual rainfall at Braidwood, the nearest town to Jackie French's property is higher than the annual rainfall in Melbourne (656 mm), Hobart (628 mm) and Adelaide (530 mm) and comparable to Perth's rainfall (850 mm). It is considerably less than the annual rainfall experienced by Brisbane (1149 mm), Sydney (1212 mm) and Darwin (1500 mm).

450 Jackie French, interviewed by the author, 8 July 2006.
451 Jackie French discusses her 'groves' technique on her personal website at www.jackiefrench.com/groves.html, last accessed 26/08/2008.
452 Permaculture and eco-gardening are discussed in more detail in Chapter 3.
453 Garden designer Edna Walling used the technique of planting fast-growing 'nursery' trees in many commissioned garden plans produced from the 1920s to the 1960s.
454 Jackie French, interviewed by the author, 8 July 2006.
455 Jackie French, *Backyard Self-Sufficiency* (Melbourne: Aird Books, 1992), p. 2.
456 Jackie French, interviewed by the author, 8 July 2006.
457 Jackie French, *Backyard Self-Sufficiency* (Melbourne: Aird Books, 1992), p. 2.
458 Jackie French, *Organic Gardening in Australia* (French's Forest: Reed, 1986).
459 Jackie French, interviewed by the author, 8 July 2006; Jackie French, *Backyard Self-Sufficiency* (Melbourne: Aird Books, 1992), p. 2.
460 Permaculturalists were also active promoters of self-sufficiency in urban areas in the 1990s.
461 Jackie French outlines this idea in a number of books, including: Jackie French, *Backyard Self-Sufficiency* (Melbourne: Aird Books, 1992); Jackie French, *Earth Gardener's Companion: A Month by Month Guide to Organic Planting, Gardening and Harvesting* (Trentham, Vic.: Earth Garden Magazine, 1990); Jackie French, *Household Self-Sufficiency: The Ultimate Guide to Making Everything from Acne and Baldness Remedies to Candles, Love Potions, Varnish and Wool Wash* (Melbourne: Aird Books, 1994); Jackie French, *Switch!: Home-Based Power, Water and Sewerage Systems for the Twenty-First Century* (Melbourne: Aird Books, 1994).
462 Jackie French, *Backyard Self-Sufficiency* (Melbourne: Aird Books, 1992), p. 6.
463 Jackie French, *Backyard Self-Sufficiency* (Melbourne: Aird Books, 1992), p. 4; Jackie French, *Household Self-Sufficiency: The Ultimate Guide to Making Everything from Acne and Baldness Remedies to Candles, Love Potions, Varnish and Wool Wash* (Melbourne: Aird Books, 1994), p. 2.
464 Jackie French, *Jackie French's Top 10 Vegetables* (Melbourne: Aird Books, 1995), p. 3.
465 Jackie French, *Natural Control of Garden Pests* (Melbourne: Aird Books, 2002), p. 7.
466 Jackie French, *Backyard Self-Sufficiency* (Melbourne: Aird Books, 1992), p. 4.
467 Jackie French, *Australian Women's Weekly*, May 1993, p. 206.
468 Jackie French, *Australian Women's Weekly*, July 1995, pp. 136–9; Jackie French, *Australian Women's Weekly*, September 2000, pp. 168–71.
469 Jackie French, *Australian Women's Weekly*, August 1994, pp. 162–5; Jackie French, *Australian Women's Weekly*, July 1995, pp. 158–61.

Chapter 5: Australian organic farming and gardening in the 2000s

470 For example David Dumaresq, Richard Greene, and Lorrae van Kerkhoff, eds, *Organic Agriculture in Australia: Proceedings of the National Symposium on Organic Agriculture, Research and Development.* RIRDC Research Paper 97/14 (Canberra: Rural Industries Research and Development Corporation, 1997); Darren Halpin, 'The Australian Organic Industry: A Profile,' (Canberra: Australian Government Department of Agriculture, Fisheries and Forestry, 2004); Rural Industries Research and Development Corporation, 'Inaugural OFA National Organics Conference 2001,' (Canberra: Rural Industries Research and Development Corporation, 2001).

471 Australian television programs featuring organic content include *Gardening Australia* and *Burke's Backyard.*

472 The main sources I have used for this chapter are interviews with current organic growers, certification documents produced by the National Association for Sustainable Agriculture Australia; Standards Australia; Australian Certified Organic (the certification arm of Biological Farmers of Australia); and a selection of the organic farming and gardening magazines, books and newsletters.

473 The Bio-Dynamic Research Institute is part of the Bio-Dynamic Agricultural Association of Australia. Bio-Dynamic Research Institute, *Demeter Bio-Dynamic Agriculture in Australia* (Bio-Dynamic Research Institute, 2005 [cited 6 November 2006]); available from www.demeter.org.au.

474 *Organic Gardener* Summer (2006/2007): p. 23; W.A. Doubleday Organic Research Association, *Newsletter* 2, no. 2 (1977): p. 23; Kristen Lyons, 'Corporate Environmentalism and Organic Agriculture in Australia: The Case of Uncle Tobys,' *Rural Sociology* 64, no. 2 (1999): p. 3.

475 Dick McNeill, interviewed by the author, 13 March 2006.

476 For a more detailed discussion of the role of NASAA in the development of certification see E. Wynen and S. Fritz, 'NASAA and Organic Agriculture in Australia', in *Organic Farming: An International History*, ed. W. Lockeretz (UK: CAB International, 2007). Wynen and Fritz claim for NASAA the role of 'defining' what it means to be organic, however, as this history demonstrates, while NASAA had a pivotal role in the regulation of organic standards the definition of what it means to be organic emerged throughout the previous 40 years.

477 Standards Australia. AS6000-2009 Organic and Biodynamic Products, Sydney, NSW. Standards Australia 2009.

478 These estimations of the number of certified organic farms in Australia include farms in conversion to organic growing, a process which takes about three years. The lower estimation is made by Darren Halpin, 'The Australian

Organic Industry: A Profile', (Canberra: Australian Government Department of Agriculture, Fisheries and Forestry, 2004), pp. 9–10. The higher estimation is made by Willer Yussefi, Helga Yussefi, and Minou Yussefi, *The World of Organic Agriculture: Statistics and Emerging Trends 2006* (Frick, Switzerland: Research Institute of Organic Agriculture, 2006), p. 25.

479 Willer Yussefi, Helga Yussefi, and Minou Yussefi, *The World of Organic Agriculture: Statistics and Emerging Trends 2006* (Frick, Switzerland: Research Institute of Organic Agriculture, 2006), p. 122.

480 Estimates of the value of Australian certified organic produce vary widely from about AUD$90 million to AUD$145 million, depending on the source of information and the means of calculation. Darren Halpin, 'The Australian Organic Industry: A Profile', (Canberra: Australian Government Department of Agriculture, Fisheries and Forestry, 2004), pp. 20–1; Willer Yussefi, Helga Yussefi, and Minou Yussefi, *The World of Organic Agriculture: Statistics and Emerging Trends 2006* (Frick, Switzerland: Research Institute of Organic Agriculture, 2006), p. 122.

481 D. Buck, C. Getz, and J. Guthman, 'From Farm to Table: The Organic Vegetable Commodity Chain of Northern California', *Sociologia Ruralis* 37, no. 3–20 (1997); J. Guthman, 'Regulating Meaning, Appropriating Nature: The Codification of Californian Organic Agriculture,' *Antipode* 30 (1998); H. Tovey, 'Food, Environmentalism and Rural Sociology: On the Organic Farming Movement in Ireland', *Sociologia Ruralis* 37 (1997).

482 S. Jordan, H. Shuji, and R. Izawa, 'Conventionalization in the Australian Organic Industry: A Case Study of the Darling Downs Region', in *Sociological Perspectives of Organic Agriculture: From Pioneer to Policy*, eds G. Holt and M. Reed (Wallingford, UK & Cambridge, USA: CABI, 2006); Kristen Lyons, 'Corporate Environmentalism and Organic Agriculture in Australia: The Case of Uncle Tobys', *Rural Sociology* 64, no. 2 (1999).

483 Hugh Campbell and Ruth Liepins, 'Naming Organics: Understanding Organic Standards in New Zealand as a Discursive Field', *Sociologia Ruralis* 41, no. 1 (2001); B. Coombes and Hugh Campbell, 'Dependent Reproduction of Alternative Modes of Agriculture: Organic Farming in New Zealand', *Sociologia Ruralis* 38, no. 2 (1998); Pernille Kaltoft, 'Values About Nature in Organic Farming Practice and Knowledge', *Sociologia Ruralis* 39, no. 1 (1999); Ulrich Kopke, 'Organic Agriculture: Maintaining Old Principles in a Changing Environment' (paper presented at the Shaping Sustainable Systems; 15th IFOAM Organic World Congress, Adelaide, 20–25 September 2005); Vonne Lund, Sven Hemlin, and William Lockeretz, 'Organic Livestock Production as Viewed by Swedish Farmers and Organic Initiators', *Agriculture and Human Values* 19, no. 3 (2002); Johannes Michelsen, 'Recent Development and Political Acceptance of Organic Farming in Europe', *Sociologia Ruralis* 41, no. 1 (2001).

484 Stewart Lockie and Darren Halpin, 'The "Conventionalisation" Thesis Reconsidered: Structural and Ideological Transformation of Australian Organic Agriculture', *Sociologia Ruralis* 45, no. 4 (2005).
485 Stewart Lockie and Darren Halpin, *ibid.*; Kristen Lyons, 'Corporate Environmentalism and Organic Agriculture in Australia: The Case of Uncle Tobys', *Rural Sociology* 64, no. 2 (1999); Kristen Lyons, 'From Sandals to Suits: Green Consumers and the Institutionalisation of Organic Agriculture', in *Consuming Foods, Sustaining Environments*, eds Stewart Lockie and Bill Pritchard (Brisbane, Australia: Australian Academic Press, 2001).
486 Stewart Lockie and Darren Halpin, 'The "Conventionalisation" Thesis Reconsidered: Structural and Ideological Transformation of Australian Organic Agriculture', *Sociologia Ruralis* 45, no. 4 (2005).
487 Laura B. DeLind, 'Transforming Organic Agriculture into Industrial Organic Products: Reconsidering National Organic Standards', *Human Organization* 59, no. 2 (2000); Kennet S.C. Lynggaard, 'The Farmer within an Institutional Environment. Comparing Danish and Belgian Organic Farming', *Sociologia Ruralis* 41, no. 1 (2001); Johannes Michelsen, 'Organic Farming in a Regulatory Perspective. The Danish Case', *Sociologia Ruralis* 41, no. 1 (2001).
488 Brenda Little, *The Australian Organic Gardening Handbook* (Padstow, NSW: Leatherwood Press, 2000), p. 7.
489 National Association for Sustainable Agriculture Australia, 'NASAA Organic Standard', (Stirling, SA: National Association for Sustainable Agriculture Australia, 2004), pp. 13, 26.
490 Brice Douglas, interviewed by the author, 4 April 2006.
491 David Dumaresq, Richard Greene, and Lorrae van Kerkhoff, eds, *Organic Agriculture in Australia: Proceedings of the National Symposium on Organic Agriculture, Research and Development*. RIRDC Research Paper 97/14 (Canberra: Rural Industries Research and Development Corporation, 1997), pp. 47–8; B. Smith, 'The Smith Family Farming Adventure', *Victorian Landcare and Catchment Management* 2008, pp. 8–9.
492 Anthony Skopp and Debbie Skopp, interviewed by the author, 30 May 2006.
493 National Association for Sustainable Agriculture Australia, 'NASAA Organic Standard', (Stirling, SA: National Association for Sustainable Agriculture Australia, 2004), p. 33.
494 Desmond Chappel, interviewed by the author, 27 May 2006; Anthony Sheldon, interviewed by the author, 6 April 2006.
495 Australian Certified Organic, 'Australian Organic Standard', (Chermside, Qld: Biological Farmers of Australia, 2006), p. 87; National Association for Sustainable Agriculture Australia, 'NASAA Organic Standard', (Stirling, SA: National Association for Sustainable Agriculture Australia, 2004), p. 33.

Standards Australia, 'AS 6000–2009 Organic and Biodynamic Products', (Sydney, NSW: Standards Australia, 2009) standard 4.1.

496 Timothy Vos, 'Visions of the Middle Landscape: Organic Farming and the Politics of Nature', *Agriculture and Human Values* 17, no. 3 (2000).

497 For example Jackie French, *Soil Food: 1372 Ways to Add Fertility to Your Soil* (Melbourne: Aird Books, 1995), pp. 64–5, 70.

498 Australian gardener Margaret Simons, in her history of compost, suggests that increasing sales of composting toilets and the use of municipal sewage in non-organic commercial plantations implies a resurgence of interest in human sewage as fertiliser as well as a productive method of waste disposal in Australia. Margaret Simons, *Resurrection in a Bucket: The Rich and Fertile Story of Compost* (Allen and Unwin, 2004), pp. 115–17.

499 Brice Douglas, interviewed by the author, 4 April 2006.

500 National Association for Sustainable Agriculture Australia, 'NASAA Organic Standard', (Stirling, SA: National Association for Sustainable Agriculture Australia, 2004), p. 13.

501 Anthony Sheldon, interviewed by the author, 6 April 2006.

502 Faidon Magkos, Arvaniti Fotini, and Antionis Zampelas, 'Organic Food: Nutritious Food or Food for Thought? A Review of the Evidence', *International Journal of Food Sciences and Nutrition* 54, no. 5 (2003); Christine M. Williams, 'Nutritional Quality of Organic Food: Shades of Grey or Shades of Green?', *Proceedings of the Nutrition Society* 61, no. 1 (2002); K. Woese *et al.*, 'A Comparison of Organically and Conventionally Grown Foods: Results of a Review of the Relevant Literature', *Journal of Science Food and Agriculture* 74 (1997); V. Worthington, 'Nutritional Quality of Organic Versus Conventional Fruits, Vegetables and Grains', *Journal of Alternative and Complementary Medicine* 7 (2001).

503 Lisbeth Grinder-Pedersen *et al.*, 'Effect of Diets Based on Foods from Conventional Versus Organic Production on Intake and Excretion of Flavonoids and Markers of Antioxidative Defence in Humans', *Journal of Agricultural and Food Chemistry* 51, no. 19 (2003); Ginerva Lombardi-Boccia *et al.*, 'Nutrients and Antioxidant Molecules in Yellow Plums (*Prunus domestica L.)* from Conventional and Organic Productions: A Comparative Study', *Journal of Agricultural and Food Chemistry* 52, no. 1 (2004); Janice Young *et al.*, 'Phytochemical Phenolics in Organically Grown Vegetables', *Molecular Nutrition and Food Research* 49 (2005).

504 Debates around the certification of aquaculture and wild-caught marine and riverine animals in the United States is discussed by Becky Mansfield, 'Organic Views of Nature: The Debate over Organic Certification for Aquatic Animals', *Sociologia Ruralis* 44, no. 2 (2004).

505 Annette McFarlane, *Organic Vegetable Gardening* (Sydney: Australian Broadcasting Corporation, 2002), p. 1. The author is quoting the Brisbane Organic Growers.

506 Australian Certified Organic, 'Australian Organic Standard,' (Chermside, Qld: Biological Farmers of Australia, 2006), p. 31, National Association for Sustainable Agriculture Australia, 'NASAA Organic Standard', (Stirling, SA: National Association for Sustainable Agriculture Australia, 2004), p. 23.

507 Brice Douglas, interviewed by the author, 4 April 2006.

508 Matthew Jamieson, interview with the author, 29 May 2006.

509 B. Smith, 'The Smith Family Farming Adventure', *Victorian Landcare and Catchment Management* 2008, p. 8.

510 Stewart Lockie and Darren Halpin, 'The "Conventionalisation" Thesis Reconsidered: Structural and Ideological Transformation of Australian Organic Agriculture', *Sociologia Ruralis* 45, no. 4 (2005): pp. 293–301; E. Wynen, *Conversion to Organic Agriculture in Australia: Problems and Possibilities in the Cereal/Livestock Industry* (Sydney: National Association for Sustainable Agriculture, 1992); E. Wynen, 'Sustainable and Conventional Agriculture in South-eastern Australia – a Comparison', in *Economic Research Report* (Melbourne: School of Economics and Commerce, La Trobe University, 1990). Another, smaller study of Australian organic horticultural farmers made similar findings about the association between organic farmers' beliefs about health and their conversion to organic production methods. S. Kosch, 'Organic Farming in Victoria' (Horticultural Project Report, Victorian College of Agriculture and Horticulture, 1995).

511 Desmond Chappel, interviewed by the author, 27 May 2006. David Dumaresq, Richard Greene, and Lorrae van Kerkhoff, eds, *Organic Agriculture in Australia: Proceedings of the National Symposium on Organic Agriculture, Research and Development.* RIRDC Research Paper 97/14 (Canberra: Rural Industries Research and Development Corporation, 1997), pp. 45–57; Matthew Jamieson, interview with the author, 29 May 2006; Leicester Jones, interviewed by the author, 28 June 2006; Dick McNeill, interviewed by the author, 13 March 2006.

512 Henk Verhoog, 'Naturalness and the Genetic Modification of Animals', *Trends in Biotechnology* 21, no. 7 (2003): pp. 294–7.

513 Australian Certified Organic, 'Australian Organic Standard', (Chermside, Qld: Biological Farmers of Australia, 2006), p. 31; National Association for Sustainable Agriculture Australia, 'NASAA Organic Standard', (Stirling, SA: National Association for Sustainable Agriculture Australia, 2004), p. 23. Standards Australia, 'AS 6000–2009 Organic and Biodynamic Products', (Sydney, NSW: Standards Australia, 2009), standards 4.8.16 and 6.8.19.

514 J. Pretty, 'The Rapid Emergence of Genetic Modification in World Agriculture: Contested Risks and Benefits', *Environmental Conservation* 28, no. 3 (2001).
515 T. Schettler, K. Barrett, and C. Raffensperger, 'The Precautionary Principle: A Guide for Protecting Public Health and the Environment', in *Life Support: The Environment and Human Health*, ed. Michael McCally (Massachusetts: MIT Press, 2002).
516 Standards Australia, 'AS 6000–2009 Organic and Biodynamic Products', (Sydney, NSW: Standards Australia, 2009), standards 4.8.16 and 6.8.19.
517 Judyth McLeod, *Botanica's Pocket Organic Gardening* (Milsons Point, NSW: Random House, 2002), p. 24.
518 Brice Douglas, interviewed by the author, 4 April 2006.
519 Anthony Sheldon, interviewed by the author, 6 April 2006.
520 Australian Certified Organic, 'Australian Organic Standard', (Chermside, Qld: Biological Farmers of Australia, 2006), p. 92; National Association for Sustainable Agriculture Australia, 'NASAA Organic Standard', (Stirling, SA: National Association for Sustainable Agriculture Australia, 2004), p. 85.
521 Standards Australia, 'AS 6000–2009 Organic and Biodynamic Products' (Sydney, NSW: Standards Australia, 2009), standard 4.5.2.
522 Jackie French, interviewed by the author, 8 July 2006; Hardy Vogtmann, '"Sustaining the Planet": Where Do We Come from and Where Do We Go?' (paper presented at the Shaping Sustainable Systems, 15th IFOAM Organic World Congress, Adelaide, 20–25 September 2005).
523 J.R.R. Tolkien, *Farmer Giles of Ham* (London: Allen & Unwin, 1974). The story was originally published in 1949.
524 Matthew Jamieson, interview with the author, 29 May 2006.
525 International Federation of Organic Agriculture, 'Principles of Organic Agriculture', (Bonn, Germany: International Federation of Organic Agriculture Movements, n.d.), p. 2.
526 Judyth McLeod, *Botanica's Pocket Organic Gardening* (Milsons Point, NSW: Random House, 2002), p. 13.
527 National Association for Sustainable Agriculture Australia, 'NASAA Organic Standard,' (Stirling, SA: National Association for Sustainable Agriculture Australia, 2004), pp. 24–5.
528 Standards Australia, 'AS 6000–2009 Organic and Biodynamic Products' (Sydney, NSW: Standards Australia, 2009), standard 47.2.
529 Australian Certified Organic, 'Australian Organic Standard', (Chermside, Qld: Biological Farmers of Australia, 2006), pp. 29, 38–40; National Association for Sustainable Agriculture Australia, 'NASAA Organic Standard', (Stirling, SA: National Association for Sustainable Agriculture Australia, 2004), pp. 13,

24–26; Standards Australia, 'AS 6000–2009 Organic and Biodynamic Products (Sydney, NSW: Standards Australia, 2009), standard 4.7.4.

530 *Organic Gardener* November/December (2007): pp. 70–2, *Organic Gardener* Summer (2006/2007): p. 78.

531 Brenda Little, *The Australian Organic Gardening Handbook* (Padstow, NSW: Leatherwood Press, 2000), p. 7.

532 *Organic Gardener* Summer (2006/2007): p. 26.

533 Biological Farmers of Australia, 'Organics, One of Our Most Viable Solutions to Climate Change', *The Organic Advantage* 2006; Tim Flannery, 'Agriculture in the Context of Climate Change', (paper presented at the Shaping Sustainable Systems; 15th IFOAM Organic World Congress, Adelaide, 20–25 September 2005); Tim Flannery, *The Weather Makers: The History and Future Impact of Climate Change* (Melbourne: Text Publishing Company, 2005), p. 256; J. Kotschi and K. Muller-Samann, 'The Role of Organic Agriculture in Mitigating Climate Change', in *International Federation of Organic Agriculture Movements* (Bonn: 2004); Rodale Institute, 'Organic Agriculture Yields New Weapon against Global Warming', (Kutztown, USA: Rodale Institute, 2003).

534 Tim Flannery, *The Weather Makers: The History and Future Impact of Climate Change* (Melbourne: Text Publishing Company, 2005), p. 256.

535 R. Lal, 'Soil Carbon Sequestration Impacts on Global Climate Change and Food Security', *Science* 304, no. 5677 (2004).

536 R. Lal, *ibid.*

537 R. Lal, *ibid.*

538 *Australian Organic News* 1, no. 6 (1992): p. 6. *Australian Organic News* was the predecessor of *Acres Australia*, the most prominent commercial organic farming magazine in Australia.

539 Dick McNeill, interviewed by the author, 13 March 2006.

540 Jackie French, interviewed by the author, 8 July 2006. It is illegal to sell produce as 'certified organic' unless it has been certified by one of the recognised organic certification organisations. However, the term 'organic' is still not legally protected in Australia. Willer Yussefi, Helga Yussefi, and Minou Yussefi, *The World of Organic Agriculture: Statistics and Emerging Trends 2006* (Frick, Switzerland: Research Institute of Organic Agriculture, 2006), p. 123.

541 According to Megg Miller, readership of *Grass Roots* has declined since its peak in the mid-1980s.

542 As listed by the magazine *Organic Gardener* Summer (2006/2007): p. 87.

543 For example in the magazines *Organic Gardening, Earth Garden* and *Grass Roots* and Judyth McLeod, *Botanica's Pocket Organic Gardening* (Milsons Point, NSW: Random House, 2002), p. 27.

544 Linda Cockburn, *Living the Good Life* (Melbourne: Hardie Grant Publishing, 2006). *Organic Gardener* Winter (2006): pp. 54–5; *Organic Gardener* Spring (2006): pp. 72–3; *Organic Gardener* Summer (2006/2007): pp. 77–8.

545 Judyth McLeod, *Botanica's Pocket Organic Gardening* (Milsons Point, NSW: Random House, 2002).

546 Megg Miller, interviewed by the author, 30 March 2006.

547 Jackie French, interviewed by the author, 8 July 2006; Megg Miller, interviewed by the author, 30 March 2006.

548 National Association for Sustainable Agriculture Australia, 'NASAA Constitution', (Stirling, SA: National Association for Sustainable Agriculture Australia, 2005), p. 2.

549 Donald Worster, 'Transformations of the Earth: Toward an Agroecological Perspective in History', *Journal of American History* 76, no. 4 (1990): p. 1093.

550 A.J. McMichael, *Human Frontiers, Environments and Disease: Past Patterns, Uncertain Futures* (Cambridge University Press, 2001), pp. xiv–xv, 331.

551 This statement paraphrases an assertion made in: David Holmgren, 'Permaculture: Sustainability Design Framework for Organic Agriculture in the Energy Descent Era' (paper presented at the Shaping Sustainable Systems; 15th IFOAM Organic World Congress, Adelaide, 20–25 September 2005).

Bibliography

Interviews

Conducted by the author

Bennett, Peter, organic gardener, garden adviser, author and broadcaster, SA, 22 February 2006.
Chappel, Desmond, organic banana farmer, Qld, 27 May 2006.
Douglas, Brice, organic beef and olive farmer, SA, 4 April 2006.
French, Jackie, organic gardener and author, NSW, 8 July 2006.
Jamieson, Matthew, organic turkey and macadamia farmer, NSW, 29 May 2006.
Jones, Leicester, organic gardener, Tas, 28 June 2006.
Mason, Ray, and Elma Mason, retired organic dairy farmers and organic gardeners, Tas, 27 June 2006.
McNeill, Dick, retired organic farmer, organic gardener and first certified Australian organic farmer, NSW, 13 March 2006.
Miller, Megg, organic gardener, author and editor, Vic, 30 March 2006.
Sheldon, Anthony, organic cereal and sheep farmer, Vic, 6 April 2006.
Skopp, Anthony, and Debbie Skopp, organic sugar cane farmers, Qld, 30 May 2006.
Stephen, David, organic gardener and founder of the Tasmanian Organic Gardening and Farming Society, Tas, 26 June 2006.
White, Graham, and Mary White, retired farmers and son and daughter-in-law of Harold White, NSW, 26 May 2006.
White, Sam, farmer and grandson of Harold White, NSW, 26 May 2006.
White, Elizabeth, retired farmer and daughter-in-law of Harold White, NSW, 26 May 2006.
Yeomans, Ken, keyline consultant and son of P.A. Yeomans, Qld, 24 May 2006.
Yeomans, Allan, manufacturer, author and son of P.A. Yeomans, Qld, 24 May 2006.

Newsletters and periodicals

Australian Organic Farming and Gardening Society, *Organic Farming Digest* 1946–1949.

Australian Organic Farming and Gardening Society, *Farm and Garden Digest* 1949–1954.

Acres Australia 1993–1994.

The Australian Gardener: a monthly journal of floriculture and horticulture 1907–1910.

Australian Organic News 1992.

Australian Women's Weekly 1990–2000.

Biological Farmers of Australia, *The Organic Advantage* 2004–2007.

Brisbane Organic Growers Group, *Newsletter* 1980–1993.

Doubleday Organic Research Association, WA, *Newsletter* 1977.

Earth Garden 1972–1988.

Grass Roots 1973–1984.

Henry Doubleday Research Association, *Newsletter* 1970–1971, 1980–1984.

Living Soil Association of Tasmania, *Newsletter* 1950–1951.

Organic Gardener 2000–2007.

Organic Farming and Gardening Society (Aust.), *Good Earth* 1966–1983.

Organic Gardening and Farming Society of Tasmania, *The Organic Gardener and Farmer* 1976–1980.

Organic Gardening and Farming Society of Tasmania, *Organic Growing* 1980–1981.

Permaculture 1978–1987.

Soil Association of South Australia, *Newsletter* 1972–1982.

Victorian Compost Society, *Victorian Compost News* 1947–1965.

Archival sources

Stretton, L.E.B. *Transcript of Evidence of the Royal Commission on the Bread Industry*, 8 June, 1949, VPRS 11910/P/1 10.

Exhibitions

Future Harvest Exhibition. Melbourne: Museum Victoria, 1997.

Books, articles, theses and reports

Adamson, William, and William Elliot. *Adamson's Australian Gardener: An Epitome of Horticulture for the Colony of Victoria*. 10th ed. Melbourne: George Robertson, 1879.

Aitken, Don. '"Countrymindedness": The Spread of an Idea'. *Australian Cultural History* 4 (1985): 34–41.

Aitken, Richard, and Michael Looker, eds. *Oxford Companion to Australian Gardens*: Oxford University Press, 2002.

Altman, Dennis. 'The Counter-Culture: Nostalgia or Prophecy?' In *Australian Society: A Sociological Introduction*, edited by A.F. Davies, S. Encel and M.J. Barry. Melbourne: Longman Cheshire, 1977.

Anderson, Deb. 'Drought, Risk and Rural Endurance: Ways of Thinking the Australian Climate'. Paper presented at the Museum Victoria History and Meaning of Things, Melbourne, 11 May 2005.

Anderson, Warwick. *The Cultivation of Whiteness*. Melbourne: Melbourne University Press, 2002.

Australian Academy of Science. *The Use of DDT in Australia*. Canberra: Australian Academy of Science, 1972.

Australian Certified Organic. 'Australian Organic Standard'. Chermside, Qld: Biological Farmers of Australia, 2006.

Balfour, E.B. *The Living Soil*. London: Faber & Faber, 1944.

Barr, N., and J. Cary. *Greening a Brown Land. The Australian Search for Sustainable Land Use*. Melbourne: Macmillan, 1992.

Belasco, W.J. *Appetite for Change: How the Counter-Culture Took on the Food Industry*. New York: Cornell University Press, 1993.

Bennett, Peter. *Australia and New Zealand Organic Gardening*. 1st ed. Frenchs Forest, NSW: Child and Associates, 1979.

Biodynamic Agriculture Australia. *What Is Biodynamics*, 2004 [cited 24 July 2006]. Available from www.biodynamics.net.au.

Bio-Dynamic Research Institute. *Demeter Bio-Dynamic Agriculture in Australia*. Bio-Dynamic Research Institute, 2005 [cited 6 November 2006]. Available from www.demeter.org.au.

Biological Farmers of Australia. 'Organics, One of Our Most Viable Solutions to Climate Change'. *The Organic Advantage* 2006, 2–3.

Blaxter, Mildred. *Health*. Cambridge, UK; Malden, USA: Polity Press, 2004.

Brisbane Organic Growers Group. *Pesticides and Alternatives: A Guide to Safer Pest Control for Gardeners and Householders*. Toowong, Queensland: Brisbane Organic Growers Group, 1978.

Brunning, F.H. *The Australian Gardener*. 19th ed. Melbourne: F.H. Brunning, 1920.

Brunning, Leslie, and Harold Alston. *The Australian Gardener: A Complete and Practical Guide Dealing with the Growing of Fruit, Flowers and Vegetables*. 30th ed. Melbourne: Robertson and Mullens, 1949.

Buck, D., C. Getz, and J. Guthman. 'From Farm to Table: The Organic Vegetable Commodity Chain of Northern California'. *Sociologia Ruralis* 37, no. 3–20 (1997).

Bunce, Michael. *The Countryside Ideal: Anglo-American Images of Landscape.* London and New York: Routledge, 1994.

Campbell, Hugh, and Ruth Liepins. 'Naming Organics: Understanding Organic Standards in New Zealand as a Discursive Field'. *Sociologia Ruralis* 41, no. 1 (2001): 22–39.

Carson, Rachel. *Edge of the Sea.* Boston: Houghton Mifflin, 1955.

——. *The Sea around Us.* London: Panther, 1951.

——. *Silent Spring.* London: Hamish Hamilton, 1963.

Carter, Paul. *Lie of the Land.* London and Boston: Faber & Faber, 1996.

Charman, Peter E., and Brian W. Murphy. *Soils: Their Properties and Management.* 2nd ed. Melbourne: Oxford University Press, 2000.

Cock, Peter. *Alternative Australia: Communities of the Future?* Melbourne: Quartet Books, 1979.

Cockburn, Linda. *Living the Good Life.* Melbourne: Hardie Grant Publishing, 2006.

Coleby, Pat. *Healthy Cattle Naturally.* Melbourne: Landlinks Press, 2002.

Commonwealth of Australia. *Official Yearbooks of the Commonwealth of Australia.* Canberra: Commonwealth Bureau of Census and Statistics, 1951–1971.

Conacher, A., and J. Conacher. *Organic Farming in Australia.* Nedlands, WA: University of WA, 1982.

Conacher, Jeanette. *Pests, Predators and Pesticides: Some Alternatives to Synthetic Pesticides.* Wembley, WA: Organic Growers Association WA, 1980.

Conford, Philip. *The Origins of the Organic Movement.* Edinburgh, UK: Floris Books, 2001.

Coombes, B., and Hugh Campbell. 'Dependent Reproduction of Alternative Modes of Agriculture: Organic Farming in New Zealand'. *Sociologia Ruralis* 38, no. 2 (1998): 127–45.

'County Palatine of Chester Local Medical and Panel Committee Medical Testament'. In *British Medical Journal Supplement*, 1939.

Cronon, William. 'A Place for Stories: Nature, History and Narrative'. *Journal of American History* 78, no. 4 (1992): 1347–76.

CSIRO. *Register of Australian Herbage Plant Cultivars: Phalaris* CSIRO, 1972 [cited 28/11/07 2007]. Available from www.pi.csiro.au/ahpc/grasses/pdf/australian.pdf.

Curthoys, Ann, and John Docker. *Is History Fiction?* Sydney: UNSW Press, 2005.

Cushing, Helen. *Beyond Organics: Gardening for the Future.* Sydney: Australian Broadcasting Corporation, 2005.

Darian-Smith, Kate, and Paula Hamilton. *Memory and History in Twentieth-Century Australia*. Melbourne: Oxford University Press, 1994.

Davison, Graeme. *The Rise and Fall of Marvellous Melbourne*. Carlton: Melbourne University Press, 1978.

DeLind, Laura B. 'Transforming Organic Agriculture into Industrial Organic Products: Reconsidering National Organic Standards'. *Human Organization* 59, no. 2 (2000): 198–208.

Dumaresq, David, Richard Greene, and Lorrae van Kerkhoff, eds. *Organic Agriculture in Australia: Proceedings of the National Symposium on Organic Agriculture, Research and Development*. RIRDC Research Paper 97/14. Canberra: Rural Industries Research and Development Corporation, 1997.

Flannery, Tim. 'Agriculture in the Context of Climate Change'. Paper presented at the Shaping Sustainable Systems; 15th IFOAM Organic World Congress, Adelaide, 20–25 September 2005.

——. *The Weather Makers: The History and Future Impact of Climate Change*. Melbourne: Text Publishing Company, 2005.

French, Jackie. *Backyard Self-Sufficiency*. Melbourne: Aird Books, 1992.

——. *Earth Gardener's Companion: A Month by Month Guide to Organic Planting, Gardening and Harvesting*. Trentham, Vic.: Earth Garden Magazine, 1990.

——. *Household Self-Sufficiency: The Ultimate Guide to Making Everything from Acne and Baldness Remedies to Candles, Love Potions, Varnish and Wool Wash*. Melbourne: Aird Books, 1994.

——. *Jackie French's Top 10 Vegetables*. Melbourne: Aird Books, 1995.

——. *Natural Control of Garden Pests*. Melbourne: Aird Books, 2002.

——. *Organic Gardening in Australia*. French's Forest: Reed, 1986.

——. *Soil Food: 1372 Ways to Add Fertility to Your Soil*. Melbourne: Aird Books, 1995.

——. *Switch!: Home-Based Power, Water and Sewerage Systems for the Twenty-First Century*. Melbourne: Aird Books, 1994.

——. *The Wilderness Garden: Beyond Organic Gardening*. Melbourne: Aird Books, 1992.

Gaynor, Andrea. 'From Chook Run to Chicken Treat: Speculation on Changes in Human–Animal Relationships in Twentieth-Century Perth, Western Australia'. *Limina* 5 (1999): 26–39.

——. *Harvest of the Suburbs: An Environmental History of Growing Food in Australian Cities*. Perth: University of Western Australia Press, 2006.

——. 'Regulation, Resistance and the Residential Area: The Keeping of Productive Animals in Twentieth-Century Perth, Western Australia'. *Urban Policy and Research* 17, no. 1 (1999): 7–16.

Grady, J. 'Working with Visible Evidence'. In *Picturing the Social Landscape: Visual Methods and the Sociological Imagination*, edited by C. Knowles and P. Sweetman. London: Routledge, 2004.

Griffiths, Tom. 'The Humanities and an Environmentally Sustainable Australia'. In *The Humanities and Australia's National Research Priorities*, report by Australian Academy of the Humanities, 13–20: Australian Academy of the Humanities, Commonwealth of Australia, 2003.

Grinder-Pedersen, Lisbeth, Salka E. Rasmussen, Susanne Bugel, Lars V. Jorgensen, Lars O. Dragsted, Vagn Gundersen, and Brittmarie Sandstrom. 'Effect of Diets Based on Foods from Conventional Versus Organic Production on Intake and Excretion of Flavonoids and Markers of Antioxidative Defence in Humans'. *Journal of Agricultural and Food Chemistry* 51, no. 19 (2003): 5671–76.

Guthman, J. 'Regulating Meaning, Appropriating Nature: The Codification of Californian Organic Agriculture'. *Antipode* 30 (1998): 135–54.

Halpin, Darren. 'The Australian Organic Industry: A Profile'. Canberra: Australian Government Department of Agriculture, Fisheries and Forestry, 2004.

Harper, D. 'Wednesday-Night Bowling'. In *Picturing the Social Landscape: Visual Methods and the Sociological Imagination*, edited by C. Knowles and P. Sweetman. London: Routledge, 2004.

Holmgren, David. *Hepburn Permaculture Gardens: 10 Years of Sustainable Living.* Hepburn: Holmgren Design Services, 1996.

——. 'Permaculture: Sustainability Design Framework for Organic Agriculture in the Energy Descent Era'. Paper presented at the Shaping Sustainable Systems; 15th IFOAM Organic World Congress, Adelaide, 20–25 September 2005.

Howard, Albert. *An Agricultural Testament.* Oxford, UK: Oxford University Press, 1940.

——. *Farming and Gardening for Health or Disease.* UK: Faber & Faber, 1945.

Howard, Albert, and Yeshwant Wad. *The Waste Products of Agriculture: Their Utilization as Humus.* UK: Oxford University Press, 1931.

Hutton, Drew, and Libby Connors. *A History of the Australian Environment Movement.* Cambridge: Cambridge University Press, 1999.

International Federation of Organic Agriculture. 'Principles of Organic Agriculture'. Bonn, Germany: International Federation of Organic Agriculture Movements, n.d.

Jones, Rebecca, and Janice Chesters. 'Muck, Bugs and Decay: The Preoccupations of Early Australian Organic Gardening'. *Studies in Australian Garden History* 2 (2006): 63–79.

Jordan, S., H. Shuji, and R. Izawa. 'Conventionalization in the Australian Organic Industry: A Case Study of the Darling Downs Region'. In *Sociological Perspectives of Organic Agriculture: From Pioneer to Policy*, edited by G. Holt and M. Reed, 142–56. Wallingford, UK and Cambridge, USA: CABI, 2006.

Kaltoft, Pernille. 'Values About Nature in Organic Farming Practice and Knowledge'. *Sociologia Ruralis* 39, no. 1 (1999): 39–53.

Keating, Jenny. *The Drought Walked Through: A History of Water Shortage in Victoria.* Melbourne: Department of Water Resources Victoria, 1992.

Kellert, Stephen R. 'The Biological Basis for Human Values of Nature'. In *Biophilia Hypothesis*, edited by E.O. Wilson and S.R. Kellert, 42–69. Island Press, 1993.

Knowles, C., and P. Sweetman. 'Introduction'. In *Picturing the Social Landscape: Visual Methods and the Sociological Imagination*, edited by C. Knowles and P. Sweetman. London: Routledge, 2004.

Kolm, J.E. 'Fertilisers'. In *Technology in Australia 1788–1988*: Australian Science and Technology Heritage Centre, 2000.

Kopke, Ulrich. 'Organic Agriculture: Maintaining Old Principles in a Changing Environment'. Paper presented at the Shaping Sustainable Systems; 15th IFOAM Organic World Congress, Adelaide, 20–25 September 2005.

Korcak, R.F. 'Early Roots of the Organic Movement: A Plant Nutrition Perspective'. *Hort Technology* 2 (1992): 263–67.

Kosch, S. 'Organic Farming in Victoria'. Horticultural Project Report, Victorian College of Agriculture and Horticulture, 1995.

Kotschi, J., and K. Muller-Samann. 'The Role of Organic Agriculture in Mitigating Climate Change'. In *International Federation of Organic Agriculture Movements*, 64–67. Bonn, 2004.

Lal, R. 'Soil Carbon Sequestration Impacts on Global Climate Change and Food Security'. *Science* 304, no. 5677 (2004): 1623–7.

Lear, Linda. *Rachel Carson: Witness for Nature*. New York: Henry Holt, 1997.

Leeper, G.W., and N.C. Uren. *Soil Science: An Introduction*. 5th ed. Melbourne: Melbourne University Press, 1993.

Leopold, A. *A Sand County Almanac*: Oxford University Press, 1987.

Little, Brenda. *The Australian Organic Gardening Handbook*. Padstow, NSW: Leatherwood Press, 2000.

Living Soil Association of Tasmania. *Compost, Why and How*. Sydney, 1946.

Lockie, Stewart, and Darren Halpin. 'The "Conventionalisation" Thesis Reconsidered: Structural and Ideological Transformation of Australian Organic Agriculture'. *Sociologia Ruralis* 45, no. 4 (2005): 284–307.

Lockie, Stewart, Kristen Lyons, and Geoffrey Lawrence. 'Constructing "Green" Foods: Corporate Capital, Risk and Organic Farming in Australia and New Zealand'. *Agriculture and Human Values* 17, no. 4 (2000): 315–22.

Lombardi-Boccia, Ginevra, Massimo Lucarini, Sabina Lanzi, Altero Aguzzi, and Marsilio Cappelloni. 'Nutrients and Antioxidant Molecules in Yellow Plums *(Prunus domestica L.)* from Conventional and Organic Productions: A Comparative Study'. *Journal of Agricultural and Food Chemistry* 52, no. 1 (2004): 90–94.

Lund, Vonne, Sven Hemlin, and William Lockeretz. 'Organic Livestock Production as Viewed by Swedish Farmers and Organic Initiators'. *Agriculture and Human Values* 19, no. 3 (2002): 255.

Lunt, Ian. *Effects of Stock Grazing on Biodiversity Values in Temperate Native Grasslands and Grassy Woodlands in South Eastern Australia: A Literature Review.* Canberra: Environment ACT, 2005.

Lynggaard, Kennet S.C. 'The Farmer within an Institutional Environment. Comparing Danish and Belgian Organic Farming'. *Sociologia Ruralis* 41, no. 1 (2001): 85–111.

Lyons, Kristen. 'Corporate Environmentalism and Organic Agriculture in Australia: The Case of Uncle Tobys'. *Rural Sociology* 64, no. 2 (1999): 251.

——. 'From Sandals to Suits: Green Consumers and the Institutionalisation of Organic Agriculture'. In *Consuming Foods, Sustaining Environments*, edited by Stewart Lockie and Bill Pritchard, 82–93. Brisbane, Australia: Australian Academic Press, 2001.

Magkos, Faidon, Arvaniti Fotini, and Antionis Zampelas. 'Organic Food: Nutritious Food or Food for Thought? A Review of the Evidence'. *International Journal of Food Sciences and Nutrition* 54, no. 5 (2003): 357–71.

Mansfield, Becky. 'Organic Views of Nature: The Debate over Organic Certification for Aquatic Animals'. *Sociologia Ruralis* 44, no. 2 (2004): 216–32.

McCalman, Janet. *Struggletown: Public and Private Life in Richmond.* Carlton, Vic: Melbourne University Press, 1985.

——. 'The Uses and Abuses of Oral History'. *Canberra Historical Journal*, no. 21 (1988): 20–25.

McFarlane, Annette. *Organic Vegetable Gardening.* Sydney: Australian Broadcasting Corporation, 2002.

McGowan, Barry. 'Chinese Market Gardens in Southern and Western New South Wales'. *Australian Humanities Review* (2005).

McLeod, Judyth. *Botanica's Pocket Organic Gardening.* Milsons Point, NSW: Random House, 2002.

McMaugh, Judy. *What Garden Pest or Disease is That?* Sydney: New Holland Publishers, 2000.

McMichael, A.J. *Human Frontiers, Environments and Disease: Past Patterns, Uncertain Futures*, 318–40. Cambridge University Press, 2001.

——. 'Population, Environment, Disease, and Survival: Past Patterns, Uncertain Futures'. *Lancet* 359 (2002): 1145–48.

McNeill, J.R. 'Observations on the Nature and Culture of Environmental History'. *History and Theory, Theme Issue* 42 (2003): 5–43.

McNeill, J.R., and V. Winiwarter. 'Breaking the Sod: Humankind, History and Soil'. *Science* 304, no. 5677 (2004): 1627–29.

Melucci, Alberto. *Nomads of the Present: Social Movements and Individual Needs in Contemporary Society.* Philadelphia: Temple University Press, 1989.

Michelsen, Johannes. 'Organic Farming in a Regulatory Perspective. The Danish Case'. *Sociologia Ruralis* 41, no. 1 (2001).

——. 'Recent Development and Political Acceptance of Organic Farming in Europe'. *Sociologia Ruralis* 41, no. 1 (2001): 3–20.

Miller, Megg, and David Miller, eds. *Grass Roots, the Early Years.* Shepparton: Night Owl Publishing, 1979.

Mollison, Bill, and David Holmgren. *Permaculture One: A Perennial Agricultural System for Human Settlements.* Melbourne: Transworld Publishers, 1978.

Moore, Andrew. *The Secret Army and the Premier.* Sydney: University of New South Wales Press, 1989.

Mulligan, Martin, and Stuart Hill. *Ecological Pioneers: A Social History of Australian Ecological Thought and Action*: Cambridge University Press, 2001.

National Association for Sustainable Agriculture Australia. 'NASAA Constitution'. Stirling, SA: National Association for Sustainable Agriculture Australia, 2005.

National Association for Sustainable Agriculture Australia. 'NASAA Organic Standard'. Stirling, SA: National Association for Sustainable Agriculture Australia, 2004.

Neve, Marjorie Hutton. *This Mad Folly: A History of Australian Pioneer Women Doctors.* Sydney: Library of Australian History, 1980.

Nitrogen Fertilisers Pty Ltd. 'Sulphate of Ammonia. Let's Introduce You …' Melbourne: Nitrogen Fertilisers Pty Ltd, n.d.

O'Hanlon, Seamus, and Tanja Luckins, eds. *Go Melbourne! Melbourne in the Sixties.* Melbourne: Circa, 2005.

Pakulski, Jan. *Social Movements: The Politics of Moral Protest.* Melbourne: Longman Cheshire, 1991.

'Pastures on New England Wool Properties'. In *Land, Water and Wool, Northern Tablelands Project Fact Sheet.* Canberra: Commonwealth Government Land and Water Australia, 2007.

Peters, Suzanne. 'The Land in Trust: A Social History of the Organic Farming Movement'. PhD, McGill University, 1979.

Powell, J.M. *Mirrors of the New World: Images and Image-Makers in the Settlement Process.* Canberra: Australian National University Press, 1977.

Pretty, J. 'The Rapid Emergence of Genetic Modification in World Agriculture: Contested Risks and Benefits'. *Environmental Conservation* 28, no. 3 (2001): 248–62.

Ratcliffe, Francis. *Flying Fox and Drifting Sand: The Adventures of a Biologist in Australia.* Sydney: Angus and Robertson, 1947.

Rayner, Jill. 'Back to the Land'. In *The Earth Garden Book: Self-Sufficiency in Australia*, edited by Irene Smith and Keith Smith, 39–40. West Melbourne: Nelson (Australia), 1975.

——. 'Getting It Straight'. In *The Earth Garden Book: Self-Sufficiency in Australia*, edited by Irene Smith and Keith Smith, 40–41. West Melbourne: Nelson (Australia), 1975.

Reed, M. 'Rebels for the Soil: The Lonely Furrow of the Soil Association 1946–2000'. PhD thesis, University of the West of England, 2004.

Reiger, Kerreen. *The Disenchantment of the Home: Modernizing the Australian Family 1880–1940*. Melbourne: Oxford University Press, 1985.

Roads, Michael J. *A Guide to Organic Living in Australia*. Launceston: Mary Fisher Bookshop, 1977.

Robin, Libby. *Defending the Little Desert: The Rise of Ecological Consciousness in Australia*. Melbourne: Melbourne University Press, 1998.

Rodale, Robert, ed. *The Basic Book of Organic Gardening*. USA: Ballentine, 1971.

Rose, Deborah Bird. 'The Ecological Humanities in Action: An Invitation'. *Australian Humanities Review*, no. 31-32 (2004).

Rural Industries Research and Development Corporation. 'Inaugural OFA National Organics Conference 2001'. Canberra: Rural Industries Research and Development Corporation, 2001.

Samuel, R., and P. Thompson. 'Introduction'. In *The Myths We Live By*, edited by R. Samuel and Paul Thompson. London: Routledge, 1990.

Schettler, T., K. Barrett, and C. Raffensperger. 'The Precautionary Principle: A Guide for Protecting Public Health and the Environment.' In *Life Support: The Environment and Human Health*, edited by Michael McCally, 239–56. Massachusetts: MIT Press, 2002.

Schoijet, Mauricio. '*Limits to Growth* and the Rise of Catastrophism'. *Environmental History* 4, no. 4 (1999): 515–30.

Scofield, A.M. 'Organic Farming: The Origin of the Name'. *Biological Agriculture and Horticulture* 4 (1986): 1–5.

Seddon, George. 'Words and Weeds: Some Notes on Language and Landscape'. In *Landprints: Reflections on Place and Landscape*, 15–27: Cambridge University Press, 1997.

Serle, Geoffrey, ed. *Australian Dictionary of Biography*. Vol. 2, *1891–1939*. Melbourne: Melbourne University Press, 1988.

Short, Rennie John. *Imagined Country: Environment, Culture and Society*. London: Routledge, 1991.

Simons, Margaret. *Resurrection in a Bucket: The Rich and Fertile Story of Compost*. Allen & Unwin, 2004.

Smith, B. 'The Smith Family Farming Adventure'. *Victorian Landcare and Catchment Management* 2008, 8–9.

Smith, Keith, and Irene Smith, eds. *The Earth Garden Book: Self-Sufficiency in Australia*. 1st ed. West Melbourne: Nelson (Australia), 1975.

Solomon, G., and T. Schettler. 'Environmental Endocrine Disruption'. In *Life Support: The Environment and Human Health*, edited by Michael McCally, 147–62. Massachusetts: MIT Press, 2002.

Sorting Phalaris Names. University of Melbourne, 2000 [cited 28/11/07 2007]. Available from www.plantnames.unimelb.edu.au/Sorting/Phalaris.

Standards Australia. *AS 6000–2009 Organic and Biodynamic Products*. Sydney, NSW. Standards Australia 2009.

Taksa, Lucy. 'The Masked Disease: Oral History, Memory and the Influenza Pandemic 1918–1919'. In *Memory and History in Twentieth-Century Australia*, edited by K. Darian-Smith and P. Hamilton. Melbourne: Oxford University Press, 1994.

The Rodale Institute. 'Organic Agriculture Yields New Weapon against Global Warming'. Kutztown, USA: The Rodale Institute, 2003.

Thomson, Alistair. 'A Past You Can Live With: Digger Memories and the Anzac Legend'. *Oral History Association of Australia Journal*, no. 13 (1991).

Thoreau, Henry David. *Walden*. Princeton, USA: Princeton University Press, 1971.

Tolkien, J.R.R. *Farmer Giles of Ham*. London: Allen & Unwin, 1974.

Touraine, Alain. *The Voice and the Eye: An Analysis of Social Movements*. Cambridge: Cambridge University Press, 1981.

Tovey, H. 'Food, Environmentalism and Rural Sociology: On the Organic Farming Movement in Ireland'. *Sociologia Ruralis* 37 (1997): 21–37.

Tremont, R.M. 'Life-History Attributes of Plants in Grazed and Ungrazed Grasslands on the Northern Tablelands of New South Wales'. *Australian Journal of Botany* 42, no. 5 (1994): 511–30.

Uglow, Jenny. *A Little History of British Gardening*. London: Pimlico, 2005.

Verhoog, Henk. 'Naturalness and the Genetic Modification of Animals'. *Trends in Biotechnology* 21, no. 7 (2003): 294–97.

Verhoog, Henk, Mirjam Matze, Edith Lammerts van Bueren, and Ton Baars. 'The Role of the Concept of the Natural (Naturalness) in Organic Farming'. *Journal of Agricultural and Environmental Ethics* 16 (2003): 29–49.

Victorian Compost Society. *The Compost Heap: The Principles and Practice of Making Compost by the 'Indore' Method as Originated by the Late Sir Alfred Howard*. Melbourne: Victorian Compost Society, 1951.

——. *Healthy Soil Is the Key to Good Health*. Victorian Compost Society, n.d.

Vogt, G. 'The Origins of Organic Farming'. In *Organic Farming: An International History*, edited by W. Lockeretz. UK: CAB International, 2007.

Vogtmann, Hardy. '"Sustaining the Planet": Where Do We Come from and Where Do We Go?' Paper presented at the Shaping Sustainable Systems; 15th IFOAM Organic World Congress, Adelaide, 20–25 September 2005.

Vos, Timothy. 'Visions of the Middle Landscape: Organic Farming and the Politics of Nature'. *Agriculture and Human Values* 17, no. 3 (2000): 245–56.

Waddell, Craig. *And No Birds Sing: Rhetorical Analyses of Rachel Carson's Silent Spring.* Carbondale: Southern Illinois University Press, 2000.

Whitby, Coralie. *Eco-Gardening.* Adelaide: Rigby, 1981.

White, H.F. *After 50 Years: Human Life and the Food Chain.* Guyra: H.F. White, 1959.

White, H.F., and C.S. Hicks. *Life from the Soil.* Melbourne: Longmans, Green and Co., 1953.

White, Harold F. *The Why and the Wherefore of Cultivation.* South Melbourne: The Pastoral Review, 1957.

Williams, Christine M. 'Nutritional Quality of Organic Food: Shades of Grey or Shades of Green?' *Proceedings of the Nutrition Society* 61, no. 1 (2002): 19–24.

Williams, Raymond. *The Country and the City.* Oxford: Oxford University Press, 1973.

——. 'Literature and Rural Society'. In *The Raymond Williams Reader*, edited by John Higgins, 109–18. Oxford: Blackwell, 2001.

Wilson, E.O. 'Biophilia and the Conservation Ethic'. In *The Biophilia Hypothesis*, edited by S.R. Kellert and E.O. Wilson, 31–41. Washington DC: Island Press, 1993.

Woese, K., D. Lange, C. Boess, and K. Berner Boegl. 'A Comparison of Organically and Conventionally Grown Foods: Results of a Review of the Relevant Literature'. *Journal of Science Food and Agriculture* 74 (1997): 281–93.

Worster, Donald. *Nature's Economy: A History of Ecological Ideas.* Melbourne: Cambridge University Press, 1992.

——. 'Transformations of the Earth: Toward an Agroecological Perspective in History'. *Journal of American History* 76, no. 4 (1990): 1087–106.

Worthington, V. 'Nutritional Quality of Organic Versus Conventional Fruits, Vegetables and Grains'. *Journal of Alternative and Complementary Medicine* 7 (2001): 161–73.

Wynen, E. *Conversion to Organic Agriculture in Australia: Problems and Possibilities in the Cereal/Livestock Industry.* Sydney: National Association for Sustainable Agriculture, 1992.

——. 'Sustainable and Conventional Agriculture in South-eastern Australia – a Comparison'. In *Economic Research Report.* Melbourne: School of Economics and Commerce, La Trobe University, 1990.

Wynen, E., and S. Fritz. 'NASAA and Organic Agriculture in Australia'. In *Organic Farming: An International History*, edited by W. Lockeretz. UK: CAB International, 2007.

Yates Garden Guide. 29th ed. Melbourne: Angus & Robertson, 1965.

Yeomans, P.A. *The Challenge of the Landscape: The Development and Practices of Keyline*. Sydney: Keyline Publishing, 1958.

Young, Ann, and Robert Young. *Soils in the Australian Landscape*. Melbourne: Oxford University Press, 2001.

Young, Janice, Xin Zhao, Edward E. Carey, Ruth Welti, Shie-Shien Yang, and Weiqun Wang. 'Phytochemical Phenolics in Organically Grown Vegetables'. *Molecular Nutrition and Food Research* 49 (2005): 1136–42.

Yussefi, Willer, Helga Yussefi, and Minou Yussefi. *The World of Organic Agriculture: Statistics and Emerging Trends 2006*. Frick, Switzerland: Research Institute of Organic Agriculture, 2006.

Index

www.ingramcontent.com/pod-product-compliance
Lightning Source LLC
LaVergne TN
LVHW061222100826
845148LV00004B/826

* 9 7 8 0 6 4 3 0 9 8 3 7 4 *